The Quran Unveiled

Dave Miller, Ph.D.

APOLOGETICS PRESS

Apologetics Press, Inc.
230 Landmark Drive
Montgomery, Alabama 36117-2752

© Copyright 2005
ISBN: 0-932859-72-0
Printed in China

Library of Congress Cataloging-in-Publication
Dave Miller (1953 -)
The Quran Unveiled
Includes bibliographic references.
ISBN 0-932859-72-0
1. Islam and religions originating in it 2. Comparative religion 3. Philosophy and theory of religion 4. Christianity and other belief systems I. Title

297–dc21   2005920481

DEDICATION

To Deb–
whose positive influence on my life
has been inestimable, profound,
and eternal

ACKNOWLEDGEMENTS

Many gracious individuals have extended their encouragement and support–too numerous to name. I am grateful to each and every one. Nevertheless, special acknowledgement is given to: James & Evelyn Byrd, Everett Chambers, Kevin & Kathy Carroll, Webb & Dorothy Cox, Lee & Kay Watts, Daryl & Vel Bond, Thomas & Doris Gardner, Eric Hall, A.C. & Marie Ivey, Margie Lindsey, James & Nancy Stephenson, and Paul & LaDon Sain.

TABLE OF CONTENTS

PREFACE

The central purpose of this study is not to provide an exhaustive treatment of Islam. Many volumes are readily available that seek to achieve this objective. Rather, the twofold purpose of this study is to provide a practical, to-the-point handbook to help Christians in their efforts to evangelize, as well as to assist Muslims in giving consideration to the contrasts and differences between New Testament Christianity and Islam.

Islam is not to be judged on the basis of how its devotees have conducted themselves over the centuries. Members of virtually every religion and philosophy, including Christianity, have committed terrible atrocities. Buddhists have set themselves on fire. People claiming to be Christians instigated the Inquisition, went on murderous crusades for land, and continue to kill each other in Northern Ireland and beyond. Muslims have hijacked planes and committed suicide bombings. The credibility, validity, and divine authenticity of any system of belief must not be determined on the basis of the failures, misconceptions, and weaknesses of its practitioners.

Instead, whether a religion has a supernatural origin must be ascertained on the basis of its **sources of authority**—its foundational fountainhead(s) from which its practice and dissemination are spawned. If a person wants to ascertain the legitimacy of Mormonism, one must study the *Book of Mormon*, the *Pearl of Great Price*, and the *Doctrine and Covenants*. If a person wishes to consider the validity of Hinduism, one must examine the Vedas. The credibility of Christianity hinges solely on the authority of the Bible, particularly the New Testament.

For Islam, the matter is equally simple. Islam's validity stands or falls on the question of the inspiration of the Quran. Though the *Hadith* are believed to be true and accurate depictions of the events in the life of Muhammad, and though they play a signifi-cant role and exert a tremendous impact on the practice of Is-lam, Islamic authorities agree that the inspired word of Allah re-sides ultimately and solely in the Quran. Hence, if the Quran possesses attributes and characteristics that are contradictory to the nature of divine inspiration, then its claim to be of supernatu-ral origin is discredited, and it is shown to be nothing more than another book among many produced by mere humans unguided by divine agency. The superstructure of Islam erected on the Quran collapses if the Quran is not the Word of God, even as the Christian religion would be discredited if the New Testament claim to be the Word of God is proven to be erroneous.

I have, to the best of my ability, made every effort to be objec-tive, honest, and unprejudiced in my attempt to examine the holy book of Islam with a view toward determining whether it comes from God. I have approached the Quran with a desire to examine its contents and attributes in a sincere desire to **know the truth**. Christians frequently are the targets of atheists who misrepresent and misunderstand the claims of the Bible in their efforts to discount its inspiration. I have genuinely attempted to avoid perpetrating the same injustice in my appraisal of the Quran. Likewise, I engaged in my own thorough reading of the Quran in order to allow it to make its full impression on my mind prior to introducing any preconceptions or prejudices held by others. I also provide the reader with **lengthy** quotations from the Quran in order to show the reader that no attempt is being made to tear verses from their context.

While the central focus of this study is the question of the va-lidity and credibility of the Quran, I have provided the reader with successive chapters on the life of Muhammad, an overview of the structure of Islam, and a brief introduction to the *Hadith* as a broader backdrop against which the Quran may be examined.

Ultimately, everyone will be judged by the Supreme Ruler of the Universe on the basis of his or her response to the evidence that is available in the world–evidence that proves the existence of the God of the Bible. As free moral agents, every accountable human being is responsible for pursuing and embracing the truth. Sufficient truth exists for every interested individual to distinguish between the true religion of God and the false religious systems that have been spawned by mere humans throughout history. May God bless you, the reader, in this critical quest of arriving at truth in order to be pleasing to Him.

Dave Miller, Ph.D.

January 1, 2005

NOTE TO THE READER

There appears to be no standardized method of transliterating Arabic words into English. I have attempted to use those spellings that both capture the flavor and approximate the sound of the Arabic, while also conforming to spellings preferred by many Islamic sources. For this reason, I have opted to refer to the holy book of Islam as the Quran rather than the Koran.

English translations of the Quran can differ in their versification. This study relies primarily on the Mentor Book edition of Pickthall's translation, following the verse divisions contained therein.

Several terms associated with Islam require an initial clarification include the following:

Allah: The Arabic word for God (literally "the God")

Islam: Means "submission to Allah"

Muslim: Means "one who submits to Allah"

A.H.–*Anno Hegira* (year of the Hegira) or **After the Hegira** ("flight"): The year Muhammad fled from Mecca to Medina (A.D. 622), marking the commencement of the Islamic (lunar) calendar

Hadith: The "traditions" that report the words and actions of Muhammad's life, considered normative for Muslims and worthy of emulation

Iblis: Satan

Injil: Gospel, i.e., the revelation/book given to **Isa** (Jesus)

Ka'bah: Means "cube" and refers to the central shrine of Islam in Mecca to which pilgrimage is made

Djinn (also jinn/genii): Spiritual creatures or demons that may or may not obey the divine will

Mosque (*masjid* in Arabic, "place of prostration"): the building in which Muslims worship, including the **Minaret** (tower from which Muslims are called to prayer by the **Mu'azzin** [or **Muezzin**]–prayer caller), the **Mihrab** (the niche that marks the *qiblah* [direction] of Mecca), and the **Minbar** (the platform/pulpit from which the Friday sermon is delivered)

Quraysh: The Arabian tribe that included Muhammad's family

Ramadan: The ninth month of the Islamic calendar during which time Muslims fast from sunrise to sunset

Shahada(s): The confessions made by Muslims affirming the oneness of Allah and the role of Muhammad as Allah's messenger

Surah: One of the 114 "chapters" in the Quran; while some translations attempt to arrange them in historical sequence, the recognized Arabic order is not chronological

Chapter 1

MUHAMMAD

The religion of Islam is inextricably linked to and centered upon the person of Muhammad. One cannot fully understand Islam and the Quran without giving consideration to the historical personage of Muhammad, his role in the formation and development of Islam, and the social milieu in which he lived. As James Beverley observed: "Muhammad is absolutely pivotal in its [Islam's–DM] origin, makeup, and ongoing life through the centuries" (1997, p. 33). In fact, "the Quran as a historical source thus presupposes a knowledge of the general outline of Muhammad's life" (Watt, 1961, p. 241). To the Muslim mind, Muhammad is the most important person in all of human history. While it is absolutely imperative to understand that Muslims do not believe that Muhammad was divine or that he is to be worshipped (Rahman, 1979, p. 33), nevertheless, Muhammad is considered to be the greatest human being–the ultimate example and model of human existence.

The major events of Muhammad's life were crystallized fairly early by Islamic sources into a generally consistent historical portrait. The principal sources used for reconstructing Muhammad's life, in addition to the biographical references to Muhammad scattered throughout the Quran, are surviving portions of the writings of three ancient biographers: (1) Muhammad ibn Ishaq, who died in A.D. 773, composed a biography for a caliph, considerable surviving remains of which have come down and were used in the annotated rescension of Abd al-Malik ibn Hisham's *The Life of Muhammad*; (2) Umar al-Waqidi of Medina, who died in A.D. 825, produced a work, surviving in an abbreviated form through his secretary, Katib, titled *The Expeditions of Muhammad*; and (3) Muhammad ibn Jarir at-Tabari, who died at Baghdad in A.D. 932, whose writings included annals of Muhammad's life and the spread of Islam (see Rodwell, 1950, p. 7). These ancient sources serve as the basis for the *Hadith*, a collection of stories, reports, and oral traditions of the actions and sayings of Muhammad handed down by followers, and eventually transcribed and compiled. No **non**-Muslim biography of Muhammad—**of ancient origin**—is extant. Hence, the non-Islamic world is dependent solely upon Islamic sources for depictions of Muhammad's life. [The biographical synopsis of the life of Muhammad that follows was gleaned from the following sources: Beverley, 1997, pp. 36-39; Braswell, 1996, pp. 11-18; Braswell, 2000, pp. 11-15; Geisler and Saleeb, 2002, pp. 70-82; Gibb, 1953, pp. 17-23; Ibn Ishaq, 1980; Nasr, 2003, pp. 48-53; Pickthall, n.d., pp. ix-xxviii; Rahman, 1982, pp. 11-24; Shorrosh, 1988, pp. 47-72. Special attention was given to the ancient Arabic accounts of Muhammad's life from the eighth and ninth centuries as reported in Lings, 1983. Unless otherwise noted, quotations of the Quran follow the translation by Mohammed Pickthall].

A BRIEF SUMMARY OF MUHAMMAD'S LIFE

The traditional date and place of Muhammad ibn Abdullah's birth is A.D. 570 in Mecca, a city located in western Saudi Arabia near the coast of the Red Sea. With the inhabitants of Arabia fragmented into tribal groupings, Muhammad was born into the Bani Hashim family clan of the Quraysh (also spelled Qureysh and

Quraish), the tribe that had long been the guardians of the Ka'bah. [The Ka'bah (meaning, "cube") is a cube-shaped building in Mecca that Arabs believe was built by Abraham and Ishmael (*Surah* 2: 125-127). Its four corners point toward the four compass points. They believe that an angel brought a celestial stone to Abraham, from where it had fallen at Abu Qubays, and that Abraham and Ishmael then placed it into the eastern corner of the Ka'bah. Allah then told Abraham to institute pilgrimage to Mecca (*Surah* 22:26-27). Over time, however, the Arabs grew idolatrous and used the facility as a shrine dedicated to many pagan deities]. The Quraysh received their sense of tribal identity from being the guardians of the Ka'bah, and hosting the annual pilgrimage made by Arabs from all over the country.

Even before Muhammad was actually born, his father, Abd Allah, son of Abd al-Muttalib, died while on a trading trip at Yathrib. His mother, Amina, in accordance with Arab custom, presented her newborn son shortly after his birth as a nursling to a Bedouin woman named Halimah, who cared for him in the desert for the next two years. Upon returning for a visit to Amina, the foster family was granted permission to keep Muhammad for another year, at which time he was returned to his mother. Amina reared Muhammad for the next three years until she, too, died when he was only six years old.

Life at Mecca

The death of Amina resulted in the boy being placed under the oversight of his grandfather, Abd al-Muttalib, whose affection soon became apparent. His grandfather took complete charge of him, and treated him with special favor. Muhammad was permitted to participate with his grandfather in activities associated with the Ka'bah as well as with the Assembly of the chief men of Mecca. This relationship was nurtured for two years, at which time the grandfather died (Muhammad was only eight). He had lost two formative influences in his life within a two-year period. His care and protection fell next to his uncle, Abu Talib, brother of Muhammad's father, who also treated him with great affection. Abu Talib's wife, Fatimah, strove to fill the void left in Muhammad's life by being a replacement for his mother—even favoring him above her own children.

Uncle Abu allowed his nephew, perhaps as early as the age of nine, to accompany him on his merchant journeys to Syria and beyond. Many biographers note that these excursions would have brought the young Muhammad into contact with Jewish and Christian influences. In fact, one Christian monk in particular, Bahira, who lived at Bostra, informed Abu Talib that great things lay in store for his nephew-son, and that he should take great care to protect him from the Jews. Other than these activities, Muhammad's childhood was spent like that of other boys of his own age, tending sheep and goats in the solitary seclusion of the hills and valleys surrounding Mecca. It was during this period that his uncles took it upon themselves to provide him with training in the use of weapons of war. In fact, he had opportunity to utilize his skills when two of his uncles took him to a battle that required his participation as a bowman. Also during this period of his life, an additional formative experience happened in which the clans of the Quraysh met in counsel to develop a system of redress by which all people could seek justice without resorting to blood feuds based on family ties. Muhammad was present, as was one who would become his closest friend, Abu Bakr.

After the age of twenty, Muhammad had increasing opportunities to travel with his kinsmen on trading expeditions. Developing his own financial savvy on these excursions enabled him eventually to take charge of the goods of merchants who entrusted him with them. He so conducted himself in the execution of these commercial transactions that he became known throughout Mecca as "al-Amin" (the Reliable or Trustworthy). His reputation did not escape the attention of Khadijah, a wealthy widow/merchant of Mecca, who relied on men to trade on her behalf. She contracted with Muhammad to supervise one of her trading caravans to Syria. His responsible behavior won the affections of his employer. Though fifteen years older than Muhammad, and married twice previously, Khadijah offered herself to him in marriage, an offer that he promptly accepted. The year was A.D. 595; Muhammad was twenty-five years of age.

So began a marriage relationship that would last for many years. In fact, Muhammad's subsequent multiple marriages would come only **after** Khadijah's death when he was fifty years old. In addition to bearing six children to Muhammad, only one of whom, Fatimah, would survive to provide him with descendants to carry on his lineage, Khadijah became an extremely important figure in Muhammad's life and in the religious direction it would take. Her economic security, comfort, psychological support, and encouragement would provide strong assurance to him in sorting out his upcoming religious experiences, and in coping with persecution from fellow Meccans.

For the next fifteen years, an interval known as the "Silent Period" (A.D. 595 to 610), Muhammad presumably carried on the usual activities that were a part of his station in life. Specifically, two pursuits occupied his attention. The first was the business responsibilities that were associated with his wife's trade caravans. The second, and more far-reaching, pursuit was his interest in contemplative pondering, meditation, and spiritual reflection. Muhammad had the habit of retreating from the hustle and bustle of city life one month a year to a cave in Mt. Hira, a desert hill a few miles north of Mecca. The month was Ramadan, the month of heat. It was at this location at the age of forty that Muhammad allegedly received his first revelation (*Surah* 96). The messenger of Allah who supposedly brought him the revelation was the angel Gabriel, who, Muhammad claimed, would bring additional revelations over the next twenty-three years.

It is believed that Muhammad received these revelations while in a quasi-sleep or trance-like state. The utterances that were the product of these trances were recorded in *Al-Quran*, which means "the lecture," "the reading," or "the recitation." The utterances that came from Muhammad when he was not under the influence of one of these ecstatic conditions are known as the *Hadith*. While the latter body of information is held in high regard by the Islamic community, and believed to represent accurate depictions of the remarks and daily occurrences in the life of Muhammad, only the Quran is considered to be the inspired word of Allah.

This first putative revelatory experience left Muhammad in an agitated state of fear and despair. His wife, Khadijah, reassured him that he was not under the influence of a jinn (an evil spirit or demon). She went immediately to her cousin, Waraqa ibn Naufal, an old man who had become a Christian and was recognized locally as a *hanif* (an Arabic word that has the English sense of "orthodox"), one who maintained belief in the one and only God of Abraham to the exclusion of idols (cf. *Surah* 6:162). He, and others of his kind at the time, possessed a strong sense of expectancy in their anticipation of a coming prophet who would turn the Arabs away from their idolatry. This belief coincided well with the Jewish community's parallel conviction that the Messiah was yet to come, having rejected the messianic claims for Jesus Christ over five centuries earlier. Known for his familiarity with the Jewish and Christian Scriptures, Waraqa believed that John 16:13, a verse that Christians apply to the Holy Spirit, referred to a future prophet. He consequently declared his conviction that the same messenger who had visited Moses had visited Muhammad, and that Muhammad had been selected as The Prophet of his people. As a result of this encouragement, for the next three years, Muhammad began to adjust himself to this newly perceived mission by preaching—but only to family and close friends (*Surah* 26:214). The first individuals to accept his prophet status were his wife, Khadijah, his ten-year-old first cousin Ali (whom he had adopted), his servant Zeyd (a former slave), and his trusted friend Abu Bakr. As time went on, additional kinsmen (mostly the young) were converted, but his four uncles showed no inclination to follow him. His protectorate uncle, Abu Talib, was not antagonistic toward Muhammad's new religious beliefs, and even allowed his two sons to convert, but he, himself, remained content with the religion of his forefathers.

Near the end of the three years, Muhammad claimed to have received another revelation commanding him to "arise and warn!" (*Surah* 74:2). This admonition caused him to begin preaching publicly in Mecca. The cornerstone feature of his message was the condemnation of the idolatry that dominated Arab culture and, in contrast, the affirmation of one God. His denigrations amounted to disparagement of the idolaters' lives as foolish, and their forefathers as infidels. In a predicament somewhat analogous to the circumstance faced by the apostle Paul in Ephesus (Acts 19:23-27), Muhammad found himself in direct conflict with the economic interests of his mother tribe, the Quraysh. As the ruling tribe of Mecca, the people of the Quraysh were the guardians of the Ka'bah, the holy place to which all Arabians made pilgrimage in the worship of their pagan deities. In addition to economic concerns, Muhammad was tampering with a cultural milieu in which greatness and immortality were achieved in **this** life—not in the life to come—revolving around the Arab ideals associated with family clans and their patriarchal structure. Once the tribal authorities recognized the threat that Muhammad posed to their religious status, social customs, and economic interests, they commenced hostilities and persecution against him and his followers.

Hostilities were greatly enhanced by divisions created within family clans due to conversions. As the number of Muslim converts increased, and the persecution intensified, Muhammad recommended that those who were able to do so should immigrate to the "Christian" country of Abyssinia. About eighty did so, and found acceptance and refuge among the Abyssinian Negus. In the meantime, Muhammad continued to denounce the Meccans for their paganism. For fear of blood-vengeance by his family clan, and out of respect for Abu Talib's rights of chieftaincy, his opponents did not attempt to kill him, though they endeavored in other ways to undermine his activities and influence. Their bitterness toward Muhammad continued to build until, in the fifth year since his announced first encounter with Gabriel, a prominent Meccan citizen, who previously had been an ardent participant in the persecution of Islam, was converted. His name was Umar ibn al-Khattab. The outraged opponents now went to greater lengths to stifle Muhammad. They rallied the family clans against Muhammad's clan—the Bani Hashim, and the clan of Muttalib (for siding with the Hashim)—even implementing a social and economic interdiction against them. During the ensuing three years, Muhammad's family members were largely marginalized and ostracized from Meccan society, and simultaneously suffered a measure of sustenance deprivation. Eventually, after two years, relatives outside the Hashim and Muttalib tired of the inconvenience created by the ban, and pressed for it to be lifted. They were successful in that the boycott was annulled and hostilities were momentarily relaxed. However, the easing of tensions was short-lived. Leaders of Quraysh attempted a new strategy by seeking to persuade Muhammad to compromise by allowing the practice of **both** religions, a ploy that Muhammad promptly refused (*Surah* 109).

Great sorrow came into Muhammad's life in A.D. 619. That year, his wife of twenty-five years, Khadijah, died at the age of sixty-five. Shortly thereafter, his protectorate uncle, Abu Talib, also died and was replaced by Abu Lahab—the one uncle that was openly hostile toward Muhammad because of his religious views. Muhammad was now more subject to persecution, since his new uncle-protectorate was not interested in shielding him from the hostilities of the other tribesmen. However, Muhammad appealed for protection from another relation, Mut'im, the chief of Nawfal, who immediately agreed to meet his request.

The next significant event in the life of Muhammad pertained to a purported trip to heaven. He went to the Ka'bah at night and fell asleep in the Hijr, the surrounding courtyard. He was awakened by Gabriel, who then showed him to a white heavenly steed with wings named Buraq. With Gabriel at his side, the steed transported him to Jerusalem, to the Temple platform, where he was met by a number of prophets, including Abraham, Moses, and Jesus. After Muhammad prayed and drank a vessel of milk, the steed transported him upward, through the seven heavens, into heaven itself, described as "the Lote Tree of the Uttermost End" (*Surah* 53:14). There Muhammad received the command that Muslims were to pray fifty prayers per day. As he began his descent back through the seven heavens, he encountered Moses, who asked him how many prayers had been required. Learning the number, Moses urged him to return to Allah and request a reduction, due to the weakness of the people. He did so, and the number was reduced to forty. Each time Moses urged him to return to receive additional reductions. When the number was lowered to five, although Moses urged him to return to Allah again, Muhammad was ashamed to do so, resulting in the Islamic practice of praying five times a day. He returned to the Rock at Jerusalem, and then on to Mecca, having accomplished the entire journey in one night. At the mosque, he related only the details of the trip to Jerusalem to those gathered, and was immediately ridiculed and mocked by his enemies, since such a trip would take at least two months by caravan. As time went by, He gradually divulged to his followers the full details of his trip to heaven (*al-mi'raj*). It is this event that led to the construction of the Dome of the Rock mosque in Jerusalem, on the former site of the Jewish Temple that was destroyed in A.D. 70 by the Romans, making this spot the third most holy site in Islam.

In the year following his wife's death, Muhammad claimed to have had two dreams in which an angel told him to marry the daughter of his best friend, Abu Bakr. Abu's daughter, A'ishah, was six years old at the time, while Muhammad was past fifty. As preparations were being made for this marriage, Muhammad married another woman, a widow named Sawdah, who was about thirty years old. The marriage to A'ishah was arranged between Muhammad and Abu and took place privately some months later—without the knowledge of A'ishah, who continued to live with her parents.

Muhammad's efforts to promulgate Muslim ideals among the Meccans continued to meet with limited success. Most of his converts were slaves, former slaves, or young people whose conversion would only further inflame parents and older kinsmen. But circumstances began to occur that would serve as a major turning point in his efforts and in his life. In A.D. 620, as persecution was reaching its zenith, six men of the tribe of Khazraj from Yathrib (a city over 200 miles to the north of Mecca), who were on pilgrimage in early June, engaged Muhammad in conversation in the valley of Mina and were soon convinced that he was, indeed, The Prophet.

Social conditions in Yathrib were ripe for receptivity. Two existing factors account for this receptivity. First, the sizable Jewish community in the city included rabbis who had been speaking of a coming Prophet among the Arabs. Second, two warring Arab tribes, the Khazraj and the Aws, were at the point in their mutually fratricidal hostilities where they sought relief from their prolonged rivalries, fearing also, in their weakened condition, exploitation by the Jewish tribes yet under their control.

The six converts to Islam returned to their city, having concluded that Muhammad was that prophet, and reported to their fellow citizens their findings. At the next season of pilgrimage in A.D. 621, five of the original six plus seven others came to meet with Muhammad and swore allegiance to him (known as the first pact of Al-Aqabah). Upon their return to Yathrib, accompanied this time by a Muslim teacher, Mus'ab, they spread the news regarding the messenger of Allah with exceptional success. When the time for pilgrimage arrived the next year, yet another delegation, composed of seventy-five Muslims, traveled to Mecca to invite Muhammad to migrate to Yathrib to be their leader. While journeying, one pilgrim (named Bara') became preoccupied with the thought that he should pray facing Mecca rather than the customary *qiblah,* Jerusalem. After all, Mecca was the site of the Ka'bah where all of Arabia made pilgrimage. And Mecca was also where the Prophet was situated, to whom they were going. So Bara' altered his direction of prayer, while the others maintained their practice of praying toward Jerusalem. Upon their arrival in Mecca, they posed the question to Muhammad regarding the propriety of praying toward Mecca. Muhammad's response was somewhat ambiguous: "You had a direction, if you had but kept to it." Bara' reinstated his former practice of praying toward Jerusalem. The meeting with Muhammad resulted in the formulation of a second pact (the Second Aqabah), in which the men pledged their loyalty and their commitment to protecting Muhammad from all opponents. This pledge included duties of war and was taken only by the males. Consequently, the First Aqabah, which contained no mention of war, became known as the "pledge of the women."

At the behest of Muhammad, Muslims began selling their property in order to leave Mecca quietly. However, tribal elements that opposed Muhammad felt that his departure would only expand his influence. They made every effort to prevent their Muslim family members from migrating—even to the point of physical restraint. Nevertheless, a steady stream of emigrants left Mecca for Yathrib. This circumstance alarmed the remaining tribal elements that perceived the potential threat of so many enemies congregating together. In the meantime, Muhammad's family protector, Mut'im, had died. The Quraysh decided the time to strike was ripe. Assassins from each clan were selected by drawing lots to attack Muhammad simultaneously in order to diffuse blame for the action equally among the clans. The bulk of the Muslims had already departed Mecca, leaving Muhammad, Abu Bakr, and Ali. Muhammad claimed to have received a revelation from Gabriel, informing him of the plot of Quraysh and instructing him to flee Mecca. On the night of the intended assassination, the assassins surrounded Muhammad's house and awaited his appearance. Muhammad requested Ali to wrap himself in Muhammad's cloak and to lie in Muhammad's bed, assuring him that no harm would follow. Muhammad then recited the Quran (*Surah* 36:9), walked out of his house, and passed through the assassins, their ability to see him supposedly temporarily removed by Allah. Meeting Abu, the two fled to the desert hills south of Mecca and hid in a cave throughout the night. By morning, the assassins, realizing that Ali was not Muhammad, left to sound the alarm. For three days, as search parties combed the area, Abu's son, 'Abd Allah, brought food at night. On the third day, Muhammad and Abu heard unfamiliar voices outside the cave. Muhammad assured Abu that Allah was with them (*Surah* 9:40). Though the pursuers came to the mouth of the cave, they did not enter, but continued their search elsewhere. After they were gone from the area, Muhammad and Abu went to the mouth of the cave and found three "miraculous" occurrences that had deterred their pursuers from entering the cave: an acacia tree had grown in the entrance, a nesting rock dove had built a nest in a hollow, and a spider had built a web across the entrance. When 'Abd Allah and three others returned that evening, the little company of Muslims embarked upon the trip to Yathrib, arriving on the twelfth day.

This event in the life of Muhammad, the Hijrah, or "flight," to Yathrib, has gone down in Islamic history as an event of such significant proportions that it constitutes the commencement of the Islamic era, and serves as the starting point of the Islamic calendar. It occurred in A.D. 622. Subsequent years are designated as "A.H."—*Anno Hegirae* (literally "year of Hijrah," meaning the year since the Hijrah). The city to which Muhammad fled, Yathrib, would become known as Al-Madinah, meaning "**the** City," i.e., the city *par excellence*, referred to in English as Medina. Muhammad's life generally is viewed in terms of two distinct phases: the Meccan years and the years at Medina. The Quran distinguishes itself in terms of its Meccan surahs and those surahs believed to have been revealed at Medina. The departure from his hometown of Mecca and his arrival in Medina signaled a significant transition and a new phase in Muhammad's life.

Life at Medina

Upon his arrival in his new abode, Muhammad promptly purchased a piece of property with a large walled courtyard to serve as the site of a mosque—an Islamic worship site. Muhammad was now in the position to shape and mold an entire community in the ways of Islam. Opposition to this aim came from two primary sources. First, Muhammad attempted to incorporate the Jewish community into a covenant of mutual obligation in the promotion of well being between Jew and Muslim, with a common aversion toward and opposition against polytheists. Initially, Muhammad's power and influence among the population of Medina was of sufficient strength that the Jews felt it politically expedient to cooperate, though their social and economic standing was threatened. However, the majority undoubtedly was unable to accept the fundamental premise that God would send a prophet who was a descendant of Ishmael–not Isaac. The second source of resistance to Muhammad's reign came from fellow Arabs who resented their own local influence being diminished by Muhammad's stature and growing popularity. Inconspicuous and subtle indications of disharmony, not lost on Muhammad, began to assert themselves, evoking from him the longest surah of the Quran–al-Baqarah (the Heifer)–*Surah 2*. One portion addressed the doubters and hypocrites–those who embraced Islam outwardly due to pressure resulting from so many others in the city doing so (vs. 8). Another verse referred to their "satans" (vs. 14)–those who were disbelievers and who sought to deter others from believing. Some of these "satans" were Jews, and the surah addressed them directly: "Many of the People of the Book desire to bring you back to unbelief after ye have believed, out of selfish envy, even after the truth hath been clearly shown them. But forgive them, and be indulgent toward them until Allah give command. Lo! Allah is Able to do all things" (*Surah 2*:109). The "Book" referred to is the Bible, i.e., the Torah and the Gospel (cf. *Surah 3*:65). While many Jews initially welcomed the potential for unity among warring factions, there had been advantages. When the Arab tribes fought with each other, the Jews could sit on the sidelines and find ways to exploit the hostilities to their own advantage. On the other hand, committing to a covenant with Muhammad obligated them to side with the Muslims in the event of war with pagan Arab tribes outside Medina.

In the meantime, Muhammad ordered the construction of two homes, attached to the eastern wall of the mosque that was still under construction going on seven months. One home was for his wife, Sawdah, and his two daughters by Khadijah, Fatimah and Umm Kulthum. Muhammad sent for them to be brought from Mecca to Medina. The other dwelling was for A'ishah, who was now nine years old. Within a month or two of her arrival from Mecca, the official wedding between she and Muhammad took place. It was a simple occasion, with no wedding feast, held in the house built for A'ishah. The couple drank from a bowl of milk and then passed it to the others who were gathered. The guests then went their way, leaving the bridegroom and bride alone. A'ishah's playmates continued to visit her and to play games even as they had prior to the wedding.

Soon after their relocation to Medina, the Prophet instigated raids against the trading caravans of the Quraysh. The revelation that Muhammad claimed to have received stated: "Sanction is given unto those who fight because they have been wronged; and Allah is indeed able to give them victory; those who have been driven from their homes unjustly only because they said: Our Lord is Allah" (*Surah* 22:39-40). Muhammad took the permission granted by the revelation to be a command, especially in view of the fact that the Muslim emigrants had fled from Mecca under duress. Another factor that spurred the Muslims on toward armed conflict was the covenant that they had made with the Jews.

For the first eleven months after the Hijrah, the raiding parties went forth, without Muhammad, but the Meccan caravans managed to elude the Muslims and bloodshed was avoided. However, when word came of an especially rich Meccan caravan returning from the north, Muhammad decided to lead two hundred men in an attack. However, inadequate intelligence thwarted the encounter, as well as the subsequent one. In the meantime, word came that a caravan was returning from the Yemen. The nine Muslims that Muhammad sent to investigate took it upon themselves to attack a small caravan of Quraysh. Returning to Medina, they were criticized by Muhammad, who had not given them specific instructions to attack—especially since it occurred during the sacred month of Rajab. Fellow Muslims, as well as

Jews, joined in the recriminations, blaming them for their violations. But then Muhammad claimed to have received another revelation: "They question thee with regard to warfare in the sacred month. Say: Warfare therein is a great transgression, but to turn men from the way of Allah, and to disbelieve in Him and in the Inviolable Place of Worship, and to expel his people thence, is a greater with Allah; for persecution is worse than killing" (*Surah* 2:217). The revelation was interpreted as ordinarily banning warfare during sacred months, with the exception being the recent incident, from which Muhammad received a fifth of the spoils.

At this same time, another revelation was given that instigated the formal shift from Jerusalem to Mecca as the place toward which worship was to be directed:

> We have seen the turning of thy face to heaven (for guidance, O Muhammad). And now verily We shall make thee turn (in prayer) toward a *qiblah* which is dear to thee. So turn thy face toward the Inviolable Place of Worship, and ye (O Muslims), wheresoever ye may be, turn your faces (when ye pray) toward it. Lo! those who have received the Scripture know that (this Revelation) is the Truth from their Lord. And Allah is not unaware of what they do (*Surah* 2:144; see also vss. 149-150).

A Mihrab (prayer-niche) in the Medina mosque that served to pinpoint the direction of Jerusalem was shifted to the south wall to face toward Mecca and the Ka'bah.

In the second year of the Hijrah, word came to Muhammad of the return from Syria of a wealthy Meccan caravan. He rallied the Muslim population of Medina to intercept it before it could reach its destination. Urgent word was sent by the caravan leader to the Quraysh to hurry to his defense. Mecca responded by marshalling a fighting force of about one thousand to confront Muhammad's three hundred five men. Both forces made for Badr and met on Friday, March 17, 623 (the 17th of Ramadan, A.H. 2). The battle is discussed in "Spoils of War" (*Surah* 8), a revelation alleged to have been given immediately after the battle. It was claimed that one thousand angels provided mostly invisible assistance to the Muslims in the fighting (*Surah* 8:9). The angels were commanded by Allah to cut off the heads of the unbelievers (vs. 12). Consequently, reports circulated that the heads of disbelievers were severed mysteriously from their bodies as they rode in battle.

Some fifty of the Quraysh were killed and about the same number were taken captive. The captives were to be kept alive to be ransomed back to their Meccan families. However, Muhammad claimed to receive a revelation of disapproval for this decision, requiring the slaughter of the captives (*Surah* 8:67). But then a revelation excused the decision and endorsed keeping them alive (vs. 68-70), although the verses are generally taken to have been a reproof, and that no quarter should have been given in that first battle. Nevertheless, two chiefs of the Quraysh, Abu Jahl and Umayyah, were executed for their stubborn defiance of Islam. When bickering broke out among the Muslims over the distribution of the spoils of war, Muhammad provided a revelation requiring equitable disposition of the booty (8:1). The next morning, the Muslims set off for Medina with captives and spoils. It became clear to Muhammad that two more of the captives, who had been the worst enemies of Islam, could not be allowed to live. They were summarily beheaded.

As remnants of the defeated Meccan army returned to Mecca, an assembly was held to decide their next action: to raise a large, powerful army from all over Arabia to march to Medina to crush the Muslims. Meanwhile, at Medina, the bulk of the Jewish population increasingly manifested their hostility toward Islam. Muhammad claimed to receive revelations warning of their treachery (*Surah* 3:118,120; 8:58). Of the three Jewish tribes in Medina, the Bani Qaynuqa now asserted themselves by spurning the covenant that they had made with Muhammad. Though they retreated into their fortress to await reinforcements, the ensuing Muslim besiegement forced them to surrender. They were then made an "example" (*Surah* 8:57) by forfeiting all their possessions and being exiled from Medina. Muhammad took possession of his legal fifth, while the rest was divided among the Muslims.

Within a year of the Battle of Badr, Muhammad took another wife, Hafsah, who had been recently widowed at the age of eighteen. A third apartment was added to the other two, occupied by Sawdah and A'ishah, that had been built adjoining the mosque.

The Meccans finally completed their preparations to take revenge on Medina and the Muslims for their defeat at Badr. The Muslims had recently captured one of the Quraysh caravans, intensifying the Meccan determination to attack Medina. They set out in A.D. 625 with an army of three thousand men, compared with Muhammad's one thousand. On the morning the two forces were to meet, three hundred of Muhammad's men turned back to Medina—"hypocrites and doubters" who had changed their minds. As forces were engaged near Uhud, the Muslims began inflicting casualties and put the Meccans to flight. The body of Muslim archers, whose volleys of arrows had prevented the advance of the Meccan cavalry, thinking that the enemy had been routed, left their post to participate in the taking of the spoils. This action enabled the enemy to reassert itself. One enemy warrior even managed to breach the ring of defenders that protected Muhammad. He struck Muhammad's helmet with a glancing blow of his sword, a blow that stunned Muhammad, wounded his cheek and shoulder, and knocked him to the ground. Word immediately spread across the battlefield that Muhammad had been killed. Recovering, Muhammad and his circle of protectors moved toward a place of safety. One horseman of Quraysh followed them and charged Muhammad, who in turn grabbed a spear and pierced his attacker in the neck, inflicting a mortal wound.

The Quraysh (who lost about twenty-two men) plundered the dead (about sixty-five Muslims) and returned to Mecca. The Muslims buried their dead, taking comfort that their fallen companions were in Paradise (*Surah* 2:153-157). As Muhammad stood among the dead, he recited: "Of the believers are men who are true to that which they covenanted with Allah. Some of them have paid their vow by death, and some of them still are waiting" (*Surah* 33:23).

One surah that addressed the circumstances of the Battle of Uhud chided those who did not obey orders (*Surah* 3:142-143), and those who thought about deserting before the battle (vs. 122). It affirmed that Islam would ultimately triumph (vss. 137-139), and then, as if Muhammad had suddenly become aware of his own mortality, the surah warned that the Muslims should remain firm even if Allah's Messenger (i.e., Muhammad) were to be killed in battle: "Muhammad is but a messenger, messengers (the like of whom) have passed away before him. Will it be that, when he dieth or is slain, ye will turn back on your heels? He who turneth back doth no hurt to Allah, and Allah will reward the thankful" (vs. 144).

In the months that followed, the potential for retaliatory raids led Muhammad to strike first against a Bedouin force, scattering them in all directions, and clarifying for others the undiminished strength of the Muslims, despite the recent defeat. Muhammad also sent an assassin to kill one particularly evil enemy of Islam— a tribal chieftain. A year after the Battle of Badr, Muhammad took in marriage another wife, Zaynab, who had been widowed by the battle. A fourth apartment was built adjoining the mosque.

Muhammad visited the Jewish tribe, Bani Nadir, to discuss a matter of mutual concern. However, as meal preparations were being made, Muhammad claimed to receive a revelation from Gabriel that the Jews were about to kill him. He arose without a word, returned to his home, and sent a messenger back to the Jews to accuse them of breaking the pact between them, and to order them out of the country. Those who refused would be beheaded. Receiving encouragement from fellow Jews and Bedouin allies to withstand Muhammad's threat, the Bani Nadir retreated behind their fortresses in defiance of Muhammad's ultimatum. The Muslims laid siege for several days with no allied assistance coming forward on behalf of the Jews. When Muhammad gave orders for some of the palm trees of the oasis to be cut down (by divine permission—*Surah* 59:5), the Jews' remaining will to resist evaporated (as the trees were crucial to the Jews' agricultural survival). They were permitted to depart into exile, forfeiting their homes and land, taking with them only what their camels could carry. They departed to the north toward Syria. The abandoned properties and possessions were confiscated by Muhammad to be given to the poor Muslims who had immigrated to Medina from Mecca (vs. 8).

Muhammad's newest wife, Zaynab, became ill and died within eight months of her marriage to the Prophet. A month later, Muhammad's cousin died, leaving his not yet thirty-year-old wife, Umm Salamah, a widow. Muhammad married her and moved her into the house vacated by Zaynab.

In the fifth Islamic year (June, A.D. 626), Muhammad led a force into the desert east of Medina to repel an impending raid. The enemy never presented itself, but Muhammad claimed to receive a revelation (the "Prayer of Fear") that permitted compromises in the appointed times of ritual prayer when a Muslim army was in the midst of military action (*Surah* 4:101-103). A month later, Muhammad led a force of one thousand men some five hundred miles to an oasis on the southern border of Syria. Marauders, especially from the Bani Kalb, had been raiding Medinan caravans and there was also the need to discourage them from joining the Quraysh in the inevitable confrontation that would eventually come between the Meccans and the Muslims. Additionally, due to the rapid spread of Islam, many Muslims were not as spiritually strong as the initial believers. Hence, Muhammad presented a revelation that relaxed the length of the nightly worship vigils (*Surah* 73:20).

It happened one day that Muhammad went to visit his adopted son. Some thirty-five years earlier, Muhammad's first wife, Khadijah, had been given as a gift a slave named Zayd ibn Harithah. Muhammad had set the fifteen-year-old Zayd free, and then adopted him as his own son, changing his name to Zayd ibn Muhammad. When Muhammad arrived at Zayd's house, Zayd's wife, Zaynab, greeted the Prophet at the door, informed him that her husband was not at home, but that Muhammad was welcome to enter. A look passed between them that both interpreted as strong feelings of romantic love. He declined her invitation to enter, so surprised was he at the strength of his feelings for her, and turning to leave, he uttered a glorification of Allah, noting how Allah exposes human hearts. When Zayd returned home, Zaynab informed her husband of the visit and Muhammad's utterance. Zayd immediately visited the prophet, offering to release his wife so that Muhammad could marry her. The Prophet declined the offer, and did so again the next day when Zayd returned with the same proposal.

There were three obstacles to Zayd's proposal to relinquish his wife to the Prophet: (1) the Islamic stance regarding the evil of divorce; (2) the Quranic limitation of four wives per man; and (3) the strong social principle that no distinction should be made between adopted sons and sons by birth. Regarding this latter concern, the Quran itself forbade men from marrying the wives of sons by birth–"sons who spring from your loins" (*Surah* 4:23). Some months passed before Muhammad claimed to receive a revelation whereupon he immediately sent a messenger to inform Zaynab that Allah had given her in marriage to Muhammad: "We gave her unto thee in marriage" (*Surah* 33:37). Since the revelation spoke of the event as an accomplished fact, no formal wedding was held. The bride (now nearly forty years old) was brought to the bridegroom (now nearly sixty) without delay. The revelation also made it clear that henceforth adopted sons should retain the name of their natural fathers and that Muhammad had no blood tie to Zayd (*Surah* 33:4-5,40). Muhammad promptly changed Zayd's name from Zayd ibn Muhammad back to Zayd ibn Harithah. The same surah gave special dispensation to Muhammad for exceeding the Quranic restriction of four wives on the basis that he is the Prophet (33:50-51). This permission was for him alone and did not extend to the rest of the Muslim community. Additionally, visitors to Muhammad's house were to limit their visiting time, speak to Muhammad's wives only with a curtain separating them, and never to marry one of Muhammad's wives (33:53). Muhammad was to be addressed in a fashion that distinguished him from his followers, and now Muslim liturgy would include expressions of love and blessings upon Muhammad (33:56).

During this period of relative peace, the Quraysh continued their preparations to launch a final and decisive assault upon the Muslims of Medina. The Bani Nadir Jews, whom Muhammad had expelled from Medina, were anxious to recover their lands. They conspired with the Meccans in their mutual determination to achieve revenge. The Jews sought assistance from the Bedouin tribes east of Medina on the plain of Najd. The Bani Asad agreed to participate, as did three clans from the Bani Ghatafan, and seven hundred from the Bani Sulaym—nearly six thousand altogether. The Jewish tribe of Qurayzah in Medina indicated their intention to maintain their pact with Muhammad. The Quraysh managed to muster four thousand from among themselves and their allies. When the Muslims received word of the advancing armies, whose arrival was expected in a week, they decided to build a trench around Medina in those sections where walls, buildings, or rock were not already present. The digging was completed in six days, and the Muslims, about three thousand strong, positioned themselves as the enemy armies approached. When the enemy arrived and saw the trench, and the Muslim archers stationed just beyond the trench whose volley arrows would be deadly for any who attempted to cross the trench, they spent several days encamped, seeking for some weakness in the Muslim defenses. They sent a Jew from the Bani Nadir who convinced the chief of the Qurayzah to renounce the pact he had made with Muhammad. The long days of Muslim diligence and alertness evoked *Surah* 33:10-11. Muhammad arranged to sow discord and distrust among the enemy forces, and, as nearly two weeks had transpired with no success, the coalition of enemy forces were on the verge of abandoning their cause. The last straw came when days of cold, wet weather wreaked further havoc on their resolve, especially a piercing east wind, causing them to head homeward. The resulting surah states: "O ye who believe! Remember Allah's favor unto you when there came against you hosts, and We sent against them a great wind and hosts ye could not see" (33:9).

After the noon prayer, Muhammad claimed that Gabriel visited him and rebuked him for laying down arms prematurely, and admonished him to rally the Muslims to confront the Bani Qurayzah for their treachery in breaking the pact with them. The besiegement of the Jewish fortress on the outskirts of Medina that ensued lasted for some twenty-five nights before the Jewish tribe agreed to surrender. The men, whose hands were bound behind their backs, were led to one side of the camp, while the women and children were led to the other, until a decision could be made regarding their fate. When the Muslims of the clan of Aws requested that the Prophet be lenient toward the Jews, Muhammad asked them if they would be satisfied if one of their own (i.e., a man of Aws) made the decision as to the Jews' fate. They agreed. So Muhammad sent for the chief of the Aws, Sa'd ibn Mu'adh, who was still recovering from battle wounds sustained at the trench. His judgment was that the men should be executed, the property divided, and the women and children made captive.

The women and children were promptly taken into Medina and lodged, while the men spent the night in the camp reciting the Torah and encouraging each other to remain firm. The next morning, Muhammad ordered long trenches to be dug in the market place. Small groups took the Jewish men, about seven hundred in all, to the trenches where they were made to sit beside the trenches that would be their graves. Muslim executioners would cut off their heads with a stroke of the sword, and another group would then be brought to the site for the same fate. The final executions were completed that night by torchlight. The women, children, and property were divided among the Muslims who participated in the siege. Muhammad chose one beautiful Jewish woman as his slave. When she converted to Islam shortly thereafter, he offered to free her and to make her his wife. But she chose to remain a slave, and died five years later.

Among the hypocrites and unbelievers in Medina were those who were otherwise sincere in their commitment, but who faltered on occasion. When such individuals repented and rectified their acts of hypocrisy, they were reinstated to the Prophet's approval on the condition of contributions from their possessions and property. The revelation Muhammad claimed to receive legislating this circumstance reads:

> And among those around you of the wandering Arabs there are hypocrites, and among the townspeople of Al-Medinah (there are some who) persist in hypocrisy whom thou (O Muhammad) knowest not. We, We know them, and We shall chastise them twice; then they will be relegated to a painful doom. And (there are) others who have acknowledged their faults. They mixed a righteous action with another that was bad. It may be that Allah will relent toward them. Lo! Allah is Relenting, Merciful. Take alms of their wealth, wherewith thou mayst purify them and mayst make them grow, and pray for them. Lo! Thy prayer is an assuagement for them. Allah is Hearer, Knower (*Surah* 9:101-103).

Some five months after the battle of the Trench, the Muslims successfully attacked a rich caravan of the Quraysh that was returning to Mecca from Syria. Early in the sixth year of the Hijrah, another successful raid was soon conducted against one of the Red Sea coastal allies of the Quraysh, the Bani Mustaliq. No more than ten were killed, but two hundred families were captured, two thousand camels, and five thousand sheep. Two of Muhammad's wives, A'ishah and Umm Salamah, had accompanied him on this expedition. As they were returning to Medina, A'ishah's onyx necklace was lost at sunset when it was too dark to search for it, so the Prophet ordered the army to camp at that location for the night so the necklace could be located at daylight. The location had no well and many were angry that the entire army had been stopped short of its intended encampment at a more hospitable site on account of a necklace. Besides, the Muslims would be unable to preface their dawn prayers with the required ablutions. But in the final hours of the night, Muhammad claimed to receive a revelation allowing dirt to be used instead of water: "And if ye be ill, or on a journey, or one of you cometh from the closet, or ye have touched women, and ye find not water, then go to high clean soil and rub your faces and your hands (therewith). Lo! Allah is Benign, Forgiving" (*Surah* 4:43).

One of the captives, a beautiful woman named Juwayriyah, asked that Muhammad intervene on her behalf on account of the high ransom price fixed by her Muslim captor. Muhammad offered to pay the full price of the ransom, instead of her father, and to marry her. She agreed, entered Islam, and married the Prophet, who built yet another apartment for her. The fact that the Prophet was now related by marriage to the Bani Mustaliq caused the other Muslims to release their captives who had not yet been ransomed–about one hundred families.

Before the army arrived back in Medina, A'ishah again lost her necklace and slipped away from the main body of travelers in search of it, only to be unintentionally left behind. When she was stumbled upon by Safwan, who himself had fallen behind, he offered her his camel to ride upon while he then led the camel back to the army. When they rode into the camp, gossip and rumors immediately spread through the camp, implying illicit behavior on the part of the couple. On their return to Medina, the rumors persisted for several weeks until Muhammad claimed to receive a revelation that denounced the talebearers and exonerated A'ishah:

> And those who accuse honorable women but bring not four witnesses, scourge them (with) eighty stripes and never (afterward) accept their testimony…. Lo! they who spread the slander are a gang among you…Unto every man of them (will be paid) that which he hath earned of the sin; and as for him among them who had the greater share therein, his will be an awful doom. Why did not the believers, men and women, when ye heard it, think good of their own folk, and say: It is a manifest untruth? Why did they not produce four witnesses? Since they produce not witnesses, they verily are liars in the sight of Allah. Had it not been for the grace of Allah and His mercy unto you in the world and the Hereafter an awful doom had overtaken you for that whereof ye murmured. Allah admonisheth you that ye repeat not the like thereof ever, if ye are (in truth) believers" (*Surah* 24:4,11-14,17).

The three who had been most active in spreading the innuendo were promptly scourged. A'ishah's father and Muhammad's close friend, Abu Bakr, who had been providing financial support to one of the three, now withdrew his support, swearing never again to assist him. However, the same surah commanded that the assistance should be reinstated and the offender forgiven (vs. 22).

In that same year during the month of Ramadan, Muhammad claimed to have a dream in which he went unopposed to the Ka'bah. He decided the dream meant that he should perform the Lesser Pilgrimage to Mecca. He set out with over a thousand fellow Muslims. The Quraysh attempted to halt the Muslim approach by sending forth two hundred horsemen. The Muslims altered their route to avoid a clash, and encamped at Hudaybiyah below Mecca. Negotiations ensued with Muhammad stressing his sole desire to achieve the pilgrimal rounds without conflict. A treaty was signed between Muhammad and the Quraysh that called for Muhammad to refrain from entering Mecca that year, on the condition that he and his followers would be permitted to do so the next year when the Quraysh would vacate the city for three days. This truce of Hudaybiyah also called for a cessation of war for ten years.

Muhammad's followers were disappointed that they were being denied the rounds. Muhammad ordered them to proceed with the sacrifices and the shaving of their heads, though these actions were to be performed only within the sacred precincts. They hesitated until Muhammad led the way. After shaving their heads, a strong wind blew their shaved hair toward Mecca and the sacred territory, which they took as a sign that Allah approved of their sacrifices. Muhammad also received a revelation, titled "Victory," as reassurance that the treaty he had made that delayed their rounds was approved (*Surah* 48). The surah confirmed the dream that Muhammad claimed to have had, as well as the "victory" of the Muslims in their intention to worship in Mecca—though delayed for a year: "Allah hath fulfilled the vision for His messenger in very truth. Ye shall indeed enter the Inviolable Place of Worship, if Allah will, secure, (having your hair) shaven and cut, not fearing. But He knoweth that which ye know not, and hath given you a near victory beforehand" (48:27; see also vs. 18).

At about this time, Muhammad's cousin/brother-in-law died. Four months later, Muhammad arranged to marry his widow— 35-year-old Umm Habibah. Another apartment was promptly built next to those of his other wives. In the meantime, Muhammad began sending letters to various rulers and monarchs, urging them to enter Islam, including those of Persia (who controlled the Yemen to the south of Mecca), Syria, and Egypt.

An attempt was made on Muhammad's life in the form of a Jewish sorcerer who cast a deadly spell on the Prophet by securing one of his hairs, tying eleven knots in it, attaching it to a date-palm sprig, and throwing it into a deep well. The spell could be broken only by untying the knots. Muhammad began to feel the ill effects of the spell and so prayed for divine intervention. He then dreamed that he was informed of the cause, which Gabriel confirmed by giving him two surahs composed of eleven verses (*Surah* 113 and 114). When the prophet sent his friend to the well with directions to recite the eleven verses of the two surahs over the well, at each verse a knot untied itself until all eleven were untied, whereupon the Prophet regained his health. He ordered the well to be filled but refrained from taking action against the sorcerer.

In the seventh year of the Hijrah, Muhammad decided the time had come to address the perceived threat of Jews who were hostile to Islam living in Khaybar. Many of the Bani Nadir who had been banished from Medina had settled there. Muhammad set out with an invading army of 1,600, while the Jews of Khaybar had 10,000 plus an additional 4,000 to be supplied by the Bani Ghatafan to aid the Jews. The information gained from a captured spy enabled the Muslims to assault the weakest fortress of the city, thereby capturing weapons and engines of war that in turn made it possible to defeat the other fortresses one by one. The Bani Ghatafan never arrived to render assistance to the Jews, as they believed they heard voices in the night that prompted them to return to their homes, imagining that their own families were in danger. The most impregnable stronghold of Khaybar was forced out when a Jew from one of the other fortresses negotiated his safety by informing Muhammad of the secret water supply. When the Muslims cut off the supply, the garrison came forth and was defeated after a savage fight.

The last stronghold to resist negotiated peace on the condition that they would abandon all their possessions and leave Khaybar. However, when their chief attempted to conceal treasure, he and his complicit cousin were executed. The Jews were allowed to remain and work their farms and orchards on the condition that they would pay an annual rent of half the produce, with the right to yet banish them reserved by Muhammad. Another oasis to the northeast, also inhabited by Jews, negotiated the same settlement when they heard of the fate of Khaybar. As the victorious Muslim army rested, a woman roasted a lamb, poisoned it, and brought it as a gift to Muhammad. As he and his companions began to eat, Muhammad spat out his first mouth full, warning the others to do the same. Only one had swallowed—and soon died. The woman was brought before Muhammad. She explained that if he were truly a prophet, he would be divinely informed of her plot. Muhammad granted her pardon. He also offered to marry Safiyyah, the seventeen-year-old widow of the chief whom he had just executed, if she would convert to Islam, or he would allow her to remain a Jewess and return to her people. She chose the former and they were married on the return march to Medina at the first rest site. On their homeward march, they detoured to yet another Jewish oasis and within three days forced its inhabitants to surrender on the same terms. The Jews remained tenants of the Muslims until their expulsion from Arabia in the caliphate (vice-regency) of Umar.

Six additional expeditions followed the campaign against Khaybar, conducted against the tribe of Hawazin and the clans of Ghatafan. Meanwhile, remaining within Medina during the nine months that followed Khaybar, Muhammad found himself facing difficulties that arose within his own household. These problems have been attributed to two factors: the increasing wealth that came to the Muslim community as a result of the campaigns against the enemies of Islam and the gradual increase in self-assertiveness by the Muslim women of Quraysh (who had come from Mecca) due to the example set by the Muslim women of Medina. The new prosperity (which resulted in expanded female appetites) and the reduced restraint caused Muhammad's wives to express to him their burgeoning expectations. At about this time, the ruler of Egypt sent a rich present to Muhammad, consisting of a variety of expensive articles, including two Coptic Christian slave girls. Muhammad decided to take the more beautiful of the two, Mariyah, for himself, lodging her in a nearby house. His wives became severely jealous, creating great unhappiness for the girl, and such torment for Muhammad that he promised his wives that he would not see the girl anymore. This circumstance resulted in the reception of a revelation by Muhammad—the "Surah of Banning" (*Surah* 66)—that reproved Muhammad for banning the girl from his life, absolved him of the oath he had taken to desist seeing her, and rebuked his wives (two in particular), even threatening the entire harem with the possibility that Muhammad might divorce them and replace them with "widows and virgin maids" (vs. 6). The surah urged all to repent in hopes that Allah would remit their evil deeds (vs. 8). Muhammad then imposed upon them a separation for one month at the end of which he went to the apartment of A'ishah (considered by all to be his favorite wife) and recited newly revealed verses to her calling upon her and his other wives to make a choice:

> If ye desire the world's life and its adornment, come! I will content you and will release you with a fair release. But if ye desire Allah and His messenger and the abode of the Hereafter, then lo! Allah hath prepared for the good among you an immense reward. ...And whosoever of you is submissive unto Allah and His messenger and doeth right, We shall give her reward twice over, and We have prepared for her a rich provision. ...obey

Allah and His messenger. ...And it becometh not a believing man or a believing woman, when Allah and His
messenger have decided an affair (for them), that they
should (after that) claim any say in their affair; and whoso
is rebellious to Allah and His messenger, he verily goeth
astray in error manifest (*Surah* 33:28-29,31,33,36).

Needless to say, A'ishah and the other wives reaffirmed their desire to maintain their status as wives of the Prophet.

When a year had passed since the signing of the treaty with
the Meccan members of the Quraysh allowing the Muslims safe
access to the Ka'bah to perform the Lesser Pilgrimage, Muhammad set out from Medina with some two thousand pilgrims. The
Quraysh vacated the city as agreed, taking up positions on the
surrounding hills overlooking the mosque. One of the Meccan
Muslims, who had never gone to Medina, spent most of the three
days with Muhammad and offered his wife's widowed sister,
Maymunah, to him in marriage, an offer the Prophet accepted.
The marriage was consummated on the return trip to Medina, a
few miles outside of Mecca. Shortly after the Lesser Pilgrimage,
three eminent men of Quraysh traveled to Medina and converted
to Islam. During this same year, the eighth year after the Hijrah,
Muhammad's eldest daughter by Khadijah, Zaynab, died. None
of his other wives had borne him children. However, his Coptic
bondmaid, Mariyah, was expecting a child soon to be born.

In the eighth year of the Hijrah, the Muslims suffered a military defeat at Mu'tah when the northern Arab tribes on the borders of Syria were reinforced by Roman imperial troops. Though
all three leaders of the expedition that were appointed by the
Prophet were killed, the Muslims managed to return to Medina
with minimal loss of life. Within a month or so, the northern
Arabs felt confident enough to launch their own initiative against
the Muslims without the help of Caesar. However, when a force
of five hundred Muslims marched north to engage them, the
hostile clans dispersed after a brief exchange of arrows. The Muslims were able to reassert Islamic influence among those on the
Syrian frontier who were more receptive to them.

THE RETURN TO MECCA

It was now abundantly apparent that the religion of Islam had established itself in Arabia as a formidable presence overshadowing all others. Several factors contributed to this growing realization. Muhammad's forces had demonstrated considerable military strength. Other tribal alliances were becoming less attractive and more hazardous. The Prophet had shown that, in addition to being dangerous and powerful, he also could be a generous and reliable ally. One significant contributor to the spread of Islam was the reassurance from the Quran, constantly recited to the believers and passed along to those whom they encountered, that Paradise—where every desire would be fulfilled—was within easy reach. This same comforting thought empowered Muslim warriors to enter battle with a fanatical resolve that gave them an immediate advantage over their foes.

An important turn of events now occurred. A skirmish broke out between two clans of Mecca—one supportive of the Muslims, the other supportive of the Quraysh. The clash resulted in a measure of collusion by Quraysh. Their involvement amounted to a breach in the pact made at Hudaybiyah that guaranteed the cessation of hostilities between themselves and Muhammad. Without informing his followers of his intention or their destination, Muhammad proceeded to gather his fighting force, including surrounding friendly tribes who joined them along the way—an army of nearly ten thousand men. They encamped on the outskirts of the sacred territory, each man lighting a campfire so that ten thousand campfires were visible to the Meccans, greatly increasing their apprehension. The Quraysh hurriedly sent one of their leaders, Abu Sufyan, along with two others, to appeal to the Prophet, but they were quickly informed that it was Quraysh who had broken the treaty. Abu's two traveling companions converted to Islam, and by morning Abu Sufyan had done the same. Muhammad told Abu Sufyan to return to Mecca and inform the Quraysh that all those would be spared who entered Abu's house, or locked themselves in their own house, or entered the mosque.

As the Muslim army approached Mecca, it was divided to enable them to enter the city from four directions. Slight resistance was met by one of the divisions from some of the Quraysh who had waited on Mt. Abu Qubays for the arrival of the Muslims. About thirty of them were killed before they fled. Muhammad then entered the city. It was the eighth year of the Hijrah (A.D. 630). After a brief respite in his tent, he mounted his camel and rode with an escort to the mosque, going straight to the Ka'bah. He touched the Black Stone with his staff as he uttered the magnification, "*Allahu Akbar, Allahu Akbar*" (Allah is most great! Allah is most great!). The words resounded throughout Mecca as the throng of Muslims repeated it. Motioning them to silence, Muhammad then made the seven rounds of the Ka'bah. Next he turned to face the 360 idols that surrounded the Ka'bah. As he rode between the Ka'bah and the circle of idols, he pointed his staff toward each idol one at a time, each time reciting *Surah* 17: 81. Each idol reportedly fell face forward as he pointed at it. He then entered the Ka'bah and gave orders for the pagan deities to be effaced.

As the Meccans who had taken refuge in the mosque and in their homes came forth and sat in groups near the Ka'bah, Muhammad addressed them in mass, asking for their reaction to the turn of events. They announced their submission to his will. He quoted *Surah* 12:92 that records the words of forgiveness spoken by Joseph to his brothers: "Have no fear this day! May Allah forgive you, and He is the Most Merciful and of those who show mercy." He gave orders for the idols to be destroyed and for all Meccan citizens to destroy any idols within their homes. He retired to the nearby hill of Safa where, many years before, he had first preached to his family. Meccans by the hundreds now came to him to pledge their allegiance and render homage to him. He gave orders for the nearby pagan temple at Nakhlah to be destroyed. Eminent Meccan citizens converted to Islam that day.

Muhammad now turned his attention to the great Arab tribe, the Bani Hawazin, who continued their resistance by assembling an army of some twenty thousand men to the east of Mecca. When the Muslims, whose numbers had now swelled by two thousand, engaged the Hawazin in battle (the Battle of Hunayn), they were initially scattered by an ambush of horsemen, with the foremost ranks fleeing to the rear. However, Muhammad rallied the Muslims and checked the onslaught of the enemy, who attempted a counterattack. This, too, was checked when Muhammad flung a handful of pebbles at the enemy as he had done at Badr. The tide suddenly changed, reportedly due to the appearance of heavenly assistance invisible to the Muslims but visible to the enemy. The surah that explains the incident reads:

> Allah hath given you victory on many fields and on the day of Huneyn, when ye exulted in your multitude but it availed you naught, and the earth, vast as it is, was straitened for you; then ye turned back in flight; then Allah sent His peace of reassurance down upon His messenger and upon the believers, and sent down hosts ye could not see, and punished those who disbelieved. Such is the reward of disbelievers. Then afterward Allah will relent toward whom He will; for Allah is Forgiving, Merciful (*Surah* 9:25-27).

Though losing many men at the outset of the battle, the Muslims lost few afterwards, while the Hawazin suffered a great slaughter. Many, including their leader, Malik, fled to the safety of the walls of Ta'if. Their women and children were made captives, and the spoils of war confiscated by the Muslims included camels, sheep, goats, and 4,000 ounces of silver. Out of his customary fifth, Muhammad distributed spoils to the recently converted Meccans (and those still unconverted) in compliance with the recently received revelation that stipulated that alms should be given to "those whose hearts are to be reconciled" (*Surah* 9:60). Several more Meccans converted at that time. When jealousy reared itself among the longstanding Muslims over the fact that recent converts and even the unconverted were receiving far more spoils than themselves, Muhammad brought them to tears by assuring them that their portion was to have the Messenger of Allah in their midst in Medina. Muhammad sent word to Malik that his family and possessions would be restored if he would become a Muslim. Malik slipped out of Ta'if at night, made his way to the Muslim camp, and entered Islam. He was then placed in charge of doing whatever he could to bring the occupants of Ta'if (a branch of the Hawazin, the Thaqif) into submission.

The Muslims returned to Medina and it was not long before Mariyah gave birth to Muhammad's son whom he named Ibrahim. During the ensuing six months, several minor expeditions were sent out from Medina in the continuing effort to spread the influence of Islam. The raid on the Bani Tayy, to the northeast of Medina, resulted in many captives and the conversion of the tribe's chief.

During this period, the Romans were successful in their expulsion of the Persians from Syria. Muhammad decided the time had come to lead a campaign against the Byzantines. He mustered the largest and best-equipped army heretofore, thirty thousand strong, and set out from Medina in October, A.D. 630, the ninth year of the Hijrah. Some who were willing to go to war were unable to participate because of a lack of sufficient equipment and turned back in tears (*Surah* 9:92). The army arrived in Tabuk, over halfway to Jerusalem, and remained there for twenty days. It was decided that the threat of imperial troops was unfounded and that the time to conquer Syria had not come. Muhammad made an agreement with a Christian and Jewish community along the eastern coast of the gulf of Aqabah to provide them with protection in exchange for an annual payment of tribute. Turning back to Medina, Muhammad sent over four hundred horsemen to the northeast of Tabuk to a stronghold on the road to Iraq. They succeeded in capturing its Christian ruler and brought him to Medina where he made an alliance with Muhammad and entered Islam.

While in Tabuk, another of Muhammad's daughters died. The funeral was held upon Muhammad's return to Medina. Meanwhile, three Muslims who had refused to participate in the northern military incursion were made outcasts for fifty days, and then forgiven on the basis of a forthcoming revelation (*Surah* 9:118).

The Hawazan leader, Malik, and his men exerted such pressure against the inhabitants of Ta'if, threatening death to any who may be caught unless he abandoned his polytheism, that the Thaqif finally decided to send a delegation to Muhammad announcing their intention to accept Islam. Their request that their pagan shrine, al-Lat, be allowed to continue for three years was rejected by the Prophet, who promptly ordered its destruction. During this ninth year of the Hijrah, the Year of Deputations (*Surah* 49), additional Arab tribes sent envoys to Muhammad declaring their willingness to repudiate polytheism in exchange for entrance into Islam. They were required to pay taxes, as were Christians and Jews.

At this point, Muhammad had firmly established himself as emperor of Arabia. During the last ten years of his life, he had personally led twenty-seven military campaigns, in nine of which there was hard fighting. Those expeditions that he planned and sent out under other leaders were thirty-eight (see Pickthall, n.d., p. xxvi).

When the time of the annual Pilgrimage drew near, Muhammad claimed to receive a new revelation (*Surah* 9), titled "Repentance." It forbade the making of any further treaties with idolaters, though treaties previously made were valid until their term ran out or were broken by the disbelievers (vs. 4). All idolaters were given four months to repent (i.e., convert to Islam) or vacate the area (vs. 2). After that, any idolaters found would be slain or taken captive (vs. 5). If an individual idolater sought protection from Muhammad, he was to be instructed in Islam and then transported to a place of safety (vs. 6). Idolaters would no longer be allowed to come near the mosque in Mecca. The Meccan Muslims were not to fear economic loss due to the expulsion of the idolaters, since Allah would compensate them (vs. 28). The gravity of this surah is evident in the fact that it is the only surah in the Quran that lacks the initial declaration: *Bismi Llahi al-Rahmani al-Rahim* ("In the name of Allah, the Beneficent, the Merciful"). This proclamation marked the end of idol worship in Arabia.

During the tenth year of the Hijrah, Muhammad remained in Medina and continued to receive deputations from those who sought to make pacts with the Muslims. Sixty Christians came from Najran and discussed many points of doctrine, including the divinity of Jesus. Muhammad claimed to receive revelation denying the divinity of Jesus and reaffirming His manhood (*Surah* 3:59-64). He called upon the Byzantine Christians to agree to invoke an imprecation on those who were not telling the truth on the matter. The Christians politely declined to take their disagreement to such a level. Muhammad made a treaty with them, providing protection by the Muslims in exchange for the payment of taxes. This same year, Muhammad endured additional sorrow. His little son, Ibrahim, the child by the Egyptian bondmaid, Mariyah, who was already walking and beginning to talk, fell ill and died.

Ancient traditional sources report that Muhammad predicted that every hundred years one who would renew Islam for the Islamic community would arise. He also predicted the coming of a caliph—the Mahdi (rightly guided)—who would reign for seven years in the latter days just prior to the return of Jesus who would return to destroy the Antichrist. One of the signs that these final things were near would be that buildings would be built higher and higher.

THE FINAL PILGRIMAGE

Muhammad, now sixty-three, proclaimed throughout Medina and beyond that he would lead the upcoming annual Pilgrimage himself—known as the "Farewell Pilgrimage." Multitudes flocked from the desert to the oasis to participate—the first to be held in hundreds of years that would not include any idolaters. Over thirty thousand men and women set out from Medina. In the tenth year of the migration, on the eleventh day of travel, Muhammad entered the mosque and performed the rituals—making the seven rounds of the Ka'bah, praying at the station of Abraham, passing seven times between Safa and Marwah (as Hagar had done when she looked for signs of any approaching help for herself and Ishmael), and entering the Ka'bah itself. Accompanied by the pilgrims, he then rode to Arafah, a hill surrounded on all sides by a valley, about thirteen miles east of Mecca. He sent a crier throughout the multitudes declaring the cessation of all blood feuds among the tribes, with the community of Islam taking precedence over all family ties. A revelation, alleged to have been received during this final pilgrimage, was thought to announce Muhammad's impending death (*Surah* 110).

On this same occasion, known as the "Day of Arafah," with the thousands of pilgrims gathered in the valley, he uttered the final passage of revelation, completing the Quran: "This day are those who disbelieve in despair of ever harming your religion; so fear them not, fear Me! This day have I perfected your religion for you and completed My favor unto you, and have chosen for you as religion AL-ISLAM" (*Surah* 5:3). The next day, he led the pilgrims to Aqabah, between Mina and Mecca, where he sacrificed the animals and called for his head to be shaved. As pilgrims gathered around him in hopes of securing one of his locks, one of his followers begged to receive the forelock. Upon receiving it, he pressed it reverently against his eyes and his lips.

During the months following the "Farewell Pilgrimage," various imposters arose claiming to be prophets on a par with Muhammad. His own followers eventually assassinated one. Another, a chief of the Bani Asad, was defeated by Muhammad's forces and chose to renounce his claims and became a force for Islam. Yet another was defeated several months later and struck down with the sword.

Toward the end of May, A.D. 632, Muhammad decided that the time had come to reverse the Muslim defeat suffered at Mut'ah. He gave orders for a campaign against the Arab tribes of Syria who had received assistance from the imperial legions. An army of three thousand was to be led by the son of one of those who had been killed in the battle. Before the army departed, Muhammad went in the early hours of the morning to Baqi al-Gharqad, the cemetery at the southeast end of Medina, to pray for forgiveness for the dead.

Within hours of this incident, Muhammad developed a severe headache. His fever increased, and those wives with whom he was next scheduled to be, relinquished their turns that he might go to the apartment of A'ishah. In the meantime, after some delay, the army went forth on the Syrian campaign as planned. At the next call to prayer, Muhammad was unable to lead, so he appointed his dearest friend and companion, Abu Bakr (father of A'ishah) to take his place. Muhammad remained in the apartment of A'ishah, with his head cradled sometimes on her lap, at other times on her breast. Though the army had been dispatched toward Syria, it had halted about three miles north of Medina upon hearing the news of Muhammad's illness. On the morning of June 8, A.D. 632, the eleventh year of Islam, the Prophet's fever abated to the extent that, though weak, he went to the mosque for the morning prayer call. The reassured army prepared to continue the northward march, while Abu Bakr went to Upper Medina to visit family. Muhammad was helped back to A'ishah's apartment where he resumed his position on his couch, his head leaning on A'ishah's breast. He soon lost consciousness, but reawakened an hour later, and recited: "with those unto whom Allah hath shown favor, of the Prophets and the saints and the martyrs and the righteous. The best of company are they!" (*Surah* 4: 69). His life slipped away and A'ishah and the other wives commenced lamentations. He was sixty-three years of age.

Receiving word of the Prophet's passing, the army returned to Medina, as did Abu Bakr. One of Muhammad's close associates, Umar, rejected the rumor of death and began chastising the people for entertaining such a notion. The disbelief that the Prophet was really dead was quelled when, in the presence of the people in the mosque, Abu Bakr recited Quranic verses that had been revealed after the Battle of Ehud: "Muhammad is but a messenger, messengers (the like of whom) have passed away before him. Will it be that, when he dieth or is slain, ye will turn back on your heels? He who turneth back doth no hurt to Allah, and Allah will reward the thankful" (*Surah* 3:144). Upon hearing this verse, it was as if those listening had heard it for the first time.

As the Muslims dispersed, a discussion immediately ensued regarding the successor of Muhammad. The Medinan Muslims favored Sa'd, until some of the Meccan Muslims arrived and joined in the discussion. The group concluded that the rightful heir to the Prophet should be Abu Bakr. Those present, with the exception of Sa'd, pledged their allegiance to Abu, acknowledging him as caliph (Arabic–*Khalifah*), his full designation being Deputy or Vice-regent for the Messenger of Allah (*Khalifat Rasul Allah*). The next morning in the mosque, Abu was described in terms of the Quranic designation "the second of two, when they two were in the cave" (*Surah* 9:40). The entire assembly swore allegiance to Abu Bakr (with one exception, Ali, who did so later). It was decided, in keeping with Muhammad's own wish to be buried where he died, to dig a grave in the floor of A'ishah's apartment near the couch on which he died, and to bury him there. This site is now at the center of the "mosque of the Prophet," the sixth to be erected on the spot, the last by a Sultan of Egypt in the sixteenth century, making Medina the second holiest city of Islam.

Chapter 2

CENTRAL TENETS

EARLY ISLAMIC HISTORY

Since Muhammad failed to designate a successor to himself, friction was bound to develop among his followers in their attempts to determine who should carry on after the Prophet's passing. Of course, it was understood that Muhammad was the **final** prophet. His successor would not be a prophet, but merely a community leader. This predicament precipitated a permanent cleavage within Islam—a breach that has never been rectified. [The details of this chapter have been extracted from Braswell, 1996; Braswell, 2000; Cragg, 2000; Nasr, 2002; Nasr, 2003; Rahman, 1979; Williams, 1961].

The initial concern that was generated at the death of Muhammad was resolved temporarily with minimal dissension. Abu Bakr was generally seen as the appropriate successor. That is not to say that unanimity was achieved. There were those who felt that leadership should be confined to a member of the Prophet's own family. His closest relative was his cousin and son-in-law, Ali, the husband of Fatimah (the daughter of Muhammad by

Khadijah) and father of the Prophet's grandchildren. Nevertheless, Bakr had been with Muhammad the longest and was Muhammad's closest friend, not to mention the fact that he was the father of Muhammad's favorite wife, A'ishah. Hence, he was named the first "caliph" (deputy or viceregent) by community consensus, and served in that capacity from A.D. 632 until his death in 634.

Prior to his passing, Abu Bakr named Umar as his successor. Umar had become a follower of Muhammad in Mecca very near the beginning. His caliphate lasted ten years (A.D. 634-644), during which time Islam expanded into Syria and Iraq by 638, Jerusalem and Egypt by 640, and parts of Persia by 642. A Persian slave, who sought revenge for his conquered people, murdered Umar in 644, but not before he appointed a council of six close Companions of the Prophet to name his successor.

Though some favored Ali, the majority of the council decided to appoint another early convert, Uthman, a more distant relative of Muhammad who had become his son-in-law. His caliphate (644-656) was responsible for Islamic military expansion into North Africa as well as the establishment of Persia as a Muslim province by 651. Possessed with the growing suspicion that leadership from within the Prophet's own family was being deliberately withheld, the discontent of those who supported Ali now escalated, their dissatisfaction fueled by what they perceived to be Uthman's inequitable treatment of some Muslims while showing favoritism to others. Amid these dissensions, Uthman rejected demands for his abdication and, in his eleventh year as caliph, was murdered by army insurgents. With the demise of Uthman, Ali was now prevailed upon to accept the caliphate, a position that he held from 656-661. He also was declared to be the first "Imam" by his followers. To Shi'ism, the Imams, though not prophets themselves, were nevertheless the spiritually inerrant replacements of Muhammad, and were related to him by blood, i.e., the descendants of Ali and Fatimah, Muhammad's daughter.

Divisions within the Islamic community (*umma*) were now firmly fixed, and unity has eluded Islam ever since the murder of Uthman. Those who supported leadership being entrusted to one of Muhammad's own family members (beginning with Ali) became known as the Shi'ites (from *shi'at 'Ali* meaning "partisans of Ali"). In contrast, those who felt that the community as a whole should determine leadership became known as the Sunni branch of Islam. Among this latter group of opponents of Ali were Muhammad's companions, Talhah and Zubayr, who, in turn, were joined by Muhammad's favorite wife, A'ishah. The two factions each had their own army. Ali established his capital at Kufa in Iraq. The cousin of Uthman, Mu'awiya, the Sunni leader who commanded the army in Syria, now sought vengeance for the death of his cousin. He manipulated Ali into seeking arbitration, which in turn caused many of Ali's supporters to desert him on the grounds that he had violated the Quran (*Surah* 49:9). These defectors accused Ali of apostasy and denounced his supporters as infidels. They formed yet another sect of Islam, the Kharijis ("Seceders," those who "stand outside"), opposing both Sunnism and Shi'ism, and succeeded in assassinating Ali in 661.

Ali was successively succeeded in Medina by his two sons, Hasan and then Husayn. Hasan became the second Imam only briefly and, on the circumstance of his being poisoned, was followed by his brother as the third Imam. The Shi'ite branch of Islam that these two sons represented became strongest in Iran, a circumstance that continues to this day, forming 93 percent of the Iranian population (see "The Largest…," 1999). The Sunnis established the Umayyad Caliphate in Damascus, lasting for ninety years. In addition to the conflict between themselves and the Shi'ites, they were faced with Bedouin rebellion against centralization of Islamic authority, as well as attempts to restore the old Meccan aristocracy. Islam spread rapidly, even while the Sunnis and the Shi'ites continued to oppose each other. In 680, the Sunni and Shi'ite forces met in the battle of Karbala in Iraq. Husayn and his entire family were brutally killed, with Husayn's head cut off and displayed in Damascus. (It later was taken to

Cairo where it was enshrined as a prominent Shi'ite holy place). This "Martyrdom of Karbala" so shocked the Muslim world that most Shi'ites, and even many Sunnis, commemorate it during the month of Muharram. To this day, the Shi'ites hold the Sunnis responsible for the death of the Prophet's grandson. The Umayyads continued the spread of Islam across North Africa. In 711, a Muslim general named Tariq invaded Spain. In 732, Islamic forces crossed the Pyrennes Mountains and entered France. Christian armies, led by Charles Martel, managed to halt the Islamic advance into Europe at the Battle of Tours. Meanwhile, Islamic forces pushed to the east of Arabia into India and to the edge of China, with Afghanistan and Pakistan coming under their control, as well as parts of Asia. Dissension, especially from the Shi'ites, began to build against the Umayyads, who were perceived more as Arab rather than Muslim rulers. With strong support from the Persians, the Banu Abbas (descendants of the Prophet's uncle) managed to defeat the Umayyads and capture Damascus. Thus ended the Umayyad caliphate.

With the advent of the Abbasid Caliphate, Islam civilization flowered and flourished. Islam's most glorious years transpired contemporaneously with the Dark Ages of Europe. A great renaissance in literature, art, science, medicine, architecture, and education commenced. Moving the capital closer to Persia, they built the city of Baghdad in 762, which soon became the greatest cultural center of the Islamic world. They controlled a vast empire from A.D. 750 to 1258. During this period, the traditional schools of Law were established and the definitive collections of *Hadith* were canonized. The Abbasid Caliphate came to an end when Mongol invaders sacked Baghdad in 1258. Various Turkish tribes began to exert ascendancy over Islam. The Ottoman Turks eventually rose to domination by 1453, bringing the Byzantine Empire to an end. Though the Ottomans claimed to be caliphs, they were actually sultans who provided staunch defense of Sunnism. The Ottoman Empire, with its seat of power at Istanbul (formerly Constantinople), maintained its influence until its decline and ultimate demise after World War I.

THE DIVISIONS

Like all religions on the planet, Islam, meaning "submission" or "surrender" (Pickthall, no date, p. 32), has experienced a multitude of divisions—a circumstance condemned by the Quran itself (*Surah* 6:160; 30:32). The most prominent division is between the Sunnis and the Shi'ites. However, many others have occurred. Just among the Shi'ites alone, multiple schisms have occurred, four being most prominent. As noted above, one division is the Kharijis. Another soon followed with the formation of the Zaydis, a name traceable to Husayn's grandson. A third sect is the Twelvers, who believe that the true Imams are in the direct line of Ali through Husayn, through a younger brother of Husayn's son Zayd (claimed by the Zaydis). The Twelvers believe that the twelfth Imam did not die, but was taken away by Allah and will return to Earth as the Mahdi at the close of human history to bring peace and justice to the world. In the absence of an Imam on Earth, the Twelve-Imam Shi'ites came to accept a monarchal form of government as a temporary substitute. However, in 1979, the Iranian Revolution challenged this tradition when Ayatollah Khomeini asserted the role of the religious scholars ('*ulama*)—the guardians and interpreters of the *Shari'ah* (Divine Law)—as the more appropriate Shi'ite rulers until the return of the Mahdi who, in the meantime, gives supernatural guidance to various leaders that arise (especially the ayatollahs). The Twelvers constitute the largest sect of the Shi'ites, and are situated mostly in Iran, although sizable Twelver communities are found in Iraq, southern Lebanon, and India.

The other division of Shi'ites is the Seveners, which traces its origin to the eldest son of the sixth Imam of the Twelvers, while the Twelvers make his younger brother their seventh Imam. The Seveners were successful in establishing a caliphate in Tunisia in 909, and in taking Egypt and building Cairo as their capital in 969. All four of these Shi'ite sects reject the Sunnis as heretics.

After the first four caliphs, many contemporaneous caliphs and dynasties arose across the Islamic world among the Sunnis, while the Shi'ites retained the Imamate. Gradually, the caliphs came to exercise only nominal authority in deference to the local king (*sultan*) who wielded the actual military and political power. The demise of the Ottoman Empire brought an end to the caliphate, resulting in a variety of individuals, often sheikhs, serving as the spiritual leaders of each local community. Thus the two primary points of contention between the two major sects of Islam are the Imamate (as it harks back to Ali and Husayn), and whether Islamic leadership belongs solely to Muhammad's male descendants. Approximately 86 to 87 percent of the Islamic world is Sunni, while the other 13 to 14 percent is Shi'ite. Less than one percent belongs to other splinter groups (e.g., Kharijis). Combined, they form the world's Muslim population, estimated to number from 1 to 1.3 billion adherents (see "Major Religions...," 2002)–the second largest religion on Earth. The nation with the largest Muslim population is Indonesia, with over 170 million Muslims, followed by Pakistan, with 136 million (see "The Largest Muslim Communities," 2000).

Another aspect of Islam that has created division has been the presence of Sufism. Sufism arose, like Christian asceticism, when the more pious members of the Islamic community felt that many Muslims were too worldly and secular in their daily behavior. They donned clothing of rough wool (*suf* in Arabic), and remained aloof from the materialistic lifestyle. Sufism is essentially mysticism, with emphasis on the experiential and esoteric components of religion. A variety of Sufi orders has arisen within Islam through the centuries. These have included the Ascetics, the Ecstatics, the Antinomians, the Poets, and the Dervishes–each emphasizing a different aspect of ascetic and mystical philosophy (see Williams, 1961, pp. 136ff.).

One other movement within Islam worthy of mention that has facilitated division is Wahhabism, the Muslim parallel to Puritans. In 18th century Saudi Arabia, the leader of this movement, Abd al-Wahhab, urged a return to the golden age of Islam when the first four caliphs led the Muslim community. Wahhabis emphasize the Arabian origins of Islam, and have remained associated with the al-Saud ruling family. They historically have been associated with warlike jihad against enemies—even Muslim enemies. Their encroachment into India during the 19th century led to fighting with the Sikhs. [Sikhs, who are noted for their turbans, practice Sikhism (a completely distinct religion from, and not to be confused with, Islam)—a monotheistic system of belief that emerged in northern India in the early 16th century, combining elements of Islam and Hinduism].

Beginning in 1099, and extending into the thirteenth century, Christian armies, acting under the orders of the pope as well as European rulers like Richard the Lionhearted, engaged in wars against the Muslims of Jerusalem and Palestine. These "Crusades" actually achieved very little success. Even the capture of Jerusalem was short lived, since the famous Kurdish Muslim general Saladin quickly retook it in 1187. The Muslims remained in control of Palestine until 1948 when a sizable portion of land was taken forcibly in order to form the modern nation of Israel. The strife between the Jews and the surrounding Muslim (and Christian Arab) neighbors by this illicit seizure has been constant and deep-seated ever since.

The negative impact on the Muslim mind of these two factors—the Crusades and the establishment of the modern state of Israel—cannot be overestimated. The average Muslim perceives Christianity to be a militaristic religion bent on dominating the world. Many Muslims view the United States, along with European nations, as imperialistic, colonialist Christian governments that wish to destroy Islam. U.S. and European support of Israel exacerbate this perception. The result is that Muslims view the Western world as morally decadent, secular, and aggressively hostile toward Islam. Their distrust of, and aversion toward, America far outweighs their feelings toward even their own evil leaders (e.g., Saddam Hussein), in much the same way that an American is more accepting of a shifty domestic politician than, say, a Chinese communist.

PARAMETERS OF ISLAMIC DOCTRINE AND PRACTICE

Despite the divisions that have occurred within Islam, certain foundational elements exist as commonalities of most every Islamic group. The central feature of Islam is the *shahadas*–the testimonials–of which there are two (sometimes viewed as one). The first affirms the absolute unity and oneness of deity: "*La ilaha illa'Llah*" ("There is no god but Allah"). The second affirms the unique and authoritative role of Allah's final human messenger and prophet, Muhammad: "*Muhammadun rasul Allah*" ("Muhammad is the messenger of Allah"). The second testimonial, in particular, distinguishes the confessor from all other religions as specifically "Muslim"–a form of the word "Islam"– meaning "one who submits/surrenders" (e.g., *Surah* 27:81,91). These testimonials constitute the very basis and essence of Islam.

In addition to the *shahadas*, the unique identity of Islam is further defined in terms of its insistence that the Quran is the verbatim Word of God. Closely related to the authoritative standing of the Quran is the honored role given to the *Hadith*–the written records of the sayings and actions of Muhammad that have been preserved and compiled by his followers in the years after his death. The *Hadith* illustrate the *Sunna*–the pattern of normative behavior established by Muhammad's own conduct. The Quran and the *Sunna* (narrated in the *Hadith*) constitute the *Shari'ah*, or Divine Law, of Islam.

The Pillars

Muslim religious practice is most visible in the devotion given to the so-called "pillars" (*arkan*) of Islam. On these basic rites rests the entire ritual structure of Islam. The first pillar consists of ritual prayers (*salat*). Wherever the Muslim may be on the globe, he or she must utter these prayers facing toward the direction of the Ka'bah in Mecca five times a day: (1) one prayer is uttered between dawn and sunrise (*Salat al-Fajr*); (2) four are said at noon (*Salat al-Zuhr*); (3) four are spoken in the afternoon (*Salat al-'Asr*); (4) three are uttered at sunset (*Salat al-Maghrib*); and (5) the final four are said in the evening before midnight (*Salat al-'Isha*). The prayers are preceded by two activities: (1) the "call to prayer" (*adhan*), a practice begun by Muhammad in Medina; and (2) ritual ablution—a precise and specified cleansing (with running water) of the hands and forearms, mouth and nostrils, face, head, and feet (cf. *Surah* 5:6). The prayer rituals (*raka'at*) entail specific body postures, movements, and words (always in Arabic) that, again, connect back to the established practice of Muhammad. The prayers may be performed anywhere, but most often take place in mosques (from *masjid* which means "place of prostration"). On Friday, corporate prayers are conducted in mosques for the entire local Islamic community.

The second pillar of Islam is the obligatory fast (*sawm*), which takes place during the holy month of Ramadan. Ramadan is the month when, according to Muslims, Muhammad began receiving Quranic revelations from Gabriel. The fast consists of complete abstinence from food and drink from dawn to sunset throughout the entire month. Consequently, most Muslims eat a meal just before dawn and another soon after sunset. Cessation of sexual intercourse is also required. Since the Islamic calendar is based on the lunar year (i.e., 354 or 355 days versus the 365 days of the solar calendar), Ramadan gradually shifts in its occurrence (making one rotation backwards through the calendar every thirty-three lunar, or thirty-four solar, years). When the month falls during the hot period of summer, refraining from drinking water during daylight hours is more difficult. Nevertheless, when rinsing his mouth for the prayers, the devoted Muslim will avoid swallowing even one drop of water.

The third pillar of Islam is pilgrimage (*hajj*). The "**great** pilgrimage" consists of traveling annually to the spatial center of the Islamic Universe—the Ka'bah in Mecca—during the Islamic lunar month of Dhu'l-hijjah. This pilgrimage is obligatory on all men and women who have the financial means to make the trip at least once during their lifetime (cf. *Surah* 3:97). The rites consist of circumambulation around the Ka'bah, specified movements, and prayers, as well as the sacrifice of an animal in Mecca and surrounding holy sites. The "**lesser** pilgrimage" (*hajj al-'umrah*) may also be made to Mecca at any time during the year, and to other holy places–especially Medina and Jerusalem.

The fourth pillar of Islam is the paying of the tithe or religious tax (*zakah*). It is to be paid by all Muslims who have the income to do so. It signifies the purification of the Muslim's wealth, making it legitimate in the eyes of Allah. The collected taxes are kept in a public treasury and used for public and religious activities, especially assistance for the needy and poor.

These four pillars constitute the basic rites of Islam. Some writers include the *shahadas* as one of the pillars to make five. Others designate the fifth pillar to be: "holy war" (*jihad*). However, Islamic sources insist that two misconceptions have developed regarding *jihad*. First, they point out that jihad refers to "**exertion** in the path of Allah." As such, *jihad* refers to the totality of effort and vigilance exerted to do the will of Allah. This exertion would certainly encompass the struggle to protect Islam and its borders–including the traditional notion of "holy war" against those who are perceived as enemies of Islam–but it extends to the war within men's souls in their efforts to bring themselves under submission to Allah. Second, *jihad* is not technically a pillar, since it involves the entirety of life–including the performance of the four pillars. Praying, fasting, tithing, and pilgrimage all require striving and exertion (*jihad*) on the part of the Muslim.

Muslims everywhere perform these rites, regardless of their group affiliation. However, additional practices are performed by the Shi'ites. The martyrdom of Husayn, as noted above, is commemorated each year during the month of Muharram. This commemoration entails well-attended religious processions in which the tragedy of Karbala is recounted and mourners beat their chests with chains. Shi'ites also emphasize pilgrimage to the tombs of the Imams and their descendants, especially to the tomb of Ali in Najaf and to the tomb of Husayn in Karbala.

The Law Schools and Spiritual Leaders

During the eighth and ninth centuries A.D., great schools of Muslim law appeared on the scene, serving as significant sources of Islamic understanding regarding the meaning of the Quran and the *Sunna*. The four great Sunni schools, named for their founders, are the Maliki, the Hanafi, the Shafi'i, and the Hanbah. Followers of the Maliki school are mostly in north and west Africa. Those who follow the Hanafi school are the Turks and the inhabitants of the Indo-Pakistani subcontinent. Adherents of the Shafi'i school are situated primarily in Egypt, Malaysia, and Indonesia. The Hanbali school is most prominent among Saudis and Syrians. The Twelvers, the majority division of the Shi'ites, have their own school, Jafari, named after the sixth Shi'ite Imam. These schools remain influential to this day, each exerting its impact on those who subscribe to its peculiar interpretations of the Law.

While Islam claims to possess no formal clergy in the Western sense, numerous individuals function as spiritual leaders within the Islamic community. These leaders generally are identified under the term *ulama*. The *ulama* include judicial figures who interpret and apply the *Shari'ah*, preachers who ascend the *minbar* to address the assembled worshippers, teachers who instruct adherents, and other persons who stand out from the average Muslim by providing leadership and spiritual counsel. The ayatollahs, for example, may publish writings on Islam, establish theological schools, or surround themselves with students who are groomed to act as leaders in mosques and Muslim communities.

The mosque serves as the primary locus of Islam. Its central feature is the prayer room with mats or rugs on the floor to facilitate the ritual standing, bending, and prostration for prayer. The *mihrab* is the niche in the wall that pinpoints the direction of Mecca (*qiblah*), toward which the prayers are to be spoken. An elevated platform provides a place for a speaker (*khatib*) to address the assembly. To the side of the mosque is one or more minarets, spiraling columns with a stairwell from which the call to prayer is sounded by the muezzin. Also, a source of water (usually fountains) is provided for the ritual purification that precedes prayer.

CONCLUSION

The basic parameters of the religion of Islam are fairly easy to discern. Like every other system of belief, it has undergone a great deal of embellishment, alteration, elaboration, and addition. However, the validity of Islam must not be judged on the basis of its imperfect practitioners or overzealous defenders. Human beings make mistakes, frequently misapprehending and misrepresenting the very ideas they have come to embrace and to which they claim allegiance. The merits of Islam must be judged on the basis of its inherent sources of authority. It is to this task that we direct ourselves in chapter 3.

Chapter 3

THE HADITH

As stated in the Preface, the authenticity, credibility, and genuineness of any religion rests solely on its sources of authority. Proof of its divine origin must exist, and that proof must be available and accessible to the unbiased, honest seeker of truth for examination. No Supreme Being would hold humans responsible for their beliefs and conduct if that Supreme Being did not provide them with sufficient evidence for His existence. Likewise, it is self-evident that He would provide conditions under which humans could have access to that information, and by which spurious and counterfeit religions could be recognized and rejected.

The Bible makes precisely these claims for God. It claims that humans can know that God exists based on available evidence **outside** the Bible (e.g., Psalm 19:1-6; Acts 14:15-17; Romans 1: 19-20). It also claims that humans can distinguish between truth and error, thereby knowing that the Bible is the Word of God (e.g., John 8:32; 1 Timothy 4:7; 2 Timothy 2:15-16; 3:15-17; Titus 1:14; 1 John 4:1). If the Quran is from God, it must possess the self-authenticating attributes and characteristics of inspiration. If it is not from God, though it may possess certain positive, even valuable, qualities, it must be rejected as disqualified to legislate human behavior in an absolute and ultimate sense. The primary purpose of the next four chapters is to examine the Quran with a view toward ascertaining whether it is, in fact, of supernatural origin.

THE *HADITH* AND THE AUTHENTICITY OF ISLAM

Before turning to this central task, brief attention is given to the *Hadith*. The reader will remember that Muslims do not claim **inerrant inspiration** for the *Hadith*–the recorded sayings and deeds of Muhammad. Nevertheless, it cannot be overemphasized that Islam places prodigious, even monumental, emphasis upon them. The accuracy that is **ascribed** to them elevates them virtually to the status of inspiration. In his book *An Introduction to the Science of Hadith*, Muslim scholar Suhaib Hasan emphasized this point rather strongly: "The Sunnah is the second source of Islamic jurisprudence, the first being the Quran. **Both sources are indispensable; one cannot practice Islam without consulting both of them**" (1994, emp. added). Muslim author Badru Kateregga made the same point: "As Muslims, our knowledge of Islam would be **incomplete and shaky** if we did not study and follow the Hadith. Similarly an outsider **cannot understand Islam** if he ignores the Hadith" (1981, p. 31, emp. added). Indeed, the average Muslim strives to pattern daily behavior after the example of the Prophet–the example that is described in the *Hadith*. Consequently, before giving treatment to the Quran, passing observations are in order regarding the impact of the *Hadith* on the attempt to evaluate Islam's credibility.

It is to be admitted that some disagreement exists even among Muslim scholars regarding the authenticity of some of the *Hadith*. Some reports of incidents in the life of Muhammad are believed–by a sizable percentage of the Islamic community–to be spurious. However, many others are set forth without hesitation by the vast majority of Muslims as completely genuine. The following four cases fit in this latter category. They are brought forward for consideration in light of the extent to which they cast doubt on the credibility of Islam.

The Prophet's Polygamy

One feature of the *Hadith* pertains to polygamy. Much has been written that is critical of Muhammad's multiple marriages. It is estimated that he had as many as nine wives simultaneously. The reported total number of wives is at least twelve: Khadijah, Sawdah, A'ishah, Hafsah, Zaynab, Umm Salamah, Zaynab, Juwariyah, Mariyah, Safyyah, Umm Habeeba, and Maymunah (Brooks, 1995, pp. 77-88). The usual Islamic response to this criticism is that Muhammad did not form these marriages out of a desire for sexual pleasure (e.g., Rahman, 1979, p. 28; Nasr, 2003, p. 52). Rather, the marriages were due to: (1) the desire to form alliances with diverse clans due to the swift expansion of Islam, bringing peace with enemies by marrying their daughters (e.g., Nasr, 2002, p. 30); (2) the need to emancipate conquered clans by linking them to Muslim family clans; and (3) Muhammad's desire to render benevolent assistance and care to widows (especially widows of men killed in battle), or to a displaced slave or captive (e.g., Pickthall, n.d., pp. 300-301). Muslim apologist Osama Abdallah offered the following justification for Muhammad's polygamy:

> Prophet Muhammad peace be upon him was a Messenger of God (filled with sympathy and mercy to people) and a leader for all Muslims. He didn't practice polygamy for the sake of sexual pleasure at all. Most of his wives were either widows (older than him in age, too) or divorced women (also most of them were either older or same age). Only one of his wives was a virgin, and he only married her because her father was his best friend. He wanted to strengthen that relationship. And it was her father who offered her to our Prophet peace be upon him anyway.

If our beloved Prophet peace be upon him really seeked [sic] sexual pleasure, then he would've married young virgins from the Muslims. Back then, people loved Prophet Muhammad peace be upon him so much, that they would literally do anything for him. Certainly fathers would've given him their young virgin daughters if he wanted to. Many people offered him their young virgin bosomed daughters anyway to raise their families' honor, but our Prophet never seeked [sic] that sexual privilege in life.

Because Prophet Muhammad peace be upon him was a smart political leader and a wonderful humble merciful true Messenger of Allah Almighty, he chose to marry the weak from his people to encourage the Muslim men to do the same; to create a balance in the Muslim society. Again, another emergency case that existed during Islam's weak times that forced the Muslims (including Prophet Muhammad peace be upon him) to practice polygamy (n.d., parenthetical items in orig.).

Another defense of Muhammad's polygamy is seen in the following general advocacy of the institution of polygamy [NOTE: "B.A.P.U.H." stands for "Blessings and peace be upon him"]:

The Prophet[B.A.P.U.H.] in his lifetime took eleven women in marriage. Majority of these marriages as described above were contracted due to cultural, social, political and moral necessity. In war when a large number of men are killed, the women outnumber men and in this situation, polygamy becomes a social and economic necessity. In case of chronically ill and infertile wife, polygamy prevents break up of marriage as the husband can contract another wife to have children. Polygamous instinct of men as compared to women is also recognised in science. Restriction of number of marriages to one for some men would most certainly encourage society to embark on adultery and prostitution. The modern world where such restrictions have been legally imposed is full of evidence to such evils.

It is universally recognised that laws, orders and limitations imposed on ordinary people are not enforced on special people chosen from among the people by themselves or by the Almighty Allah. Let us first take the rights of the leaders chosen by people such as kings, presidents, prime ministers, chief justices and general managers. They all enjoy special privileges, usually defined by the constitution or parliament of the country. When we do not object to these privileges given to ordinary men, how can we question the privileges given to the prophets? ("Polygamy," n.d.).

Notice that the latter remarks justify Muhammad's excessive polygamy on the basis of his special status as the prophet of Allah.

Of course, no one is in a position to know what was in Muhammad's mind at the time these relationships were formed. Hence, no one can **prove** his motives to be legitimate or illegitimate. If Muhammad's polygamy is justifiable on the grounds that he was simply extending assistance to war widows, why not allow **all** Muslim men to take as many widowed wives as Muhammad? Even Muhammad could not accommodate all the widows of war. If their deprived and needy status was truly the issue, surely Allah would want **all** widows to be cared for—thus opening the door to Muslim men besides Muhammad marrying more than four wives. The same may be said if polygamy is justifiable on the grounds of forming political alliances. Why not allow **all** Muslim men to assist with the strengthening of alliances as well as the emancipation of conquered clans?

Regardless, these alleged justifications do not account for all of Muhammad's marriages. A'ishah was only six years old when Muhammad claimed to receive dreams instructing him to marry her. He was past fifty. What possible rationale can be offered to legitimize this intention? Certainly not "to strengthen the relationship with his best friend"! Much is made of the fact that Muhammad did not consummate the marriage at this point. Yet, it is admitted that he did so within three years when A'ishah was nine. But whether he did so or not, the propriety of such a marriage, both in terms of the age of the child as well as the disparity in their respective ages, is appalling, repugnant, and, to say the least, unacceptable to the unbiased observer.

An even greater objection centers on Muhammad's conduct with regard to the wife of Zayd. Zayd was a freed slave whom Muhammad had adopted and reared as his own son. Seeing Zaynab, Zayd's wife, in her home (some say partially unclad) during Zayd's absence, sparked the circumstances that led to Zayd divorcing his wife in order to accommodate Muhammad's desire to have her. The shock waves that reverberated across the community elicited a string of curt, even stinging, revelations: (1) *Surah* 33:37, which declared the marriage of Muhammad to Zaynab as a "done deal"; (2) *Surah* 33:4-5,40, which clarified the previous revelation that forbade men from marrying the wives of sons by birth (4:23). The new revelation insisted that adopted sons were not included in the previous prohibition; (3) *Surah* 33: 50-51, which granted special dispensation to Muhammad to exceed the Quran's restrictive limitation of no more than four wives (4:3); and (4) *Surah* 33:53, which made three sweeping declarations. First, it chided visitors to Muhammad's home for delaying their departure and overstaying their welcome. The guests who came to celebrate Muhammad's marriage to Zaynab lingered longer than the Prophet preferred, delaying his desire to be alone with his newest wife. Second, it required all future conversations with Muhammad's wives to be conducted with a veil or curtain separating the guest from the wife. Third, no Muslim was ever to marry one of Muhammad's wives. Also, henceforth, Muslims were to invoke blessings on Muhammad (vs. 56).

Once again, for the unbiased, objective observer, this event brings the credibility of Muhammad and his revelations into serious question. In the first place, the Bible consistently represents God as impartial and perfect in justice (e.g., Deuteronomy 10:17; Acts 10:34; Romans 2:11; Ephesians 6:9; Colossians 3: 25; 1 Peter 1:17). The God of the Bible simply would not grant special dispensation to one man over others. He would not exempt one person from a law while expecting others to keep it. Prophets and inspired spokesmen of God in the Bible were never given the right to sidestep laws of God—let alone laws that **all** men are under obligation to obey.

Second, how can Zaynab's divorce from Zayd be morally justifiable on **any** grounds? Observe carefully the wording of the surah that speaks to this point:

> And it becometh not a believing man or a believing woman, when Allah and His messenger have decided an affair (for them), that they should (after that) claim any say in their affair; and whoso is rebellious to Allah and His messenger, he verily goeth astray in error manifest. And when thou saidst unto him on whom Allah hath conferred favor and thou hast conferred favor: Keep thy wife to thyself, and fear Allah. And thou didst hide in thy mind that which Allah was to bring to light, and thou didst fear mankind whereas Allah had a better right that thou shouldst fear Him. So when Zeyd had performed the necessary formality (of divorce) from her, We gave her unto thee in marriage, so that (henceforth) there may be no sin for believers in respect of wives of their adopted sons, when the latter have performed the necessary formality (of release) from them. The commandment of Allah must be fulfilled. There is no reproach for the Prophet in that which Allah maketh his due (*Surah* 33:36-38).

One cannot help but be suspicious. This surah is worded the way one would expect it to be worded if it was produced by a man, unguided by God, who was seeking to justify his desire for another man's wife. Likewise, the unbiased observer surely is stunned, incredulous, and dismayed at the lax attitude toward divorce. Absolutely no justification existed for Zayd to divorce his wife—except to make her available to Muhammad, under the guise that it was an unhappy marriage (see Pickthall, p. 300).

What a far cry from the teaching of the New Testament. Jesus declared in no uncertain terms: "Whoever divorces his wife, **except for sexual immorality**, and marries another, commits adultery; and whoever marries her who is divorced commits adultery" (Matthew 19:9, emp. added). Jesus gave one, and only one, reason for divorce in God's sight. In fact, even the Old Testament affirmed that God "hates divorce" (Malachi 2:16). The teaching of the Bible on divorce is a higher, stricter, nobler standard than the one advocated by the Quran. The two books, in fact, **contradict each other** on this point.

Separate from the question of Muhammad's motives for contracting multiple marriages (whether to unite clans or aid widows), the more pressing question pertains to whether polygamy, itself, is a legitimate social institution–i.e., is it sanctioned by God? It certainly is true that plural marriages were commonplace in the Old Testament. Some prominent men of the Bible are said to have contracted multiple marriages, including Abraham, Jacob, David, and Solomon. Yet, this circumstance is simply reported (along with other violations of divine law) without any indication that God approved of it. One does not find the Bible stating explicitly that polygamy is God's will. But that is precisely what the Quran does: "And if ye fear that ye will not deal fairly by the orphans, marry of the women, who seem good to you, two or three or four; and if ye fear that ye cannot do justice (to so many) then one (only) or (the captives) that your right hands possess" (*Surah* 4:3).

In contrast, quite the opposite is the case in the Bible. God ordained the institution of marriage at the very beginning of the Creation. He enjoined strict heterosexual monogamy (e.g., Genesis 2:24). Whatever human beings did throughout the centuries prior to Christ's advent in their relaxation of the divine will on this point, the fact remains that God legislated one man for one woman for life. Disobedient man introduced polygamy into the world (Genesis 4:19). God tolerated (not endorsed) this sordid state of affairs prior to Christ. [NOTE: God used the Jews in His redemptive scheme to bring Christ into the world (e.g., Romans 9-11). This dependence on the physical descendants of Abraham did not imply endorsement of their sinful departures from His will in their personal lives–though He continued to work through them and even bless them. Each individual Jew's eternal salvation will be based on his or her own choices and actions.] But with the institution of New Testament Christianity, God's original intention for the human race received definitive reconfirmation and reinstatement: "Let each man have his own wife, and let each woman have her own husband" (1 Corinthians 7:2). Polygamy is sinful. Every New Testament passage that addresses the marriage relationship presupposes **monogamy** (e.g., Matthew 5:31-32; Mark 10:1-12; Ephesians 5:22-33; 1 Timothy 3:2; Titus 1:6; Hebrews 13:4).

Even as the church is represented as the bride of Christ (e.g., Ephesians 5:23-32), Jesus would no more have multiple brides than He would endorse men having multiple wives. In fact, God would be guilty of being a respecter of persons if He allowed men to have a plurality of wives, while disallowing women from having a plurality of husbands. Likewise, who could successfully deny that polygamy is damaging to the psyche and self-worth of women?

The *Hadith* confirm that Muhammad's polygamy created jealousy, bickering, and bitter rivalry among his wives (see Brooks, 1995, p. 83). In fact, the Quran itself reflects this turmoil on the occasion of Muhammad adding to his harem the Coptic Christian slave girl, Mariyah. The bitter jealousy of his wives caused him to separate from her initially, only to reinstate her standing when the newly received surah commanded him to do so (*Surah* 66). The result was that Muhammad lived a month with Mariyah—undoubtedly spiting his other wives. Another surah then followed that reprimanded the wives, and ordered them to make a choice as to whether they desired to be married to Muhammad (*Surah* 33). Was this special treatment extended to Mariyah, which punished the other wives by depriving them of their usual turn with Muhammad, a violation of the equal-treatment clause of the Quran (Shorrosh, 1988, p. 65; cf. Lings, 1983, pp. 276-279)? Additionally, the consensus of the Islamic community has ever been that A'ishah was Muhammad's favorite wife, and that she received preferential treatment—a circumstance in direct violation of the Quran. The prophet's polygamy is unquestionably a "difficulty" that the Christian mind (i.e., one guided by the New Testament) finds objectionable.

Credence Given to Spells

The *Hadith* report a most curious incident regarding the power of spells. The traditional sources give the following account:

In these same weeks after the return of the pilgrims there was an attack on the Prophet's life by a means which had not yet been used against him. In every generation of the Jews in Arabia there could be found one or two adepts in the science of magic; and one of these was amongst the Jews still living in Medina, Labid by name, an expert sorcerer who had also instructed his daughters in the subtle art lest his own knowledge should die with him. Labid now received a heavy bribe to put as deadly a spell as he could upon the Prophet. For this purpose he needed some combings of his hair, which he or one of his daughters contrived to procure, possibly through the intermediary of an entirely innocent person. He tied eleven knots in the hair, and his daughters breathed imprecations upon each knot. Then he attached it to a sprig from a male date-palm which had on it the outer sheath of the pollen, and threw it into a deep well. The spell could only be undone by the untying of the knots.

The Prophet was soon aware that something was seriously wrong. On the one hand his memory began to fail him, while on the other hand he began to imagine that he had done things which in fact he had not done. He was also overcome with weakness, and when food was pressed upon him he could not bring himself to eat. He prayed God to cure him, and in his sleep he was conscious of two persons, one sitting at his head and the other at his feet. He heard one of them inform the other of the exact cause of his infirmity and of the name of the well. When he woke Gabriel came to him, and confirming his dream he gave him two *surahs* of the Koran, one of which contains five verses and the other six. The Prophet sent 'Ali to the well, telling him to recite over it the two *surahs*. At each verse one of the knots untied itself until all were untied and the Prophet recovered his full strength of mind and body.

The first of the two surahs is:

> *Say: I take refuge in the Lord of daybreak from the evil of that which He hath created, and from the evil of dusk when it dimmeth into night, and from the evil of the women who breathe upon knots, and from the evil of the envier when he envieth (Surah 113).*

The second is:

> *Say: I take refuge in the Lord of men, The King of men, the God of men, from the evil of the stealthy whisperer, who whispereth in the breasts of men; from jinn and from men (Surah 114)* [Lings, p. 261].

It certainly is to be expected that the local Arabs who were contemporaries of Muhammad would be superstitious—believing in and practicing witchcraft, sorcery, and divination. People infected with such thinking are reflected even in the Bible—people who were out of touch with God's view. However, the Bible never gives credence to such superstitions by implying that they have any validity. On the contrary, the Bible depicts them as aberrant and bogus (e.g., 2 Thessalonians 2:9—"lying [i.e., counterfeit] wonders"). In stark contrast, the *Hadith* (by reporting Muhammad's own belief that a spell was responsible for his illness), and, by implication, the Quran (for providing two surahs that assist in warding off the perceived threat of spells) unwittingly attest to a belief in such nonsense.

The Direction of Prayer

Muslims the world over always face Mecca when they pray. But this practice has not always been the case. Muhammad, himself, originally prayed toward **Jerusalem**. The issue first arose prior to the Hijrah when one early Medinan pilgrim took it upon himself to alter the *qiblah* from Jerusalem to Mecca. The *Hadith* report the circumstances that brought about the eventual change:

> Not long after Mus'ab's departure, some of the Muslims of Yathrib set out upon the Pilgrimage as had been arranged between him and them, in all seventy-three men and two women, hoping to make contact with the Prophet. One of their leaders was a Khazrayite chief named Bara', and during the first days of the journey a preoccupying

thought came over him. They were on their way towards Mecca wherein was the House of God, the Ka'bah, the greatest centre of pilgrimage for the whole of Arabia; and therein was also the Prophet, to whom they were going, and it was there that the Koran had been revealed, and thither their souls were moving ahead of them in aspiration. Was it then right or reasonable, when the time came for prayer, that they should turn their backs on that direction and face towards the north, towards Syria? This may have been more than a mere thought, for Bara' had only a few more months to live, and men who are near to death are sometimes gifted with premonitions. However that may be, he told his companions what was in his mind, whereupon they said that as far as they knew the Prophet was wont to pray towards Syria, that is towards Jerusalem, and they did not wish to differ from him. "I shall pray towards the Ka'bah," said Bara', and he did so throughout the journey, while all the others continued to pray towards Jerusalem. They remonstrated with him to no avail, except that when they arrived in Mecca he had some misgivings and he said to Ka'b ibn Malik, one of his younger clansmen—and one of the more gifted poets of Yathrib: "Son of my brother, let us go to the Messenger of God and ask him about what I did on this journey, for doubts have fallen into my soul through my seeing that ye were against me." So they asked a man in Mecca where they could find the Prophet, whom they did not even know by sight. "Know ye his uncle 'Abbas?" said the man, and they replied that they did, for 'Abbas was a frequent visitor to Yathrib and was well known there. "When ye enter the Mosque," said their informant, "he is the man sitting beside 'Abbas." So they went to the Prophet, who said, in answer to the question of Bara': "Thou hadst a direction, if thou hadst but kept to it." Bara' took to praying towards Jerusalem once more, in order to do as the Prophet did, though the answer he had received could have been taken in more than one sense (Lings, pp. 110-111).

The ambiguous response that Muhammad offered left the pilgrim feeling that he needed to reinstate his former practice of praying toward Jerusalem—even as Muhammad himself continued to do. Thus, the practice remained until a year or so after the Hijrah and the resettlement of the Muslims in Medina.

It was in this same moon of Sha'ban that there came a Revelation of great ritual importance. Its opening words refer to the Prophet's extreme care to face in the right direction for prayer. In the Mosque the direction was set by the Mihrab, the prayer-niche in the Jerusalem wall; but when he was outside the town he would check his direction by the sun if it were day and by the stars at night.

We have seen the turning of thy face unto the sky; and now We shall turn thee a way that shall well please thee. So turn thou thy face towards the Inviolable Mosque; and wheresoever ye may be, turn ye your faces toward it (Surah 2:144).

A Mihrab was forthwith made in the south wall of the Mosque, facing towards Mecca, and the change was accepted with joy by the Prophet and his Companions. From that day Muslims have turned in the direction of the Ka'bah for the performance of the ritual prayer, and by extension for other rites (Lings, p. 137).

Several questions are in order. Why did Muhammad and his early followers initially perform their prayers facing Jerusalem? Had Allah instructed them to do so? Or were they simply the products of their environment in which Jewish influence prevailed? Geiger argued that the switch was made from Mecca (which pagan Arabs practiced) to Jerusalem to appease the Jews, in the vain hope that they might accept his prophethood, but then was switched back when Muhammad realized they were not to be appeased (1896, p. 14). In any case, why would God suddenly alter the direction from Jerusalem to Mecca (*Surah* 2:144)? The verse seems to indicate the reason to be that it was because Mecca was dear to Muhammad. Are we to understand that God would establish the focal point of worship, for all people for all time, based on the preferential whim of a prophet? Since God is not subject to time, and since He would have anticipated the central importance of Mecca (or Muhammad's preference), why did He not establish the proper *qiblah* early in Muhammad's reception of revelation?

Apparently, Muhammad's contemporaries were equally skeptical of this sudden transition. The Quran's attempt to explain the reversal reflects the extent to which questions were raised and challenges presented. To the objective observer, the belabored explanation is strained, unconvincing, and patently self-serving.

> And they say: Be Jews or Christians, then ye will be rightly guided. Say (unto them, O Muhammad): Nay, but (we follow) the religion of Abraham, the upright, and he was not of the idolaters. Say (O Muslims): We believe in Allah and that which is revealed unto us and that which was revealed unto Abraham, and Ishmael, and Isaac, and Jacob, and the tribes, and that which Moses and Jesus received, and that which the Prophets received from their Lord. We make no distinction between any of them, and unto Him we have surrendered. And if they believe in the like of that which ye believe, then are they rightly guided. But if they turn away, then are they in schism, and Allah will suffice thee (for defence) against them. He is the Hearer, the Knower. (We take our) colour from Allah, and who is better than Allah at colouring. We are His worshippers. Say (unto the People of the Scripture): Dispute ye with us concerning Allah when He is our Lord and your Lord? Ours are our works and yours your works. We look to Him alone. Or say ye that Abraham, and Ishmael, and Isaac, and Jacob, and the tribes were Jews or Christians? Say: Do ye know best, or doth Allah? And who is more unjust than he who hideth a testimony which he hath received from Allah? Allah is not unaware of what ye do. Those are a people who have passed away; theirs is that which they earned and yours that which ye earn. And ye will not be asked of what they used to do. **The foolish of the people will say: What hath turned them from the *qiblah* which they formerly observed?** Say: Unto Allah belong the East and the West. He guideth whom He will unto a straight path. Thus We have appointed you a middle nation, that ye may be witnesses

against mankind, and that the messenger may be a witness against you. And We appointed the *qiblah* **which ye formerly observed** only that We might know him who followeth the messenger, from him who turneth on his heels. In truth it was a hard (test) save for those whom Allah guided. But it was not Allah's purpose that your faith should be in vain, for Allah is full of pity, Merciful toward mankind. We have seen the turning of thy face to heaven (for guidance, O Muhammad). And now verily We shall make thee turn (in prayer) toward a *qiblah* which is dear to thee. So turn thy face toward the Inviolable Place of Worship, and ye (O Muslims), wheresoever ye may be, turn your faces (when ye pray) toward it. Lo! **those who have received the Scripture know that (this Revelation) is the Truth from their Lord.** And Allah is not unaware of what they do. And even if thou broughtest unto those who have received the Scripture all kinds of portents, they would not follow thy *qiblah*, nor canst thou be a follower of their *qiblah*; nor are some of them followers of the *qiblah* of others. And if thou shouldst follow their desires after the knowledge which hath come unto thee, then surely wert thou of the evildoers. Those unto whom We gave the Scripture recognise (this revelation) as they recognise their sons. But lo! a party of them knowingly conceal the truth. It is the Truth from thy Lord (O Muhammad), so be not thou of those who waver. And each one hath a goal toward which he turneth; so vie with one another in good works. Wheresoever ye may be, Allah will bring you all together. Lo! Allah is Able to do all things. And whencesoever thou comest forth (for prayer, O Muhammad) turn thy face toward the Inviolable Place of Worship. Lo! it is the Truth from thy Lord. Allah is not unaware of what ye do. Whencesoever thou comest forth turn thy face toward the Inviolable Place of Worship; and wheresoever ye may be (O Muslims) turn your faces toward it (when ye pray) so that men may have no argument against you, save such of them as do injustice—Fear them not, but fear Me!—and so that I may complete My grace upon you, and that ye may be guided (*Surah* 2:135-150, emp. added).

The author of the Quran quite obviously felt pressure to formulate a plausible explanation that would account for why, after having been praying toward Jerusalem, he now (quite conveniently) was reverting to Mecca. The reader can discern in the explanation the underlying accusations of duplicitous inconsistency that must have been raised by his opponents.

More important, as noted earlier in this chapter, God would not specify a physical location on Earth as a "holy shrine" to which humans are to give homage. While the Old Testament indicates that during the exile, Daniel prayed three times one day facing Jerusalem (Daniel 6:10), the Law of Moses enjoined no such requirement. Nor do we have any indications whatsoever that Jesus practiced or enjoined such a thing. It would make far more sense to require believers to face toward the sky—upwards toward God. Neither Jerusalem nor Mecca and the Ka'bah merits any such allegiance.

Al-Mir'raj

Muhammad's purported trip to heaven (*al-mir'raj*) lacks the characteristics and markings of authenticity, and has about it an unmistakable apocryphal flavor. In fact, it smacks of outright myth and outlandish fairytale. The story begins when Muhammad visited the Ka'bah at night and fell asleep. Here is the incident as reported in the traditional early Arabic accounts from the eighth and ninth centuries:

> "Whilst I was sleeping in the Hijr," he said, "Gabriel came to me and spurred me with his foot whereupon I sat upright, yet I saw nothing and lay down once again. A second time he came; and a third time, and then he took me by the arm and I rose and stood beside him, and he led me out to the gate of the Mosque, and there was a white beast, between a mule and an ass, with wings at his sides wherewith he moved his legs; and his every stride was as far as his eye could see."

> The Prophet then told how he mounted Buraq, for so the beast was named; and with the Archangel at his side, pointing the way and measuring his pace to that of the

heavenly steed, they sped northwards beyond Yathrib and beyond Khaybar, until they reached Jerusalem. Then they were met by a company of Prophets—Abraham, Moses, Jesus and others—and when he prayed on the site of the Temple, they gathered together behind him in prayer. Then two vessels were brought before him and offered him, one of wine the other of milk. He took the vessel of milk and drank from it, but left the vessel of wine, and Gabriel said: "Thou hast been guided unto the path primordial, and hast guided thereunto thy people, O Muhammad, and wine is forbidden you."

Then, as had happened to others before him—to Enoch and Elijah and Jesus and Mary—Muhammad was taken up out of this life to Heaven. From the rock in the centre of the site of the Temple he again mounted Buraq, who moved his wings in upward flight and became for his rider as the chariot of fire had been for Elijah. Led by the Archangel, who now revealed himself as a heavenly being, they ascended beyond the domain of earthly space and time and bodily forms, and as they passed through the seven Heavens he met again those Prophets with whom he had prayed in Jerusalem. But there they had appeared to him as they had been during their life on

earth, whereas now he saw them in their celestial reality, even as they now saw him, and he marvelled at their
transfiguration. Of Joseph he said that his face had the
splendour of the moon at its full, and that he had been
endowed with no less than the half of all existing beauty.
Yet this did not diminish Muhammad's wonderment at
his other brethren, and he mentioned in particular the
great beauty of Aaron. Of the Gardens that he visited in
the different Heavens he said afterwards: "A piece of
Paradise the size of a bow is better than all beneath the
sun, whereon it riseth and setteth; and if a woman of the
people of Paradise appeared unto the people of earth,
she would fill the space between Heaven and here below with light and with fragrance." Everything he now
saw, he saw with the eye of the Spirit; and of his spiritual
nature, with reference to the beginnings of all earthly
nature, he said: "I was a Prophet when Adam was yet
between water and clay."

The summit of his ascent was *the Lote Tree of the Uttermost
End.* So it is named in the Koran, and, in one of the oldest
commentaries, based on the sayings of the Prophet, it is
said: "The Lote Tree is rooted in the Throne, and it marks
the end of the knowledge of every knower, be he Archangel or Prophet-Messenger. All beyond it is a hidden
mystery, unknown to any save God Alone." At this summit of the universe Gabriel appeared to him in all his
archangelic splendour, even as he was first created. Then,
in the words of the Revelation: *When there enshrouded the
Lote Tree that which enshroudeth, the eye wavered not nor did it
transgress. Verily he beheld, of all the signs of his Lord, the greatest (Surah* 53:16-18). According to the commentary, the
Divine Light descended upon the Lote Tree and enshrouded it and all else beside, and the eye of the Prophet
beheld it without wavering and without turning aside
from it. Such was the answer—or one of the answers—to
the supplication implicit in his words: "I take refuge in
the Light of Thy Countenance."

At the Lote Tree the Prophet received for his people the
command of fifty prayers a day; and it was then that he
received the Revelation which contains the creed of Is-

lam: *The messenger believeth, and the faithful believe, in what hath been revealed unto him from his Lord. Each one believeth in God and His angels and His books and His messengers: we made no distinction between any of His messengers. And they say: we hear and we obey; grant us, Thou our Lord, Thy forgiveness; unto Thee is the ultimate becoming (Surah 2:185).*

They made their descent through the seven Heavens even as they had ascended. The Prophet said: "On my return, when I passed Moses–and what a good friend he was unto you!–he asked me: 'How many prayers have been laid upon thee?' I told him fifty prayers every day and he said: 'The congregational prayer is a weighty thing, and thy people are weak. Return unto thy Lord, and ask Him to lighten the load for thee and thy people.' So I returned and asked my Lord to make it lighter, and He took away ten. Then I passed Moses again, and he repeated what he had said before, so I returned again, and ten more prayers were taken from me. But every time I returned unto Moses he sent me back until finally all the prayers had been taken from me except five for each day and night. Then I returned unto Moses, but still he said the same as before; and I said: 'I have returned unto my Lord and asked Him until I am ashamed. I will not go again.' And so it is that he who performeth the five in good faith and in trust of God's bounty, unto him shall be given the meed of fifty prayers."

When the Prophet and the Archangel had made their descent to the Rock at Jerusalem, they returned to Mecca the way they had come, overtaking many southbound caravans. It was still night when they reached the Ka'bah (Lings, pp. 101-103, italics in orig.).

A believer in the Bible has no problem with the **miraculous** element of the story. The Bible is filled with the miraculous. But the miracles of the Bible have plausible purpose and meaning attached to them–i.e., to confirm or authenticate the spoken Word (see Miller, 2003c). They do not reek of fairytales. While the entire episode raises incredulous eyebrows in itself, the details of the trip serve only to strengthen this initial impression. Why does the steed have **wings**? Why does the steed have a **name**? Why fly first to **Jerusalem** before ascending to heaven, rather than making the trip to heaven directly from Mecca? Why meet up with **Abraham, Moses, and Jesus** in Jerusalem before proceeding? Why should the central purpose of the trip be to ascertain **the number of prayers** to be uttered by Muslims, when many other facets of religious practice besides prayer would surely merit as much, if not more, attention on such a momentous trip?

Allah's initial requirement of fifty prayers per day is surely ludicrous to the person who is acquainted with the God of the Bible. The God of the Bible would not place such a mandate on humans. In fact, the time and effort that would be required to achieve this requirement would hamper—if not physically prevent—performance of the many other aspects of godly living that are equally necessary to please God. The number is typical of what an **un**inspired human would first "float" in an effort to achieve compliance with a final lesser amount. Couple this accommodation with the allowance of **dirt** as a substitute for **water** in the prefatory ablutions to the prayers (*Surah* 4:43; 5:6), and the credulity of Islam is stretched even farther. The God of the Bible would not so act. Water immersion is stipulated in the New Testament as prerequisite to salvation (e.g., Matthew 29:19; Mark 16:16; John 3:5; Acts 2:38). If dirt may be substituted for water in regard to prayer, surely some other substance would be allowable in place of water immersion. However, **no such substitution is permissible**.

The emphasis on location, wherein a site is set aside and revered as a holy spot to be visited, also reflects negatively upon the credibility of the account. Mosaic religion in the Old Testament certainly singled out Jerusalem as the central point of Jewish worship. After all, the land had been promised to the genetic descendants of Abraham (Genesis 12:7; 13:15; 15:7,18), and that was where the permanent Temple eventually was built to carry out atonement procedures (2 Samuel 7:13; 1 Kings 5:5; 2 Chronicles 5:1). However, God repudiated the misconception that evolved among the Jews that "holy sites" held any validity in the observance of Bible religion (2 Samuel 7:4ff.; Isaiah 66:1;

Matthew 23:16ff.; Acts 7:48; 17:24). The locations, objects, and events of Mosaic religion were, in fact, "types and shadows" that merely pointed to the higher spiritual realities that would come with Christianity (Colossians 2:17; Hebrews 8:5; 9:23ff.; 10:1).

Corrupt forms of Judaism and Christianity, to which Muhammad would have been exposed in the sixth and seventh centuries, placed unbiblical emphasis on "holy sites" and ritualistic tradition. Rather than seeing through these travesties, and recognizing them as the result of human invention unsanctioned by the Bible, Muhammad instead copied and adapted the concept as fundamentally legitimate. In fact, selecting Jerusalem as the point from which he claimed to have ascended to heaven demonstrates that Muhammad possessed a regard for the city that was formed by contemporaneous Jews and/or Christians—a regard that demonstrates a misunderstanding of the stature of the city from the **biblical** point of view. Jesus spoke to this issue very clearly in His interaction with the Samaritan woman:

> The woman said to Him, "Sir, I perceive that You are a prophet. Our fathers worshiped on this mountain, and you Jews say that in Jerusalem is the place where one ought to worship." Jesus said to her, "Woman, believe Me, the hour is coming when you will neither on this mountain, nor in Jerusalem, worship the Father. You worship what you do not know; we know what we worship, for salvation is of the Jews. But the hour is coming, and now is, when the true worshipers will worship the Father in spirit and truth; for the Father is seeking such to worship Him. God is Spirit, and those who worship Him must worship in spirit and truth" (John 4:19-24).

His declaration discounts the legitimacy of so-called "holy" places, shrines, and temples. Under New Testament Christianity, there is no place on Earth that is more "holy" than any other place. Only corrupt forms of Judaism and/or Christianity would fail to grasp this conception.

Similarly, the extent to which Muhammad's notions were the result of corrupt Christian sources is further seen in the fact that the *Hadith* liken his purported trip to heaven "to others before him" including Enoch, Elijah, Jesus, and Mary. The Bible does represent both Enoch and Elijah as having been taken miraculously by God into eternity without experiencing physical death (Genesis 5:24; 2 Kings 2:11; Hebrews 11:5). Of course, they did not return to Earth. Neither is it recorded that they entered into the presence of God in heaven (John 3:13; cf. Lyons, 2003a). On the other hand, Jesus ascended in bodily form at the end of His life on Earth with no intention of setting foot on the Earth again, and is in heaven at the right hand of God (Luke 24:51; Acts 1:2,9-11; 1 Thessalonians 4:17; Mark 16:19; Romans 8:34). Apart from these three personages, the Bible gives absolutely no indication that the earthly mother of Jesus, Mary, circumvented physical death or ascended to heaven. This notion was derived from the corrupt brand of Christianity propagated by Catholicism that advocates the doctrine of the "Bodily Assumption of Mary" (Abbott, 1966, p. 90). The *Hadith* exemplify the fact that Muhammad was unwittingly deceived by the corrupt forms of Judaism and Christianity to which he was exposed.

CONCLUSION

Many additional reported incidents in the *Hadith* could be considered that bring the credibility of Islam into question in the mind of an honest, objective seeker of truth. But these instances are sufficient to illustrate the point. Nevertheless, the ultimate test rests with the Quran itself. The religion of Islam depends upon the inspiration of the Quran for its authenticity and legitimacy, even as Christianity depends upon the inspiration of the Bible. If the Quran manifests attributes that are inconsistent with its claim of divine inspiration, then it is demonstrated to be the work of man—not God. The reader is invited to give consideration to the evidences set forth in the subsequent chapters that call into question the Quran's claim to inspiration.

Chapter 4

JEWISH ORIGINS

The Quran (meaning "recitation") originally made its appearance in Arabic–the language of the Arabs who lived in the Arabian Peninsula in the sixth and seventh centuries A.D. It is divided into 114 "surahs" (a designation that is roughly equivalent to the Bible's own current division into "chapters") and over 6,000 verses. It is thought that eighty-six surahs were revealed in Mecca, and twenty-eight in Medina (Braswell, 2000, p. 24), although the traditional order of the Quran is not chronological. The process took place over a twenty-three year period (A.D. 610-632), allegedly "through the agency of the archangel of revelation, Gabriel" (Nasr, 2002, p. 22; cf. *Surah* 2:97; 26:192-195; 42:51-52). Whereas the Bible consists of a collection of distinct books (with no chapter or verse divisions in its originally released form), each with its own inspired author, purpose, theme, and historical setting, the Quran is a collection of self-contained surahs. Muslims claim that the Quran is "pure Divine Word" that "flowed through the Prophet's heart" (Rahman, 1979, p. 33). An editorial "we" is used throughout to represent Allah speaking. [More will be said about the text of the Quran in chapter 6.]

THE INFLUENCE OF
EXTRABIBLICAL JUDAISM

In the quest to ascertain whether the Quran is of divine origin, the first evidence that calls the credibility of the Quran into question is its extensive reliance on uninspired contemporaneous Jewish sources. While much has been written on the influence of uninspired sources on the production of the Quran, including Jewish, Christian (especially Syriac [Gibb, 1953, pp. 25-27] and the Apocrypha [Rodwell, 1950, p. 119, notes #3,4]), Zoastrian, Arabian, et al. (e.g., Bell, 1925; Geiger, 1896; Goldsack, 1907; Jenkinson, 1931; Mingana, 1927; Tisdall, 1905), the present study confines itself to a sampling of the demonstrable links to Judaism.

The issue is not whether the Quran shares content in common with uninspired, secular sources. An inspired book would naturally be expected to allude to matters that are of relevance to, and being discussed by, people at large. It would be expected to make pronouncements and speak authoritatively on its own, though its affirmations are coincidentally concomitant with those of an uninspired nature. It might even incorporate into itself statements that are also made in uninspired sources simply because those statements are true (cf. Smith, 2003; Jackson, 2002). To do so does not leave the book open to the charge of being uninspired, or guilty of plagiarism, even as it is faulty to postulate that since a human and a cow share in common possession of a head, eyes, ears, nose, and legs, the one must have come from the other. Rather, the central issue is whether the features of the Quran that are shared in common with uninspired Jewish sources are of such a nature as to prove that the Quran is of human origin.

Arabia in the sixth and seventh centuries was essentially oral in its social interaction, i.e., the population relied primarily, if not exclusively, on oral traditions and story-telling for its daily social interaction. Muslims insist that Muhammad himself was illiterate (e.g., Pickthall, p. xi; cf. *Surah* 7:157). Though an unproven claim, it nevertheless illustrates the widespread recognition that Arabians at the time were in the same general condition as their medieval European counterparts. During those Dark Ages, roving minstrels, wandering poets, and lyricists supplied the population with a steady diet of literary amusement. The Arabs of Muhammad's day included a sizeable Jewish community, especially in Yathrib (Medina), whose religious viewpoints would have been widely circulated and hence well known. As wealthy and successful merchants, whose staunch monotheism stood out in stark contrast to the pagan, polytheistic Arab majority, the Jews of Arabia unquestionably exerted a powerful influence on Muhammad's Arabia. The author of the Quran clearly reflects a healthy respect for the Jews (e.g., *Surah* 2:146; 6:20)– even though this respect eventually took a back seat to Muhammad's determination to bring them into submission to Islam.

The brand of Judaism to which Muhammad was exposed, like Christianity at the time, was a corrupt one. Literally centuries of legend, myth, and fanciful folklore had accumulated among the Jews, reported in the Talmud, the Midrash, and the Targumim. These three Jewish sources were replete with **uninspired** rabbinical commentary and speculation. These tales and fables would have existed in Arabia in oral form as they were told and retold at Bedouin campfires, among the traveling trade caravans that crisscrossed the desert, and in the towns, villages, and centers of social interaction from Yemen in the southern Arabian Peninsula, to Abyssinia to the west, and Palestine, Syria, and Persia to the north.

The evidence indicates that Muhammad had frequent contact with Arabian Jews–a fact conceded even by Muslim scholars (e.g., Pickthall, p. 32). The Quran itself verifies this contact repeatedly. For example, on one occasion Muhammad defended his claim to prophethood by insisting that the Scriptures of the Jews predicted his own coming: "And lo, it is in the Scriptures of the men of old. Is it not a token for them that **the doctors of the Children of Israel** know it?" (*Surah* 26:197, emp. added). Muhammad obviously had sufficient interaction with the Jews, even learned ones, to justify claiming them as verification of his own views. This appeal to the Jews—in an attempt to bolster his own credibility and deflect the charge of having invented his revelations—is common in the Quran (e.g., 3:69,75; 5:44,63; 10: 94-95; 16:103; 25:4-5; 46:9-10). These Jews undoubtedly would have related popular Jewish stories from the rabbinical literature of the day—a strictly **oral** transference. The evidence indicates "the Jews of Arabia were not learned men, and that they were better acquainted with the fables of the Talmud than with the Bible" (Tisdall, 1905, p. 92). Since Muhammad likely had no direct contact with the Bible, he would have assumed that the tales told by the Jews were, in fact, accurate **biblical** accounts.

If the author of the Quran was not actually inspired of God, one would expect him to acquire his ideas either from his own fertile imagination, from external sources, or from both. Due to his respect for the powerful Jewish tribes, and his desire to gain their assent to his claim to be an extension of the previous Jewish prophets, one naturally would expect Muhammad to incorporate (with embellishment and modification) Jewish tales that were current among his contemporaries, into his Quranic utterances. Of course, one would not necessarily expect to find these Talmudic and Midrash stories transferred to the Quran word for word, for three reasons: (1) he naturally would alter them sufficiently to create the illusion of the stories having been acquired by him independent of contemporaneous circulation; (2) his acquaintance with the stories most surely would have come through word of mouth—secondhand oral sources—rather than written documents; and (3) they came to him from Hebrew into Arabic, and now, in the present attempt to compare them, both must be examined in English. Keep in mind that when a story is transmitted orally, one would expect many of the original details to be dropped or modified. One would fully expect the hearer of these stories, in this case ostensibly Muhammad, to key into those points that intrigued his own unique individuality and that appealed to his own peculiar mental patterns as memorable. Sayfush-Shaytaan alluded to this tendency:

When an individual comes into contact with a story, they understand it in light of so many past experiences. The fact that each individual leads a wholly unique life makes for different understandings (no matter how minor) of the same story. **This change in understanding will cause the story to enter an altered state** when it is related to the next link in the chain of transmitters (n.d., emp. added).

Nevertheless, despite these indirect and diluted transferals, the evidence that the Quran contains a considerable amount of borrowed material from **uninspired** Talmudic sources, rabbinical oral traditions, and Jewish legends—stories that abound in puerile, apocryphal, absurd, outlandish pablum—is self-evident and unmistakable. In the words of Charles Torrey: "It is perfectly evident that Mohammed's source was an already fixed collection of Jewish tales, existing at Mekka, in whatever manner he may have received them" (1933).

[NOTE: In order to facilitate objectivity and impartiality, the following treatment of the Quran rests on two Muslim translations. The primary text employed is that of Mohammed Pickthall, originally published in London in 1930, one of the most widely used translations done by an English man of letters who converted to Islam. His translation faithfully represents the sense of the original, though his use of archaic English tends to be cumbersome for the average reader. Pickthall's translation was diligently compared with that of Abdullah Yusuf Ali, a highly readable and extremely popular translation, originally published in 1934 in Lahore, Pakistan. Additional translations occasionally consulted and compared include those of George Sale (originally published in London in 1734), J.M. Rodwell (published in London in 1861), and N.J. Dawood—an Iraqi Jew born in Baghdad (also published in London in 1956). Unless otherwise noted, the translations from the Talmud, Midrash, and other Jewish literature were done by the highly respected and widely reputed Jewish German scholar Louis Ginzberg, outstanding Talmudist of the twentieth century, whose monumental multi-volume se-

ries, *The Legends of the Jews* (1909-1939), was a compendium of
the best-known and most widely circulated extrabiblical Jewish
legends, culled and collected from the original rabbinical Talmudic, Midrashim, and Targumim literature, as well as from additional legendary sources.]

The reader is invited to give consideration to the following
samples, wherein Jewish legend and the Quran coincide:

Abraham and the Idols

As one would expect, the Quran has a great deal to say about
Abraham. Once again, much of what it says is not found in the
Bible. However, many of the details are found among the contemporaneously circulating rabbinical stories of the Jewish community. For example, the Quran asserts that Abraham experienced a hostile encounter with his father over idol worship: "Remember when Abraham said unto his father Azar: Takest thou
idols for gods? Lo! I see thee and thy folk in error manifest" (*Surah*
6:75; cf. vss. 76-84). The fuller account is found in *Surah* 21:

> And We verily gave Abraham of old his proper course,
> and We were Aware of him, when he said unto his father
> and his folk: What are these **images unto which ye pay
> devotion**? They said: We found our fathers worship-
> pers of them. He said: Verily ye and your fathers were in
> plain error. They said: Bringest thou unto us the truth, or
> art thou some jester? He said: Nay, but your Lord is the
> Lord of the heavens and the earth, Who created them;
> and I am of those who testify unto that. And, by Allah, I
> shall circumvent your idols **after ye have gone away**
> and turned your backs. Then he **reduced them to frag-
> ments**, all save the chief of them, that haply they might
> have recourse to it. They said: **Who hath done this to
> our gods?** Surely it must be some evil-doer. They said:
> We heard a youth make mention of them, who is called
> Abraham. They said: Then bring him (hither) before the
> people's eyes that they may testify. They said: Is it thou
> who hast done this to our gods, O Abraham? He said:
> But this, **their chief hath done it**. So question them, if
> they can speak. Then gathered they apart and said: Lo!

ye yourselves are the wrong-doers. And they were utterly confounded, and they said: Well thou knowest that **these speak not**. He said: Worship ye then instead of Allah that which cannot profit you at all, nor harm you? Fie on you and all that ye worship instead of Allah! **Have ye then no sense?** They cried: **Burn him** and stand by your gods, if ye will be doing. We said: **O fire, be coolness and peace for Abraham**. And they wished to set a snare for him, but We made them the greater losers. And **We rescued him** and Lot (and brought them) to the land which We have blessed for (all) peoples (*Surah* 21:51-71; cf. 19:41-49, emp. added).

The rabbinic version of this incident that circulated prior to the advent of Islam (Sayfush-Shaytaan, 2002) was eventually codified in *Midrash Breishit Rabbah* (38:13):

And Haran died in front of Terach his father. R. Hiyya the grandson of R. Ada of Yafo [said]: **Terach was an idolater.** One day **he went out somewhere**, and put Avraham in charge of selling [the idols]. When a man would come who wanted to purchase, he would say to him: "How old are you"? [The customer] would answer: "Fifty or sixty years old." [Avraham] would say: "Woe to the man who is sixty years old and desires to worship something one day old." [The customer] would be ashamed and leave. One day a woman came, carrying in her hand a basket of fine flour. She said: "Here, offer it before them." Abraham seized a stick, and **smashed all the idols**, and placed the stick in the hand of the biggest of them. When his father came, he said to him: **"Who did this to them?"** [Avraham] said: "Would I hide anything from my father? A woman came, carrying in her hand a basket of fine flour. She said: "Here, offer it before them." When I offered it, one god said: "I will eat first," and another said, "No, I will eat first." Then **the biggest of them** rose up and smashed all the others. [His father] said: "Are you making fun of me? **Do they know anything?**" [Avraham] answered: **Shall your ears not hear what your mouth is saying?** He took [Avraham] and handed him over to Nimrod. [Nimrod] said to him: "Let us worship the fire." [Avraham] said to him: "If so, let us worship the water which extinguishes the fire." [Nimrod] said to him: "Let us worship the water." [Avraham] said to him: "If so, let us worship the clouds which bear the water." [Nimrod] said to him: "Let us worship the clouds." [Avraham] said to him: "If so, let us worship the wind which scatters the clouds." [Nimrod] said to him: "Let us worship the wind." [Avraham] said to him: "If so, let us worship man who withstands the wind." [Nimrod] said to him: "You are speaking nonsense; I only bow to the fire. **I will throw you into it.** Let the God to Whom you bow come and save you from it." Haran was there. He said [to himself] "Either way; If Avraham is successful, I will say that I am with Avraham; If Nimrod is successful, I will say that I am with Nimrod." Once **Avraham went into the furnace and was saved**, they asked [Haran]: "With which one are you [allied]"? He said to them: "I am with Avraham." They took him and threw him into the fire and his bowels were burned out. He came out and died in front of Terach his father. This is the meaning of the verse: And Haran died in front of Terach (Sayfush-Shaytaan, n.d., emp. added; cf. Ginzberg, 1909, 1:195-202).

Observe the points of commonality (as indicated by boldface type) between the midrashic account and that found in the Quran: (1) Abraham's father and kinfolk are depicted as idol worshippers; (2) Abraham smashes the idols into pieces; (3) this action is taken while the idolaters are absent; (4) the question is raised as to who was responsible; (5) when confronted, Abraham blames the demolition on the biggest idol; (6) it is admitted by his accuser(s) that the idols cannot speak/know; (7) Abraham raises a question that convicts his accuser(s)' of their own disbelief in idols; (8) Abraham is subjected to being burned; (9) he is divinely protected from the effects of the fire. In the ancient midrashic accounts (*Pesachim* 118a; *Shemoth Rabbah* 8:5; *Devarim Rabbah* 2:29; et al.), Gabriel prepares to rescue Abraham by asking him, "Abraham, shall I save thee from the fire?" Abraham's response is, "God in whom I trust, the God of heaven and earth, will rescue me." God was so impressed with Abraham's zeal that He decided to intervene Himself, and commanded the fire, **"Cool off and bring tranquility to my servant Abraham."** A literal rendering of the words would be **"May cooling and comfort be granted to My servant Abraham"** (Ginzberg, 1909, 1:201; 1925, 5:212). Observe how closely the Quranic account resembles the midrashic account: "O fire, **be coolness and peace for Abraham"** (*Surah* 21:69). Once again, the parallel between the Quranic account and the midrashic legend is too striking to be coincidental. The author of the Quran undoubtedly heard this story from discussions with Jews, who left him with the impression that the story was biblical.

The Quranic account is clearly adapted to coincide with the cultural circumstances Muhammad was then facing, i.e., resistance from his contemporaries to monotheism due to the entrenched practice of polytheism inherited from their Arab ancestors. The author of the Quran placed his own homiletical admonitions into the mouth of a biblical character, in this case Abraham: "We found our fathers worshippers of them. He said: Verily ye and your fathers were in plain error" (*Surah* 21:53-54; cf. 9: 114; 26:70-76; 29:16; 37:85; 43:26; 60:4).

Joseph

While the Quran is laced with many allusions to incidents and characters reported in the Bible, *Surah* 12 is the only surah that is devoted in its entirety to a single character: Joseph. The differences from the Bible narrative are striking. On the other hand, multiple commonalities exist between the Quran's version and those propagated by Jewish folklore. The following ten major correlating features (and several additional sub-features) are commended to the reader's attention.

In the first place, whereas the Bible indicates that Jacob sent Joseph to check on the well-being of his brothers (Genesis 37: 14), the Quran represents Joseph's brothers as requesting that Jacob allow Joseph to accompany them on their outing the following day for the purpose of **recreation**: "They said: O our father! Why wilt thou not trust us with Joseph, when lo! we are good friends to him? Send him with us to-morrow that he may **enjoy himself and play**. And lo! we shall take good care of him" (*Surah* 12:11-12, emp. added). Post-biblical, pre-Quranic Jewish literature (*Midrash Breishit Rabbah* 84:8-10; *Mishle* 26:99; et al.) states: "Once the brethren of Joseph led their father's flocks to the pastures of Shechem, and they intended **to take their ease and pleasure there**" (Ginzberg, 1910, 2:10, emp. added). Both accounts share in common the unbiblical allusion to recreation being part of the reason for the trip away from home.

Second, whereas the Bible states that the brothers claimed that Joseph was devoured by "a wild beast" (Genesis 37:20,33), the Quran places into the mouths of both Jacob and his sons the precise identity of the alleged predator:

> He said: Lo! in truth it saddens me that ye should take him with you, and I fear lest **the wolf** devour him while ye are heedless of him. They said: If **the wolf** should devour him when we are (so strong) a band, then surely we should have already perished. Then, when they led him off, and were of one mind that they should place him in the depth of the pit, We inspired in him: Thou wilt tell them of this deed of theirs when they know (thee) not. And they came weeping to their father in the evening. Saying: O our father! We went racing one with another, and left Joseph by our things, and **the wolf** devoured him, and thou believest not our sayings even when we speak the truth (*Surah* 12:13-17, emp. added).

Uninspired Jewish legend (*Yashar Wayesheb* 85a-85b) had already supplied this obscure detail:

> The sons of Jacob set out on the morrow to do the bidding of their father, while he remained at home and wept and lamented for Joseph. In the wilderness they found **a wolf**, which they caught and brought to Jacob alive, saying: "Here is the first wild beast we encountered, and we have brought it to thee. But of thy son's corpse we saw not a trace." Jacob seized **the wolf**, and, amid loud weeping, he addressed these words to him: "Why didst thou devour my son Joseph...?" To grant consolation to Jacob, God opened the mouth of the beast, and he spake:

"As the Lord liveth, who hath created me, and as thy soul liveth, my lord, I have not seen thy son, and I did not rend him in pieces...." Astonished at the speech of **the wolf,** Jacob let him go, unhindered, whithersoever he would, but he mourned his son Joseph as before (Ginzberg, 1910, 2:25, emp. added).

Third, the Quran claims that Joseph was retrieved from the pit, into which his brothers had placed him, not by the brothers as the Bible reports (Genesis 37:28), but by a passing caravan: "And there came a caravan, and they sent their waterdrawer. He let down his pail (into the pit). He said: Good luck! Here is a youth. And they hid him as a treasure, and Allah was Aware of what they did" (*Surah* 12:19). Once again, Jewish folklore (*Yashar Wayesheb* 81b-82a) is the source of this detail:

While the brethren of Joseph were deliberating upon his fate, seven Midianitish merchantmen passed near the pit in which he lay. They noticed that many birds were circling above it, whence they assumed that there must be water therein, and, being thirsty, they made a halt in order to refresh themselves. When they came close, they heard Joseph screaming and wailing, and they looked down into the pit and saw a youth of beautiful figure and comely appearance. They called to him, saying: "Who art thou? Who brought thee hither, and who cast thee into this pit in the wilderness?" **They all joined together and dragged him up**, and took him along with them when they continued on their journey (Ginzberg, 2:15, emp. added).

Fourth, Joseph's sale price is represented in the Quran as a meager remuneration–a mere pittance–without specifying the exact amount: "And they sold him for **a low price**, a number of silver coins; and **they attached no value to him**" (*Surah* 12:20, emp. added). The Bible reports the actual amount (twenty pieces of silver) without offering an evaluative comment on whether such a price was high or low (Genesis 37:28). However, Jewish legend (*Tanchuma Wayesheb* 2; *Midrash Hagadol* 564; et al.), which retained the specific biblical amount, supplied the additional detail regarding comparative value:

The price paid for Joseph by the Midianites was twenty pieces of silver, enough for a pair of shoes for each of his brethren. Thus "they sold the righteous for silver, and the needy for a pair of shoes." For so handsome a youth as Joseph **the sum paid was too low by far**, but his appearance had been greatly changed by the horrible anguish he had endured in the pit with the snakes and the scorpions. He had lost his ruddy complexion, and he looked sallow and sickly, and the Midianites were justified in paying **a small sum** for him (Ginzberg, 2:16, emp. added).

Fifth, the Quran gives considerable attention to the events involving Potiphar's wife's attempted sexual seduction of Joseph. The reader is urged to read the Bible account and observe its simplicity and dignity, as well as its avoidance of superfluous embellishment so typical of human curiosity and human propensity for invention and elaboration (Genesis 39:7-20). In stark contrast to this majestic account, the Quran serves up an eyebrow-raising rendition [the reader is urged to pay special attention to the words in boldface type for points of comparison]:

And she, in whose house he was, asked of him an evil act. She bolted the doors and said: Come! He said: I seek refuge in Allah! Lo! he is my lord, who hath treated me honourably. Wrong-doers never prosper. She verily desired him, and **he would have desired her if it had not been that he saw the argument of his Lord.** Thus it was, **that We might ward off** from him evil and lewdness. Lo! he was of Our chosen slaves. And they raced with one another to the door, and **she tore his shirt from behind**, and they met her lord and master at the door. She said: What shall be his reward, who wisheth evil to thy folk, save prison or a painful doom? (Joseph) said: She it was who asked of me an evil act. And **a witness of her own folk** testified: If his shirt is torn from before, then she speaketh truth and he is of the liars. And **if his shirt is torn from behind**, then she hath lied and he is of the truthful. So when he saw his shirt torn from behind, he said: Lo! this is of the guile of you women.

Lo! the guile of you is very great. **O Joseph! Turn away from this**, and thou, (O woman), ask forgiveness for thy sin. Lo! thou art of the sinful.

And women in the city said: The ruler's wife is asking of her slave-boy an ill deed. Indeed he has **smitten her to the heart with love**. We behold her in plain aberration. And when she heard of their sly talk, she sent to them and prepared for them a cushioned couch (to lie on at the feast) and **gave to every one of them a knife** and said (to Joseph): Come out unto them! And **when they saw him they exalted him and cut their hands**, exclaiming: Allah Blameless! This is not a human being. This is no other than some gracious angel. She said: This is he on whose account ye blamed me. I asked of him an evil act, but he proved continent, but if he do not my behest he verily shall be imprisoned, and verily shall be of those brought low. He said: O my Lord! Prison is more dear than that unto which they urge me, and if Thou fend not off their wiles from me I shall incline unto them and become of the foolish. So his Lord heard his prayer and fended off their wiles from him. Lo! He is Hearer, Knower. And it seemed good to them (the men-folk) after they had seen **the signs (of his innocence) to imprison him for a time** (*Surah* 12:23-35, emp. added).

This account contains many details that are completely foreign to the biblical record. However, one who is familiar with the legends and folklore prominent among Jews in the sixth century A.D. is not the least surprised at these curious additions to the original, authentic account found in the Bible. In the rabbinical folklore, the discussions of Potiphar's wife (whose name is even provided–Zuleika) place exceptional emphasis (*ad nauseam*) on her intense, sustained obsession with Joseph (see Ginzberg, 2:39-52). They depict her as being completely given over to doing everything within her power to secure Joseph's sexual submission–everything from threatening to have him thrown into prison, to offering to murder her own husband (2:42). This overemphasis is undoubtedly preserved and reflected in the Quran's own allusion to the Egyptian women's comment: "And women in the city said: The ruler's wife is asking of her slave-boy an ill deed. Indeed **he has smitten her to the heart with love**. We behold her in plain aberration" (*Surah* 12:30, emp. added). Muslim translator, Abdullah Yusuf Ali, renders the verse even more emphatically: "Ladies said in the City: 'The wife of the (great) Aziz is seeking to seduce her slave from his (true) self: Truly **he has inspired her with violent love**: we see she is evidently going astray'" (1934, p. 146, emp. added). Jewish sources are the origin of the exaggerated emphasis on the woman's passion.

The Quran suggests that in facing the sexual advances of Potiphar's wife, Joseph was tempted to give in to his own sexual impulses—if it had not been for "the argument of his Lord" (i.e., Allah) who intervened and "warded off from him evil and lewdness." What was this "argument" of Allah that prevented Joseph from succumbing to Potiphar's wife? The Quran does not elaborate. But the rabbinical legends supply unmistakable clarification (*Sotah* 36b; Jerusalem Talmud *Horayoth* 2,46d; *Tanchuma Wayesheb* 9; *Yashar Wayesheb* 88a; *Midrash Breshit Rabbah* 87:7; 98:20; *Midrash Shemuel* 5, 63; *Midrash Shir* 1:1; et al.). On one occasion, she made elaborate preparations in hopes of ensnaring him upon his return from outdoors duties:

> Then Zuleika stood before him suddenly in all her beauty of person and magnificence of raiment, and repeated the desire of her heart. It was the first and the last time that Joseph's steadfastness deserted him, but only for an instant. **When he was on the point of complying** with the wish of his mistress, the image of his mother Rachel appeared before him, and that of his aunt Leah, and the image of his father Jacob. The last addressed him thus: "In time to come the names of thy brethren will be graven upon the breastplate of the high priest. Dost thou desire to have thy name appear with theirs? Or wilt thou forfeit this honor through sinful conduct? For know, he that keepeth company with harlots wasteth his substance." **This vision of the dead, and especially the image of his father, brought Joseph to his senses**, and his illicit passion departed from him (Ginzberg, 2:46-47, emp. added).

Without this clarification, the Quranic account is seen to be piece-meal, puzzling, and incomplete. It leaves the distinct impression that something is missing. Familiar with the Jewish legend, the author of the Quran merely had to insert a vague reference to the incident in order to achieve credibility for the purported revelation he was presenting to his contemporaries, who instantly would have recognized the allusion.

Additionally, the Quran speaks of Joseph making a mad dash for the door—with Potiphar's wife in hot pursuit. She tore his shirt "from behind." Of course, the biblical account says no such thing. It indicates that she grabbed his outer tunic, but he allowed it to slip off of his body intact (Genesis 39:12). Nothing is said of the garment being torn—let alone being torn **from behind**. Once again, the Jewish sources (*Midrash Hagadol* 589; Abkir in *Midrash Yalkut* 145-146; *Yashar Wayesheb* 88a-89a; *Midrash Breishit Rabbah* 87:8; *Targum Yerushalmi* 39:14; et al.) account for the added details in the following excerpts:

> Joseph fled forth, away from the house of his mistress.... But hardly was he outside when the sinful passion again overwhelmed him, and he returned to Zuleika's chamber. Then the Lord appeared unto him, holding the Eben Shetiyah in His hand, and said to him: "If thou touchest her, I will cast away this stone upon which the earth is founded, and the world will fall to ruin." Sobered again, Joseph started to escape from his mistress, but Zuleika **caught him by his garment**, and she said: "As the king liveth, if thou wilt not fulfil my wish, thou must die," and while she spoke thus, she drew a sword with her free hand from under her dress, and, pressing it against Joseph's throat, she said, "Do as I bid thee, or thou diest." Joseph ran out, **leaving a piece of his garment** in the hands of Zuleika as he wrenched himself loose from the grasp of the woman with a quick, energetic motion. Zuleika's passion for Joseph was so **violent** that, in lieu of its owner, whom she could not succeed in subduing to her will, she kissed and caressed **the fragment of cloth left in her hand** (Ginzberg, 2:47, emp. added).

Realizing that Joseph might report her actions, Zuleika decided to protect herself by accusing him first. She spoke first to some of the other males in the household:

> You had scarcely gone away to the festival when he entered the house, and making sure that no one was here he tried to force me to yield to his lustful desire. But **I grasped his clothes, tore them**, and cried with a loud voice (Ginzberg, 2:48, emp. added).

The men immediately report the information to Potiphar, who has Joseph flogged unmercifully and then brought to trial before priests who sat as judges. The test that these priestly judges apply in an effort to ascertain Joseph's guilt or innocence bears a striking resemblance to the one given in the Quran:

> The judges ordered the garment of Joseph to be brought which Zuleika had in her possession, and they **examined the tear** therein. It turned out to be on **the front part of the mantle**, and they came to the conclusion that Zuleika had tried to hold him fast, and had been foiled in her attempt by Joseph, against whom she was now lodging a trumped up charge. They decided that Joseph had not incurred the death penalty, but they condemned him to incarceration, because he was the cause of a stain upon Zuleika's fair name. **Potiphar himself was convinced of Joseph's innocence**, and when **he cast him into prison**, he said to him, "I know that thou art not guilty of so vile a crime, but I must put thee in durance, lest a taint cling to my children" (Ginzberg, 2:49-50, emp. added).

Observe that the judges found Joseph innocent of Zuleika's accusations based upon the location of the tear in Joseph's garment. While the Quran represents the tear as being on the back, this section of the Jewish Midrash places the tear in the front. But the matter is clarified in the midrashic accounts (*Targum Yerushalmi, Hadar, Da'at, Midrash Aggada, Pa'aneah, Shu'aib* on Gen. 47:22; et al. cf. Ginzberg, 1925, 5:362 note 340):

> It was the priests that made the suggestion to examine Joseph's torn garment, which his mistress had submitted as evidence of his guilt, and see whether the rent was

in front or in back. **If it was in back, it would show his innocence–he had turned to flee, and his temptress had clutched him so that the garment tore. But if the tear was in front, then it would be a proof of his guilt**–he had used violence with the woman, and she had torn the mantle in her efforts to defend her honor. **The angel Gabriel came and transferred the rent from the fore part to the back,** and the Egyptians were convinced of Joseph's innocence, and their scruples about raising him to the kingship were removed (Ginzberg, 2: 107, emp. added).

Not only does this Jewish report explain the origin of the Quranic account, it also gives insight as to why **Gabriel** is the sole revealer of revelation to Muhammad. A perusal of Jewish folklore reveals that Gabriel occupied a prominent position in his angelic role, surpassing and eclipsing the other angels (see the listing of citations in Ginzberg, 1938, 7:172-174). Whereas Gabriel is afforded exceptional visibility in both the Quran and the Jewish legends, in the totality of the sixty-six books of the Bible, Gabriel is mentioned **only four times**–and only in two books (Daniel 8: 16; 9:21; Luke 1:19,26)!

Also in both accounts, Potiphar is convinced of Joseph's innocence. In the Quran, he begs Joseph to let the entire matter pass, while in the Midrash he admits Joseph's innocence and excuses himself for what he must do. In both accounts Joseph still goes to prison–in the Jewish account in order to protect the reputations of Zuleika and her children, while the Quran omits the reason with the vague assertion: "And it seemed good to them (the menfolk) after they had seen the signs (of his innocence) to imprison him for a time" (*Surah* 12:35). Notice also that the Quran affirms for a second time that Joseph was close to succumbing to the sexual advances of Zuleika (and her friends), and so begged Allah to arrange for him to go to prison: "He said: O my Lord! Prison is more dear than that unto which they urge me, and if Thou fend not off their wiles from me **I shall incline unto them and become of the foolish**" (vs. 33, emp. added). This is a different Joseph than the one described in the biblical account.

Still another link is seen in the brief reference in the Quran to the fact that when Joseph attempted to counter her accusation by declaring his own innocence in the presence of Potiphar, someone within her household came to his defense: "(Joseph) said: She it was who asked of me an evil act. And a witness of her own folk testified" (*Surah* 12:26). Who was this in-house person who came to Joseph's aid? The Quran does not say. But the rabbinical sources do (*Yashar Wayesheb* 88a-89a; *Midrash Aggada*, Gen. 41:45; Abkir in *Midrash Yalkut* 146):

> Potiphar gave credence to her words, and he had Joseph flogged unmercifully. While the cruel blows fell upon him, he cried to God, "O Lord, Thou knowest that I am innocent of these things, and why should I die today on account of a false accusation by the hands of these uncircumcised, impious men?" **God opened the mouth of Zuleika's child**, a babe of but eleven months, and he spoke to the men that were beating Joseph, saying: "What is your quarrel with this man? Why do you inflict such evil upon him? Lies my mother doth speak, and deceit is what her mouth uttereth. This is the true tale of that which did happen," and the child proceeded to tell all that had passed–how Zuleika had tried first to persuade Joseph to act wickedly, and then had tried to force him to do her will. The people listened in great amazement. But the report finished, the child spake no word, as before. Abashed by the speech of his own infant son, Potiphar commanded his bailiffs to leave off from chastising Joseph, and the matter was brought into court, where priests sat as judges (Ginzberg, 2:49, emp. added).

It is at this point that the Jewish sources assign the discussion regarding the location of the tear in Joseph's garment to the judges, whereas the Quran places the same discussion in the mouth of the household witness.

Yet another parallel between the Quran and Jewish commentary in the telling of the story of Potiphar's wife is the reference to her female friends–the women of the city. At first, they are critical of her obsession with Joseph. Zuleika handles their gossip by inviting them to her home:

And women in the city said: The ruler's wife is asking of her slave-boy an ill deed. Indeed he has smitten her to the heart with love. We behold her in plain aberration. And **when she heard of their sly talk, she sent to them** and **prepared for them a cushioned couch** (to lie on at the feast) and **gave to every one of them a knife** and said (to Joseph): **Come out unto them!** And **when they saw him they exalted him and cut their hands,** exclaiming: Allah Blameless! **This is not a human being. This is no other than some gracious angel.** She said: This is he **on whose account ye blamed me. I asked of him an evil act, but he proved continent** (*Surah* 12:31-32, emp. added).

The Quranic account is puzzling. Why did Zuleika give them knives? And why did they cut their hands upon seeing Joseph enter the room? These details make no sense—unless the author had heard an oral account of the Jewish folklore on the matter (*Sepher Hayashar* 87a-87b; *Tanchuma Wayesheb* 5; cf. Abkir in *Midrash Yalkut* 146; *Midrash Hagadol* 590):

When Zuleika could not prevail upon him, to persuade him, her desire threw her into a grievous sickness, and all the women of Egypt came to visit her, and they said unto her, "Why art thou so languid and wasted, thou that lackest nothing? Is not thy husband a prince great and esteemed in the sight of the king? Is it possible that thou canst want aught of what thy heart desireth?" Zuleika answered them, saying, "**This day shall it be made known unto you whence cometh the state wherein you see me.**"

She commanded her maid-servants to prepare food for all the women, and **she spread a banquet before them** in her house. **She placed knives upon the table** to peel the oranges, and then **ordered Joseph to appear**, arrayed in costly garments, and wait upon her guests. **When Joseph came in, the women could not take their eyes off him, and they all cut their hands with the knives,** and the oranges in their hands were covered with blood, but they, not knowing what they were doing, continued to look upon the beauty of Joseph without turning their eyes away from him.

Then Zuleika said unto them: "What have ye done? Behold, I set oranges before you to eat, and you have cut your hands." All the women looked at their hands, and, lo, they were full of blood, and it flowed down and stained their garments. They said to Zuleika, "**This slave in thy house did enchant us, and we could not turn our eyes away from him on account of his beauty**." She then said: "**This happened to you that looked upon him but a moment**, and you could not refrain yourselves! **How, then, can I control myself in whose house he abideth continually**, who see him go in and out day after day? How, then, should I not waste away, or keep from languishing on account of him!" And the women spake, saying: "It is true, who can look upon this beauty in the house, and refrain her feelings? But he is thy slave! Why dost thou not disclose to him that which is in thy heart, rather than suffer thy life to perish through this thing?" Zuleika answered them: "**Daily do I endeavor to persuade him, but he will not consent to my wishes**. I promised him everything that is fair, yet have **I met with no return from him**, and therefore I am sick, as you may see" (Ginzberg, 2:44-45, emp. added).

The multiple parallels are unmistakable. Notice the following nine (as indicated in boldface type above): In both accounts: (1) Potiphar's wife seeks to justify her lovesick condition to the women; (2) she does so by inviting them to a banquet; (3) each is given a knife as part of the table place setting; (4) she orders Joseph to make an appearance; (5) on seeing Joseph's handsome appearance, the women cut their hands with the knives; (6) the women verbally extol Joseph's looks; (7) Potiphar's wife verbalizes her sense of exoneration; (8) she verbally reaffirms to them that she attempted to seduce him; (9) but he refused to consent.

Sixth, the Quran indicates that, as a matter of fact, Jacob knew all along that Joseph was not actually dead—a fact he divulged in a conversation with his sons: "They said: By Allah, thou wilt never cease remembering Joseph till thy health is ruined or thou art of those who perish! He said: I expose my distress and anguish only unto Allah, and **I know from Allah that which ye know not**" (*Surah* 12:85-86, emp. added). A few verses later, when Jacob received the report of Joseph having revealed himself to his brothers, the Quran reports his reaction: "Said I not unto you that **I know from Allah that which ye know not?**" (vs. 96, emp. added). This notion flatly contradicts the biblical account, but it coincides perfectly with Jewish sources (*Soferim* 21; *Targum Yerushalmi* Gen. 37:33; *Midrash Breishit Rabbah* 84:21; 91:1,6; *Yashar Wayesheb* 85a; *Tanchuma Mikkez* 5; *Aggadat Bereshit* 69,136-138; *Midrash Hagadol* 632,635; et al.), which, as one would expect, provide extensive expansions of the concept that the author of the Quran would naturally have condensed and compressed:

> It is a law of nature that however much one may grieve over the death of a dear one, at the end of a year consolation finds its way to the heart of the mourner. But the disappearance of a living man can never be wiped out of one's memory. Therefore the fact that he was inconsolable **made Jacob suspect that Joseph was alive**, and he did not give entire credence to the report of his sons. His vague suspicion was strengthened by something that happened to him. He went up into the mountains, hewed twelve stones out of the quarry, and wrote the names of his sons thereon, their constellations, and the months corresponding to the constellations, a stone for a son, thus, "Reuben, Ram, Nisan," and so for each of his twelve sons. Then he addressed the stones and bade them bow down before the one marked with Reuben's name, constellation, and month, and they did not move. He gave the same order regarding the stone marked for Simon, and again the stones stood still. And so he did respecting all his sons, until he reached the stone for Joseph. When he spoke concerning this one, "I command you to fall down before Joseph," they all prostrated themselves. He tried the same test with other things, with trees and sheaves, and always the result was the same, and Jacob **could not but feel that his suspicion was true, Joseph was alive**.... And as God kept the truth a secret from Jacob, Isaac did not feel justified in acquainting him with his grandson's fate, **which was well known to him, for he was a prophet**. Whenever he was in the

company of Jacob, he mourned with him, but as soon as he quitted him, he left off from manifesting grief, **because he knew that Joseph lived** (Ginzberg, 2:26-27, emp. added).

The famine, which inflicted hardships first upon the wealthy among the Egyptians, gradually extended its ravages as far as Phoenicia, Arabia, and Palestine. Though the sons of Jacob, being young men, frequented the streets and the highways, yet they were ignorant of what their old home-keeping father Jacob knew, that corn could be procured in Egypt. **Jacob even suspected that Joseph was in Egypt.** His prophetic spirit, which forsook him during the time of his grief for his son, yet manifested itself now and again in dim visions, and he was resolved to send his sons down into Egypt (Ginzberg, 2: 68, emp. added).

One can see how the author of the Quran, hearing such detailed fabrications of biblical topics, and relying strictly on his memory of what he had heard, would naturally compress the narrative while simultaneously confusing and mixing some of the particulars. Whereas in the Quranic account, Jacob claims to have known all along that Joseph was alive, in the Jewish fables, Jacob, whose prophetic powers were dulled from grieving, suspicioned that Joseph was still alive, while Isaac, being a prophet, knew for certain that he was. The biblical record coincides with neither account.

Seventh, Jacob advised his sons on their second journey to Egypt not to enter the city by the same gate.

And he said: O my sons! **Go not in by one gate; go in by different gates.** I can naught avail you as against Allah. Lo! the decision rests with Allah only. In Him do I put my trust, and in Him let all the trusting put their trust. And when they entered in the manner which their father had enjoined, it would have naught availed them as against Allah; **it was but a need of Jacob's soul** which he thus satisfied; and lo! **he was a lord of knowledge** because We had taught him; but most of mankind know not (*Surah* 12:67-68, emp. added).

As usual, the Quran alludes to puzzling details without providing any explanation or clue to their significance. Why require the sons to avoid entering together through a single gate? The requirement was not an injunction of Allah, but merely a preference of Jacob due to his "knowledge." What knowledge? The rabbinical writings solve the mystery (*Midrash Breishit Rabbah* 91:6; *Midrash Hagadol* 635; *Midrash Mikkez 99b; Midrash Yalkut* 148; *Targum Yerushalmi* Gen. 42:5; et al.) by mentioning both the original admonition of Jacob as well as a subsequent reporting of the words in a letter he sent to the viceroy of Egypt:

> And as he knew that they were likely to attract attention, on account of their heroic stature and handsome appearance, **he cautioned them against going to the city all together through the same gate**, or, indeed, showing themselves all together anywhere in public, **that the evil eye be not cast upon them** (Ginzberg, 2:68, emp. added).

Jacob also put a letter addressed to the viceroy of Egypt into the hands of his son. The letter ran thus: "From thy servant Jacob, the son of Isaac, the grandson of Abraham, prince of God, to the mighty and wise king Zaphenathpaneah, the ruler of Egypt, peace! I make known unto my lord the king that the famine is sore with us in the land of Canaan, and I have therefore sent my sons unto thee, to buy us a little food, that we may live, and not die. My children surrounded me, and begged for something to eat, but, alas, I am very old, and I cannot see with mine eyes, for they are heavy with the weight of years, and also on account of my never-ceasing tears for my son Joseph, who hath been taken from me. I charged my sons **not to pass through the gate all together at the same time**, when they arrived in the city of Egypt, **in consideration of the inhabitants of the land, that they might not take undue notice of them**. Also I bade them go up and down in the land of Egypt and seek my son Joseph, mayhap they would find him there" (Ginzberg, 2:78, emp. added).

The midrashic accounts allude to the fact that Jacob did not want his many sons to call attention to themselves by clumping all together when they entered the city, lest they evoke jealousy from the citizens of the city. Pickthall includes a footnote in his translation of this section of the Quran that reads: "There is a prevalent superstition in the East that the members of a large family ought not to appear all together, for fear of the ill luck that comes from envy in the hearts of others" (p. 179). The Quran aligns itself with rabbinical writings in this regard.

Eighth, the Quran indicates that when the brothers returned to Egypt a second time, Joseph took Benjamin aside privately and revealed his identity to his little brother: "And when they went in before Joseph, he took his brother unto himself, saying: Lo; I, even I, am thy brother, therefore sorrow not for what they did" (*Surah* 12:69). The rabbinical writings (*Yashar Mikkez* 104b-105a) divulge this same detail:

> Joseph ordered his magic astrolabe to be brought to him, whereby he knew all things that happen, and he said unto Benjamin, "I have heard that the Hebrews are acquainted with all wisdom, but dost thou know aught of this?" Benjamin answered, "Thy servant also is skilled in all wisdom, which my father hath taught me." He then looked upon the astrolabe, and to his great astonishment he discovered by the aid of it that he who was sitting upon the throne before him was his brother Joseph. Noticing Benjamin's amazement, Joseph asked him, "What hast thou seen, and why art thou astonished?" Benjamin said, "I can see by this that Joseph my brother sitteth here before me upon the throne." And **Joseph said: "I am Joseph thy brother!** Reveal not the thing unto our brethren. I will send thee with them when they go away, and I will command them to be brought back again into the city, and I will take thee away from them. If they risk their lives and fight for thee, then shall I know that they have repented of what they did unto me, and I will make myself known unto them. But if they forsake thee, I will keep thee, that thou shouldst remain with me. They shall go away, and I will not make myself known unto them" (Ginzberg, 2:83, emp. added).

[NOTE: If the author of a book, who claims to be conveying information that he has received from God, was, in fact, actually speaking, not from divine revelation, but from his own uninspired memories of stories he had heard from his contemporaries, thereby relying on his own fallible memory to recall details of legends that he had heard only orally by word of mouth, one would expect him to remember the general outlines of story plots, along with the most prominent characters integral to those plots whose names would have been verbalized repeatedly as the story was being told. On the other hand, one also would expect the author to have difficulty remembering (and consequently omit from his own accounts) the names of less prominent characters. This is precisely what we find in the Quran. For example, in the lengthy surah (111 verses) on the life story of Joseph, **not one of Joseph's brothers is mentioned by name**! Other than Joseph only, Jacob, Abraham, and Isaac are mentioned—as one would expect in view of the fact that the Jews everywhere repeatedly refer to the three patriarchal forefathers of the Jews. No allusion is made to the professions of the butler and baker, but instead they are referred to only as "young men" and "fellow prisoners." Benjamin is identified only as "a brother of yours from your father." The Midianites and Ishmaelites are simply "a caravan." Potiphar is simply "he of Egypt who purchased him," and Potiphar's wife is "she in whose house he was" and "the ruler's wife." The only location alluded to is Egypt. In stark contrast, the Bible's account of Joseph gives the names of people—Potiphar, Judah, Reuben, Simeon, Benjamin, Bilhah, Zilpah, Jacob's alternate name—Israel, Joseph's alternate name—Zaphnath-Paaneah, Asenath (Joseph's wife), Poti-Pherah (Asenath's father), Manasseh, Ephraim, Ishmaelites, Midianites, Egyptians, Hebrews, and also the names of locations—Egypt, Dothan, Shechem, Hebron, Gilead, the land of the Hebrews, Canaan, On, and Goshen. All of these designations are conspicuously absent in the Quran's account. These are precisely the kind of details one would expect a borrower to omit when attempting to recall from memory.]

Ninth, in contrast to the Bible, the Quran gives an alternate explanation as to why Joseph had to remain in prison an additional two years after interpreting the dreams of the chief butler and the chief baker:

> O my two fellow-prisoners! As for one of you, he will pour out wine for his lord to drink; and as for the other, he will be crucified so that the birds will eat from his head. Thus is the case judged concerning which ye did inquire. And he said unto him of the twain who he knew would be released: Mention me in the presence of thy lord. But **Satan caused him to forget to mention it** to his lord, so he (Joseph) stayed in prison for some years (*Surah* 12: 41-42, emp. added).

The Bible says nothing as to the reason why the chief butler's memory failed to the extent that he forgot about Joseph (Genesis 40:23), though it does indicate that when Pharaoh had his dreams, the chief butler acknowledged fault for having forgotten him (Genesis 41:9). Where did the Quran get its information that the butler's lapse in memory was due to external intervention? The Jewish rabbis circulated their own explanation (*Midrash Breishit Rabbah* 88:7; 89:2-3; *Tanchuma Wayesheb* 9; *Tehillim* 105,451; *Midrash Hagadol* 594-595,598-599,610; *Targum Yerushalmi* Gen. 40:14,23; *Yashar Wayesheb* 91b)—an explanation that roughly parallels and expands on the Quran's account:

> Properly speaking, Joseph should have gone out free from his dungeon on the same day as the butler. He had been there ten years by that time, and had made amends for the slander he had uttered against his ten brethren. However, he remained in prison two years longer. "Blessed is the man that trusteth in the Lord, and whose hope is the Lord," but **Joseph had put his confidence in flesh and blood**. He had prayed the chief butler to have him in remembrance when it should be well with him, and make mention of him unto Pharaoh, and the butler forgot his promise, and therefore Joseph had to stay in prison two years more than the years originally allotted to him there. **The butler had not forgotten him intentionally, but it was ordained of God that his memory**

should fail him. When he would say to himself, If thus and so happens, I will remember the case of Joseph, the conditions he had imagined were sure to be reversed, or if he made a knot as a reminder, an angel came and undid the knot, and Joseph did not enter his mind (Ginzberg, 2:54-55, emp. added).

While it is true that the Quran attributes the chief butler's lapse in memory to Satan, and the Jews attributed it to God, the two views agree that the butler was subjected to an external, supernatural force that prevented him from remembering.

Tenth, the Quran claims that when Joseph's cup was discovered in Benjamin's bag, a statement about being a thief was uttered: "They said: If he stealeth, a brother of his stole before" (*Surah* 12:77). This curious remark parallels the rabbinical writings (*Midrash Breishit Rabbah* 102:9; *Tanchuma Mikkez* 10; *Midrash Hagadol* 653; *Yashar Mikkez* 105a):

He searched all the sacks, and in order not to excite the suspicion that he knew where the cup was, he began at Reuben, the eldest, and left off at Benjamin, the youngest, and the cup was found in Benjamin's sack. In a rage, his brethren shouted at Benjamin, "O **thou thief and son of a thief!** Thy mother brought shame upon our father by her thievery, and now thou bringest shame upon us" (Ginzberg, 2:85, emp. added).

The Jewish writing makes Benjamin and his mother (i.e., Rachel–Genesis 31:19) the thieves, while the Quran makes Benjamin and his brother the thieves. Nevertheless, the connection is apparent.

These several examples are sufficient to establish the point. The uninspired Jewish expansions on the story of Joseph are far more extravagant than even the Quran, supplying numerous curious details on which the Bible is completely silent. But the Quran's frequent ties to Jewish folklore, in contradistinction to the Bible, is apparent to the unbiased investigator.

The author of the Quran must have been self-conscious regarding the amount of material he manufactured with regard to Joseph. He must have feared the charge of fabrication, and so sought both to bolster his own credibility, while defending his own lengthy expansions. He spends the closing ten verses of the surah defending his version of the story, aligning himself with past messengers of Allah, offering a threat to those who do not accept him, and declaring his version a confirmation of the existing account found in the Bible:

> This is of the tidings of the Unseen which We inspire in thee (Muhammad). Thou wast not present with them when they fixed their plan and they were scheming. And though thou try much, most men will not believe. Thou askest them no fee for it. It is naught else than a reminder unto the peoples.... When the messengers despaired and thought that they were denied, then came unto them Our help, and whom We would was saved. And our wrath cannot be warded from the guilty. In their history verily there is a lesson for men of understanding. **It is no invented story** but a confirmation of the existing (Scripture) and a detailed explanation of everything, and a guidance and a mercy for folk who believe (*Surah* 12:102-104,111, emp. added).

Solomon and the Queen of Sheba

In order to be objective and completely fair, a lengthy section of the Quran is reproduced below, followed by the parallel Jewish account, so that the reader may realize the extent to which the Quran depended on Jewish folklore for its own content. Patience is needed to work through these lengthy sections in order to achieve an honest comparison. The story of Solomon and Sheba is given in *Surah* 27 as follows [the reader is advised to take special notice of the boldface type]:

> And Solomon was David's heir. And he said: O mankind! Lo! we have been taught the language of birds, and have been given (abundance) of all things. This surely is evident favour. And **there were gathered together** unto Solomon **his armies of the jinn** and humankind, **and of the birds**, and they were set in battle order; till, when they reached the Valley of the Ants, an ant exclaimed: O ants! Enter your dwellings lest Solomon and his armies crush you, unperceiving. And (Solomon)

smiled, laughing at her speech, and said: My Lord, arouse
me to be thankful for Thy favour wherewith Thou hast
favoured me and my parents, and to do good that shall
be pleasing unto Thee, and include me in (the number
of) Thy righteous slaves. And he sought **among the birds**
and said: How is it that I see not **the hoopoe**, or is he
among the absent? I verily **will punish him with hard
punishment or I verily will slay him**, or he verily shall
bring me a plain excuse. But he was not long in coming,
and he said: I have found out (a thing) that thou appre-
hendest not, and **I come unto thee from Sheba** with
sure tidings. Lo! **I found a woman ruling over them**,
and she hath been given (abundance) of all things, and
hers is a mighty throne. I found her and her people wor-
shipping the sun instead of Allah; and Satan maketh their
works fair-seeming unto them, and debarreth them from
the way (of Truth), so that they go not aright: so that they
worship not Allah, Who bringeth forth the hidden in the
heavens and the earth, and knoweth what ye hide and
what ye proclaim, Allah; there is no God save Him, the
Lord of the tremendous Throne.

(Solomon) said: We shall see whether thou speakest truth
or whether thou art of the liars. **Go with this my letter**
and throw it down unto them; then turn away and see
what (answer) they return, (The Queen of Sheba) said
(when she received the letter): O chieftains! Lo! there
hath been thrown unto me a noble letter. Lo! **it is from
Solomon**, and lo! it is: In the name of Allah the Beneficent, the Merciful; **Exalt not yourselves against me**,
but **come unto me** as **those who surrender**. She said:
O chieftains! Pronounce for me in my case. I decide
no case till ye are present with me. They said: We are
lords of might and lords of great prowess, but **it is for
thee to command**; so consider what thou wilt command.
She said: Lo! kings, when they enter a township, ruin it
and make the honour of its people shame. Thus will they
do. But lo! I am going **to send a present unto them**,
and to **see with what (answer) the messengers return**. So when (the envoy) came unto Solomon, (the King)
said: What! Would ye help me with wealth? But that which

Allah hath given me is better than that which He hath given you. Nay it is ye (and not I) who exult in your gift. Return unto them. We verily shall come unto them with hosts that they cannot resist, and we shall drive them out from thence with shame, and they will be abased. He said: O chiefs! Which of you will bring me her throne before they come unto me, surrendering? A stalwart of the Jinn said: I will bring it thee before thou canst rise from thy place. Lo! I verily am strong and trusty for such work. One with whom was knowledge of the Scripture said: I will bring it thee before thy gaze returneth unto thee. And when he saw it set in his presence, (Solomon) said: This is of the bounty of my Lord, that He may try me whether I give thanks or am ungrateful. Whosoever giveth thanks he only giveth thanks for (the good of) his own soul: and whosoever is ungrateful (is ungrateful only to his own soul's hurt). For lo! my Lord is Absolute in independence, Bountiful. He said: Disguise her throne for her that we may see whether she will go aright or be of those not rightly guided.

So, when **she came**, it was said (unto her): Is thy throne like this? She said: (It is) as though it were the very one. And (Solomon said): We were given the knowledge before her and we had surrendered (to Allah). And (all) that she was wont to worship instead of Allah hindered her, for she came of disbelieving folk. It was said unto her: Enter the hall. And when she saw it **she deemed it a pool** and **bared her legs**. (Solomon) said: Lo! it is a hall, made smooth, **of glass**. She said: My Lord! Lo! I have wronged myself, and I surrender with Solomon unto **Allah, the Lord of the Worlds** (*Surah* 27:16-44, emp. added).

Now compare this account with the one found in the Jewish second *Targum of Esther*, also called *Targum Sheni*, whose composition predated the production of the Quran ("Is the Quran's Story...?").

Again, when King Solomon's heart was merry with his wine, **he commanded** to bring the beasts of the field and **the fowls** of the air and the creeping things of the

earth and **the jinns** and the spirits and the night-goblins
to dance before him, in order to show his greatness to all
the kings who were prostrating themselves before him.
And the king's scribes summoned them by their names,
and they all assembled and came unto him, except the
prisoners and except the captives and except the man
who took charge of them. At that hour **the cock of the
desert** was enjoying himself **among the birds and was
not found.** And the king commanded concerning him
that they should bring him by force, and **wished to destroy him.** The cock of the desert returned to King Solomon's presence and said to him, "Hearken, my lord the
king of the earth, incline thine ear and hear my words. Is
it not three months ago that I took counsel in my heart
and formed a firm resolution with myself that I would
not eat, and would not drink water, before I had seen the
whole world and flown about in it? And I said, Which
province or kingdom is there that is not obedient to my
lord the king? **I beheld and saw a fortified city**, the
name of which is Qitor, in an eastern land. The dust is
heavy with gold, and silver is like dung in the streets, and
trees have been planted there from the beginning; and
from the Garden of Eden do they drink water. There are
there great multitudes with garlands on their heads. From
there are plants from the Garden of Eden, because it is
near unto it. They know how to shoot with the bow, but
cannot be slain with the bow. **One woman rules over
them all**, and her name is the Queen of Sheba. Now if it
please thee, my lord the king, this person will gird up my
loins, and I shall rise up and go to the fortress of Qitor, to
the city of Sheba; I shall 'bind their kings with chains
and their nobles with links of iron,' and shall bring them
unto my lord the King." And the saying was pleasing before the king, and the king's scribes were called, and **they
wrote a letter** and fastened the letter to the wing of the
cock of the desert. And he arose and went up high into
the sky and bound on his tiara and grew strong, and flew
among the birds. And they flew after him. And they went
to the fortress of Qitor, to the city of Sheba. And it came
to pass at morning time that the Queen of Sheba went

forth by the sea to worship. And the birds darkened the sun; and she laid her hand upon her garments and rent them, and she became surprised and troubled. And when she was troubled, the cock of the desert came down to her, and she saw, and lo! a letter was fastened to his wing. She opened and read it. And this was what was written in it: "**From me, King Solomon.** Peace be to thee, peace be to thy nobles! Forasmuch as thou knowest that the Holy One, blessed be He! has made me King over the beasts of the field, and over the fowls of the air, and over jinns and over spirits and over night-goblins, and all the kings of the East and the West and the South and the North come and inquire about my health (peace): now, **if thou art willing and dost come** and inquire after my health, well: I shall make thee greater than all the kings that bow down before me. And **if thou art not willing and dost not come nor inquire after my health, I shall send against thee kings and legions and horsemen**. And if thou sayest, 'What kings and legions and horsemen has King Solomon?'—the beasts of the field are kings and legions and horsemen. And if thou sayest, 'What horsemen?'—the fowls of the air are horsemen, my armies are spirits and jinns, and the night-goblins are legions that shall strangle you in your beds within your houses: the beasts of the field shall slay you in the field; the birds of the air shall eat your flesh from off you." And when the Queen of Sheba heard the words of the letter, again a second time she laid her hand upon her garments and rent them. **She sent and called the elders and nobles**, and said to them, "Do ye not know what King Solomon has sent to me?" They answered and said, "**We do not know King Solomon nor do we make any account of his kingdom**." But she was not contented, nor did she hearken unto their words, but she sent and called all the ships of the sea and **loaded them with offerings and jewels and precious stones**. And she sent unto him six thousand boys and girls, and all of them were born in the same (one) year, and all of them were born in one month, and all of them were born in one day, and all of them were born in one hour, and all of them were of the same stature, and all of them were of the same figure, and all of them were clad in purple garments. And **she wrote a letter and sent it to King Solomon** by their hands. "From the fortress of Qitor to the land of Israel is seven years journey. Now through thy prayers and through thy petitions which I entreat of thee, I shall come to thee at the end of three years." And it came to pass at the end of three years **that the Queen of Sheba came to King Solomon**. And when King Solomon heard that the Queen of Sheba had come, he sent unto her Benaiah the son of Jehoiada, who was like the dawn that rises at morningtime, and resembled the Star of Splendour (Venus) which shines and stands firm among the stars, and was similar to the lily which stands by the watercourses. And when the Queen of Sheba saw Benaiah, son of Jehoiada, she alighted from the chariot. Benaiah, son of Jehoiada, answered and said to her, "Why hast thou alighted from thy chariot?" She answered and said to him, "Art not thou King Solomon?" He answered and said to her, "I am not King Solomon, but one of his servants who stand before him." And forthwith she turned her face behind her and uttered a parable to the nobles, "If the lion has not appeared to you, ye have seen his offspring, and if ye have not seen King Solomon ye have seen the beauty of a man who stands before him." And Benaiah, son of Jehoiada, brought her before the king. And when the king heard that she had come to him, he arose and went and sat in a crystal house. And when the Queen of Sheba saw that the king sat in a crystal house, she considered in her heart and said that **the king sat in water**, and **she gathered up her garment** that she might cross over, and he saw that she had hair on **her legs**. The king answered and said unto her, "Thy beauty is the beauty of women, and thy hair is the hair of a man; and hair is beautiful for a man, but for a woman it is disgraceful." The Queen of Sheba answered and said to him, "My lord the king, I shall utter to thee three parables, which if thou explain to me, I shall know that thou art a wise man, and if not, thou art as the rest of men." (Solomon solved all three problems.) And she said, **"Blessed be the Lord thy**

God who delighted in thee to seat thee upon the throne of the kingdom to do judgment and justice." And she gave unto the king good gold and silver.... And the king gave her all that she desired (Tisdall, 1905, pp. 84-89, emp. added).

If the reader will take note of the boldface type in both passages, a minimum of seventeen points of commonality will be seen to exist between the two accounts: (1) Solomon rules over armies of jinns and birds; (2) these creatures were ordered to gather before him; (3) one bird is absent; (4) the bird is threatened with punishment/destruction for being absent; (5) when the bird appears before Solomon, it justifies its absence on the basis of its visit to Sheba; (6) a woman rules over the land of Sheba; (7) a letter is sent by the bird to the queen; (8) she identifies the letter as being from Solomon; (9) the letter commands her to visit Solomon; (10) the letter contains a threat that she must not show hostility/resistance toward Solomon; (11) she confides in her nobles to receive their counsel; (12) the nobles have no helpful recommendation to make; (13) the queen prefaces her visit to Solomon by sending both a message and gifts to him; (14) the queen visits Solomon; (15) when she sees Solomon in his palace, the floor surface appears to be water or glass; (16) she lifts up her garment to cross over, thus baring her legs; and (17) she offers praise to Solomon's God.

The reader is urged to compare both of these apocryphal embellishments of Sheba's visit to Solomon with the accurate one depicted in 1 Kings 10:1-13 and 2 Chronicles 9:1-12. The biblical account provides a simple, unadorned narrative of the queen's visit to Jerusalem, having as its obvious purpose to illustrate the fame, wealth, and wisdom of Solomon. The Quranic narrative, on the other hand, has as its purpose to show the queen's conversion to Islam. The story is laced with the admonitions regarding submission and the oneness of Allah that one would expect from Muhammad. A comparison of the Bible on the one hand and the Quran on the other further illustrates the stark contrast between an inspired account and the efforts of uninspired writers to create the illusion of inspiration (see also Jameel, n.d.).

Hot Flood Waters

The Quran alludes to Noah several times. Two such allusions are noted here due to their connection to Jewish accounts. One pertains to the contemporaries of Noah mocking him as he constructed the ark, while the other describes the condition of the floodwater:

> And it was inspired in Noah, (saying): No one of thy folk will believe save him who hath believed already. Be not distressed because of what they do. Build the ship under Our Eyes and by Our inspiration, and speak not unto Me on behalf of those who do wrong. Lo! they will be drowned. And he was building the ship, and every time that chieftains of his people passed him, **they made mock of him**. He said: Though ye make mock of us, yet we mock at you even as ye mock; And ye shall know to whom a punishment that will confound him cometh, and upon whom a lasting doom will fall. (Thus it was) till, when Our commandment came to pass and **the oven gushed forth water** (*Surah* 11:36-40, emp. added).

> And We verily sent Noah unto his folk, and he said: O my people! Serve Allah. Ye have no other god save Him. Will ye not ward off (evil)? But the chieftains of his folk, who disbelieved, said: This is only a mortal like you who would make himself superior to you. Had Allah willed, He surely could have sent down angels. We heard not of this in the case of our fathers of old. He is only a man in whom is a madness, so watch him for a while. He said: My Lord! Help me because they deny me. Then We inspired in him, saying: Make the ship under Our eyes and Our inspiration. Then, when Our command cometh and **the oven gusheth water**, introduce therein of every (kind) two spouses, and thy household save him thereof against whom the Word hath already gone forth. And plead not with Me on behalf of those who have done wrong. Lo! they will be drowned. And when thou art on board the ship, thou and who so is with thee, then say: Praise be to Allah Who hath saved us from the wrongdoing folk! (*Surah* 23:23-28, emp. added).

The Bible makes no reference to the reactions of Noah's contemporaries to his work. Nor does it give any indication of the temperature of the floodwaters. Jewish sources (*Midrash Tanchuma* 5; *Rosh Hashanah* 12a; *Sanhedrin* 108b; *Zebahim* 113b; *Yerushalmi Sanhedrin* 10,29b; et al.) provide the basis for both allusions:

> Even after God had resolved upon the destruction of the sinners, He still permitted His mercy to prevail, in that He sent Noah unto them, who exhorted them for one hundred and twenty years to amend their ways, always holding the flood over them as a threat. As for them, **they but derided him**. When they saw him occupying himself with the building of the ark, they asked, "Wherefore this ark?"

> The crowd of sinners tried to take the entrance to the ark by storm, but the wild beasts keeping watch around the ark set upon them, and many were slain, while the rest escaped, only to meet death in the waters of the flood. The water alone could not have made an end of them, for they were giants in stature and strength. When Noah threatened them with the scourge of God, they would make reply: "If the waters of the flood come from above, they will never reach up to our necks; and if they come from below, the soles of our feet are large enough to dam up the springs." But God bade each drop pass through Gehenna before it fell to earth, and the hot rain scalded the skin of the sinners. The punishment that overtook them was befitting their crime. As their sensual desires had made them hot, and inflamed them to immoral excesses, so they were chastised **by means of heated water** (Ginzberg, 1:153,158-159, emp. added; Simon, 1938).

Moses

The Quran makes several references to Moses. After all, Moses was a lawgiver—a provider of revelation—with whom Muhammad would naturally have wanted to identify himself. The Quranic embellishments of various incidents in the life of Moses are apparent and amusing. For example, the Bible indicates that when Pharaoh's daughter found Moses in the river, Moses' sister offered to locate a nurse for the child from among the Hebrew women. Pharaoh's daughter agreed, and told the sister to make the necessary arrangements (Exodus 2:7-9). The Quran claims that Allah had actually forbidden Moses being suckled by a foster mother: "And We had before forbidden fostermothers for him, so she said: Shall I show you a household who will rear him for you and take care of him? So We restored him to his mother" (*Surah* 28:12-13). Jewish Talmudic and Midrash literature explains the Quran's allusion in *Sotah* (12b) and *Shemot Rabbah* (1:25): "The Holy One, Blessed is He, said: 'Shall the mouth that will one day speak to me suckle anything unclean?'" ("Pharaoh's Magicians," n.d.; Cohen, 1936). These minute details from Jewish folklore arise frequently in the Quran.

The Quran provides its own version of the events that took place at the base of Mt. Sinai where the Israelites gathered to receive the Law of Moses from God. The following three examples pertain to events at the Sinai encampment.

The Lowing of the Golden Calf

> O Children of Israel! We delivered you from your enemy, and We made a covenant with you on the holy mountain's side, and sent down on you the manna and the quails, (Saying): Eat of the good things wherewith We have provided you, and transgress not in respect thereof lest My wrath come upon you; and he on whom My wrath cometh, he is lost indeed. And lo! verily I am Forgiving toward him who repenteth and believeth and doeth good, and afterward walketh aright. And (it was said): What hath made thee hasten from thy folk, O Moses? He said: They are close upon my track. I hastened unto Thee that Thou mightest be well pleased. He said: Lo! We have tried thy folk in thine absence, and As-**Samiri** hath misled them. Then Moses went back unto his folk, angry and sad. He said: O my people! Hath not your Lord promised you a fair promise? Did the time appointed then appear too long for you, or did ye wish that wrath from your Lord should come upon you, that ye broke tryst with me? They said: We broke not tryst with thee of our own will, but we were laden with burdens of ornaments of the folk, then cast them (in the fire),

for thus As-**Samiri** proposed. Then he produced for them
a calf, of saffron hue, which **gave forth a lowing sound**.
And they cried: This is your God and the God of Moses,
but he hath forgotten. See they not, then, that it returneth
no saying unto them and possesseth for them neither
hurt nor use? And Aaron indeed had told them beforehand: O my people! Ye are but being seduced therewith,
for lo! your Lord is the Beneficent, so follow me and obey
my order. They said: We shall by no means cease to be
its votaries till Moses return unto us. He (Moses) said: O
Aaron! What held thee back when thou didst see them
gone astray, that thou followedst me not? Hast thou then
disobeyed my order? He said: O son of my mother! Clutch
not my beard nor my head! I feared lest thou shouldst
say: Thou hast caused division among the Children of
Israel, and hast not waited for my word. (Moses) said:
And what has thou to say, O **Samiri**? He said: I perceived
what they perceive not, so I seized a handful from the
footsteps of the messenger, and then threw it in. Thus
my soul commended to me. (Moses) said: Then go! And
lo! in this life it is for thee to say: Touch me not! and lo!
there is for thee a tryst thou canst not break. Now look
upon thy god of which thou hast remained a votary. Verily we will burn it and will scatter its dust over the sea
(*Surah* 20:80-97, emp. added).

Beyond the obvious differences in detail from the biblical version (not the least of which is that in the Bible Aaron made the
calf–Exodus 32:2-4), this account offers at least two peculiarities
that suggest rabbinical influence. In the first place, the golden
calf is represented as making a lowing sound (also *Surah* 7:148).
This circumstance is included in the traditions of the Talmud
where Pirke Rabbi Eliezer stated: "The **calf came forth lowing** and the Israelites beheld it. R. Jehuda saith, Samael entered
into it and lowed in order to mislead Israel" (as quoted in Rodwell, 1950, p. 99, emp. added).

In the second place, Samiri is included in the Quranic account
as the instigator of the idolatrous incident. Since the rabbinical
account alludes to the involvement of a "Samael" (the Jewish

name for the angel of death–Tisdall, 1905, p. 113) in the affair, some have surmised this person to be the Samiri referred to in the Quran. However, a more likely explanation lies in the fact that "Samiri" is the Arabic word for "Samaritan" (Goldsack, 1907, p. 17). The author of the Quran very likely had been made forcefully aware of the longstanding hostility between the Jews and the Samaritans. In view of the fact that even the Muslim commentators refer to the Samaritans as the people who say, "Touch me not" (Rodwell, p. 99; Geiger, 1896, p. 131), it appears evident that the Quran's mention of Samiri was a reference to the Samaritans. Observe carefully how this conclusion is further supported by the surah's own reference to Samiri being banished ("Then go!"), with the accompanying judgment sentence: "In this life it is for thee to say: Touch me not!" (vs. 97). Of course, every student of biblical history knows that the Samaritan race did not come into existence until over seven centuries later in the eighth century B.C. (2 Kings 17:24-29; cf. Graetz, 1891, 1:285; Ewing, 1956, 4:2673-2674; Kelso, 1976, 5:244-247). The Bible account says nothing about either Samael or the Samaritan.

[As a side note, the reader also will observe that Muslim translator Pickthall's rendering of the calf as "saffron hue" evades the fact that the Arabic word *jasad*, by his own admission (p. 132, note), can refer only to a body of flesh and blood. Muslim translator Ali sidesteps the point by translating it as "image" (pp. 102, 203), as did Dawood (1976, pp. 230,258). Sale rendered it "a corporeal calf" (n.d., pp. 93,172), while Rodwell translated it "corporeal" in one of the instances and "ruddy like gold" in the other (1950, pp. 99,306). The Quran actually affirms that the calf possessed a fleshly **body**.]

Israelites Killed and Raised

Another incident at the base of Mt. Sinai that arose from Jewish folklore also is alluded to in the Quran:

> And when Moses said unto his people: O my people! Ye have wronged yourselves by your choosing of the calf (for worship) so turn in penitence to your Creator, and

kill (the guilty) yourselves. That will be best for you with your Creator and He will relent toward you. Lo! He is the Relenting, the Merciful. And when ye said: O Moses! We will not believe in thee till we see Allah plainly; and even while ye gazed the **lightning seized you**. Then We **revived you after your extinction**, that ye might give thanks (*Surah* 2:54-56, emp. added).

The People of the Scripture ask of thee that thou shouldst cause an (actual) Book to descend upon them from heaven. They asked a greater thing of Moses aforetime, for they said: Show us Allah plainly. The storm of **lightning seized them** for their wickedness. Then (even after that) they chose the calf (for worship) after clear proofs (of Allah's Sovereignty) had come unto them. And We forgave them that! (*Surah* 4:153, emp. added).

These passages affirm that, on account of their impious insistence that Allah authenticate Moses as His messenger by showing Himself, God struck dead several Israelites with lightning at the base of Mt. Sinai, and then brought them back to life: "We raised you up after your death" (Ali, p. 5). In the biblical account, thunder and lightning were emitted from the top of the mountain, so frightening the people that they requested that God not speak directly to them. No one was **killed** as a result, not to mention **resurrected** (Exodus 19:16; 20:19; cf. Deuteronomy 5:22-26). Once again, the Quran sides with Jewish mythology (*Sanhedrin* 5):

The Israelites desired two things of God, that they might see His glory and hear His voice; and both were granted them, as it is written: "Behold the Lord our God hath showed us His glory and His greatness, and we have heard His voice out of the midst of the fire." Then they had no power to bear it; for when they came to Sinai and He appeared to them, **their soul departed at His speech**, as it is written: "My soul went forth when he spake." The Law (the Torah) however interceded with God for them saying: "Would a king marry his daughter and slay all his household?" The whole world rejoices (on account of thy appearance), and shall thy children (the Israelites) die? At once **their souls returned to them**, therefore it is written: "The Law of the Lord is perfect, restoring the soul" (Geiger, pp. 129-130, emp. added; cf. Ginzberg, 1911, 3:195).

In stark contrast to the biblical account, the Quran aligns itself with a Jewish fable in claiming that Israelites at the base of Mt. Sinai died and were resurrected due to their encounter with God.

Mt. Sinai Lifting Upward

At least three times the Quran alludes to the idea of Mt. Sinai being situated **above** the Israelite nation as they were encamped to receive the Law of Moses: "And (remember, O children of Israel) when We made a covenant with you and caused the Mount to tower above you, (saying): Hold fast that which We have given you, and remember that which is therein, that ye may ward off (evil)" (*Surah* 2:63). "And when We made with you a covenant and caused the Mount to tower above you, (saying): Hold fast by that which We have given you..." (*Surah* 2:93); "And when We shook the Mount above them as it were a covering, and they supposed that it was going to fall upon them (and We said): Hold fast that which We have given you..." (*Surah* 7:171). Various Muslim commentators verify this incident, describing it as necessary in order to threaten the Jews with being crushed if they refused to accept the commandments being given to them (Tisdall, 1905, p. 109).

The legend of the "ascent of Sinai" is found in several contemporaneous Jewish sources (e.g., *Midrash Shir* 44a; *Tehillim* 75,337; *Tanchuma Noah* 3; *Nispahim* 55; et al.). They speak of the heavens opening and Mt. Sinai, freed from Earth, rising into the air, so that its summit towered into the heavens (Ginzberg, 1911, 3:93-94). From the Babylonian Talmud, the Jewish tractate *Abodah Zarah* (2b) represents God as saying: "I covered you over with the mountain like a lid" (Mishcon, 1935). The same concept is alluded to in *Sabbath* (88a): "These words teach us that the Holy One, blessed be He, inverted the mountain above them like a pot, and said unto them, 'If ye receive the law, well: but if not, there shall your grave be'" (Freedman, 1938b). Once again, no such folklore is found in the original, authentic account reported in the Bible (Exodus 19:9-25; 20:18-21).

Interestingly enough, the origin of this curious circumstance is traceable to a Jewish misunderstanding of the Hebrew adjective (*tagh-tee*) in Exodus 19:17, and the preposition (*tah-ghath*) in Deuteronomy 4:11 and Exodus 32:19. The terms describe the positioning of the Israelites in relation to the mountain. English versions can reflect the same confusion. For example, the King James translators rendered the Exodus phrase: "and they stood at **the nether part** of the mount." "Nether" is a Middle English word that meant beneath, below, or under. The Deuteronomy phrase was rendered: "and ye came near and stood **under** the mountain." While both underlying Hebrew terms are broad in the range of meanings attached to them, and can include the notion of being underneath, nevertheless, the proper translation of the passages in reference to the Israelites' location is unquestionably "at the foot of" (see Weingreen, 1959, p. 88; Harris, et al., 1980, 2:967-969; Gesenius, 1847, p. 862; Keil and Delitzsch, 1976, 1:103,225,311). The fact is that Mt. Sinai did not "tower above" or "over" the Israelites. The Jewish legend that was generated by this misunderstanding was obviously circulated among the Jews and beyond, eventually making its way to the ears of the author of the Quran who mistook it as a bona fide biblical incident.

Two additional events in the life of Moses to which the Quran alludes involve Korah, as well as Pharaoh's magicians whom Moses faced in Egypt:

The Conversion of the Egyptian Magicians

The Quran indicates that Pharaoh's magicians were so impressed with the miracles performed by Moses and Aaron, that they abandoned their paganism and converted to Islam:

> And the wizards came to Pharaoh, saying: Surely there will be a reward for us if we are victors. He answered: Yea, and surely ye shall be of those brought near (to me).

They said: O Moses! Either throw (first) or let us be the first throwers? He said: Throw! And when they threw they cast a spell upon the people's eyes, and overawed them, and produced a mighty spell. And We inspired Moses (saying): Throw thy staff! And lo! it swallowed up their lying show. Thus was the Truth vindicated and that which they were doing was made vain. Thus were they there defeated and brought low. And **the wizards fell down prostrate, crying: We believe in the Lord of the Worlds, the Lord of Moses and Aaron.** Pharaoh said: Ye believe in Him before I give you leave! Lo! this is the plot that ye have plotted in the city that ye may drive its people hence. But ye shall come to know! Surely I shall have your hands and feet cut off upon alternate sides. Then I shall crucify you every one. They said: Lo! We are about to return unto our Lord! Thou takest vengeance on us only forasmuch as we believed the tokens of our Lord when they came unto us. Our Lord! Vouchsafe unto us stedfastness and make us die as men who have surrendered (unto Thee) (*Surah* 7:113-126, emp. added).

Moses said unto them: Woe unto you! Invent not a lie against Allah, lest He extirpate you by some punishment. He who lieth faileth miserably. Then they debated one with another what they must do, and they kept their counsel secret. They said: Lo! these are two wizards who would drive you out from your country by their magic, and destroy your best traditions; So arrange your plan, and come in battle line. Whoso is uppermost this day will be indeed successful. They said: O Moses! Either throw first, or let us be the first to throw? He said: Nay, do ye throw! Then lo! their cords and their staves, by their magic, appeared to him as though they ran. And Moses conceived a fear in his mind. We said: Fear not! Lo! thou art the higher. Throw that which is in thy right hand! It will eat up that which they have made. Lo! that which they have made is but a wizard's artifice, and a wizard shall not be successful to whatever point (of skill) he may attain. **Then the wizards were (all) flung down prostrate, crying: We believe in the Lord of Aaron and Moses.** (Pharaoh) said: Ye put faith in him before I give you leave. Lo! he is your chief who taught you magic. Now surely I shall cut off your hands and your feet alternately, and I shall crucify you on the trunks of palm trees, and ye shall know for certain which of us hath sterner and more lasting punishment. They said: We choose thee not above the clear proofs that have come unto us, and above Him Who created us. So decree what thou wilt decree. Thou wilt end for us only the life of the world. Lo! **we believe in our Lord**, that He may forgive us our sins and the magic unto which thou didst force us. **Allah is better and more lasting** (*Surah* 20:61-73, emp. added).

And it was said unto the people: Are ye (also) gathering? (They said): Aye, so that we may follow the wizards if they are the winners. And when the wizards came they said unto Pharaoh: Will there surely be a reward for us if we are the winners? He said: Aye, and ye will then surely be of those brought near (to me). Moses said unto them: Throw what ye are going to throw! Then they threw down their cords and their staves and said: By Pharaoh's might, lo! we verily are the winners. Then Moses threw his staff and lo! it swallowed that which they did falsely show. And **the wizards were flung prostrate, crying: We believe in the Lord of the Worlds, the Lord of Moses and Aaron**. (Pharaoh) said: Ye put your faith in him before I give you leave. Lo! he doubtless is your chief who taught you magic! But verily ye shall come to know. Verily I will cut off your hands and your feet alternately, and verily I will crucify you every one. They said: It is no hurt, for lo! unto our Lord we shall return. Lo! we ardently hope that our Lord will forgive us our sins because **we are the first of the believers** (*Surah* 26:39-51, emp. added).

In the Bible's depiction of the scene, while the magicians make an admission that the third plague (lice) was due to "the finger of God" (Exodus 8:19), no inkling whatsoever is given that would lead one to conclude that the magicians ever considered conversion. On the other hand, the rabbinical sources show the prevailing view circulated among the Jews of Muhammad's day.

For example, *Shemot Rabbah* (42:6) notes that Moses accepted Egyptian proselytes into Israel. *Midrash Tanchuma* (on *Parshat Ki Tissa*) refers to Jannes and Jambres (assumed to be the names of Pharaoh's magicians—cf. 2 Timothy 3:8) as being among those who exited Egypt with the Israelites, and who, according to the *Zohar*, became Jews (as quoted in "Pharaoh's Magicians," n.d.). They were, in fact, participants in the Golden Calf episode (Ginzberg, 1911, 3:120; cf. 3:363).

Korah's Keys

The Korah of the Bible was an Israelite who led a rebellion against the leadership authority of Moses and Aaron (Numbers 16). In the Quran, he is represented as a man who had been blessed by Allah with wealth:

> Now Korah was of Moses' folk, but he oppressed them; and We gave him so much treasure that the stores thereof would verily have been a burden for a troop of mighty men (*Surah* 28:76).

Pickthall's translation of the Arabic differs slightly from Ali's on a noteworthy word. Whereas Pickthall renders the term "stores," Ali renders it "keys" (as do Dawood, Sale, and Rodwell): "such were the treasures We had bestowed on him, that **their very keys would have been a burden** to a body of strong men." The Jewish Babylonian Talmud contains the origin of this point as well in both *Sanhedrin* (110a) and *Pesachim* (119a): "Rabbi Levi said: The **keys of Korah's treasure house were a load** for three hundred white mules, though all the keys and locks were of leather" (Shacter, 1935; Freedman, 1938a).

The Burial of Abel

One additional sample will serve to place closure on this brief analysis. The Quran reports a most curious incident with regard to Cain and Abel. Since Cain committed human history's first murder, it would naturally be of interest to the inquiring mind to consider how the first human beings reacted to the phenomenon, and first occurrence, of death.

But recite unto them with truth the tale of the two sons of Adam, how they offered each a sacrifice, and it was accepted from the one of them and it was not accepted from the other. (The one) said: I will surely kill thee. (The other) answered: Allah accepteth only from those who ward off (evil). Even if thou stretch out thy hand against me to kill me, I shall not stretch out my hand against thee to kill thee, lo! I fear Allah, the Lord of the Worlds. Lo! I would rather thou shouldst bear the punishment of the sin against me and thine own sin and become one of the owners of the Fire. That is the reward of evil-doers. But (the other's) mind imposed on him the killing of his brother, so he slew him and became one of the losers. Then Allah sent **a raven scratching up the ground, to show him how to hide his brother's naked corpse.** He said: Woe unto me! Am I not able to be as this raven and so hide my brother's naked corpse? And he became repentant. For that cause We decreed for the Children of Israel that whosoever killeth a human being for other than manslaughter or corruption in the earth, it shall be as if he had killed all mankind, and whoso saveth the life of one, it shall be as if he had saved the life of all mankind. Our messengers came unto them of old with clear proofs (of Allah's sovereignty), but afterwards lo! many of them became prodigals in the earth (*Surah* 5:27-32, emp. added).

The Jewish legend that formed the basis of the Quran's treatment of Abel's burial—a legend that would have circulated from ancient times before being codified in a formalized Talmudic or Midrash entry ("The Murder...")—most assuredly was reiterated in the hearing of the author of the Quran. It is found in *Tanchuma Bereshit* (10), *Pirke Rabbi Eliezer* (21), *Midrash Breishit Rabbah* (22:8), et al., and appears in the following form:

Nature was modified also by the burial of the corpse of Abel. For a long time it lay there exposed, above ground, because Adam and Eve knew not what to do with it. They sat beside it and wept, while the faithful dog of Abel kept guard that birds and beasts did it no harm. On a sudden, the mourning parents observed how **a raven scratched the earth away** in one spot, and then hid a dead bird of his own kind in the ground. Adam, **following the ex-**

ample of the raven, buried the body of Abel, and the raven was rewarded by God. His young are born with white feathers, wherefore the old birds desert them, not recognizing them as their offspring. They take them for serpents. God feeds them until their plumage turns black, and the parent birds return to them. As an additional reward, God grants their petition when the ravens pray for rain (Ginzberg, 1909, 1:113, emp. added).

Notice that the Quran attributes the burial of Abel to Cain, while the rabbinical account assigns the task to Adam. In either case, the role the raven plays in both accounts is too comparable to be coincidental (cf. Slavonic *2 Enoch* 4:91). Either the author of the Quran copied the Jewish legend, or the author of the Jewish legend copied the Quran. I will let the reader be the judge.

CONCLUSION

The process of comparing Jewish folklore with the Quran could go on interminably. An occasional link between two sources might be explainable on legitimate grounds that would refute the charge of collusion. However, the Quran's reliance on uninspired Jewish sources is extensive and specific. Indeed, the Quran is literally riddled with such indications–if the reader cares to endure the tedium necessary to ferret them out. The author of the Quran demonstrated considerable ignorance of the Bible, but a striking acquaintance with Jewish legends. The present study foregoes the considerable additional evidence that verifies a comparable borrowing from **non**-Jewish sources. For the unbiased investigator who is willing to expend the time and effort, the proof is available, and it is decisive.

It cannot be overemphasized that Muhammad likely had very little, if any, contact with the actual Bible. His contact with the Bible was dependent on the representations presented to him by the Jews. The Jews, in turn, seemed to be more enamored with rabbinic folklore and legend rather than in actually expounding the biblical text. Consequently, in detail after detail where the Quran differs with the biblical record, it coincides with the Jewish legends that were current in Muhammad's day.

The usual Muslim responses to this allegation are that: (1) the Bible has been corrupted over the centuries, and that the Quran provides the accurate, correct accounts; and (2) the appearance of the Quran predated the invention of the Jewish legends that were, in turn, borrowed from the Quran. But these responses are insufficient and inadequate. The first claim would mean that the Quran has more in common with Jewish legend than it does with the Bible! Even the Jews themselves have never claimed inspiration for the Talmudic and Midrash folklore that accumulated over the centuries preceding the advent of the Quran. The Muslim defense also would mean that the Jewish myths, legends, and uninspired rabbinical commentary have been preserved with greater care than the Bible itself! Anyone who has given consideration to the preservation of the Bible (i.e., the science of textual criticism), would find such an assertion to be laughable and reflective of abject ignorance of the facts. The Jews have been vindicated in their meticulous preservation of the Old Testament text—a fact confirmed by the discovery of the Dead Sea Scrolls in 1945. The New Testament has been verified to be the best-attested book from antiquity (see Appendix 1).

The second claim is thwarted by the fact that while the science of dating ancient writings is somewhat precarious, and some allowance may be made for the official recording of some Jewish legends after the appearance of the Quran, one cannot place **all** borrowed Jewish legends in this category. The bulk of the Talmudic (both Palestinian/Jerusalem and Babylonian), Midrashim, and Targumim literature circulated literally centuries before the birth of Muhammad and the arrival of the Quran, eventually assuming final codified form by about A.D. 500 (Rodkinson, 1918, 1:22; "Talmud...", 2004; Hertz, 1934, p. xiii; "Gemara [Talmud]"; "Jewish Literature..."; "Talmud," 2003; "Rabbinic Chart"). Even if a few of them were not committed to an official written status until later, their presence and widespread circulation prior to the Quran has been firmly established. What is more pertinent, the parallels between the Quran and these legends are of such a nature that it is apparent to the objective researcher that the Jewish legends provide the context to items that the Quran otherwise leaves undecipherable. In the words of the highly respected Talmudist Louis Ginzberg, commenting on an incident in the life of Joseph that is found in both the Quran and the Midrash, "the **Jewish** origin of the legend as given in *Tanchuma* is **beyond dispute**" (1925, 5:340, note 118, emp. added).

The single fact of the Quran's borrowing from Jewish sources is sufficient to pronounce the Quran the production of an uninspired author(s). Nevertheless, additional evidences are available for consideration in the chapters that follow.

Chapter 5

INTERNAL AND HISTORICAL INACCURACIES

The Quran claims to be free from internal discrepancy: "Will they not then ponder on the Quran? If it had been from other than Allah they would have found therein much incongruity" (*Surah* 4:82). This acknowledgment—that the existence of "incongruity" in any book that claims to be of divine origin would nullify its claim—is commendable and self-evident to the rational individual. But does the Quran live up to its claim? Much has been written on this aspect of the Quran. Many charges have been leveled against the credibility of the Quran, and Muslim apologists have attempted to respond to several of these criticisms. This chapter addresses only a fraction of the many discrepancies that have been identified.

INHERITANCE LAWS

The Quran provides legislation to assist in the disposition of a deceased Muslim's estate. However, the directives are not only confusing, they are self-contradictory. The reader is requested to bear with the following tedious reading:

Allah chargeth you concerning (the provision for) your children: to the male the equivalent of the portion of two females, and **if there be women (daughters—Ali) more than two, then theirs is two-thirds of the inheritance**, and if there be one (only) then the half. **And to his parents a sixth of the inheritance (each—Ali)**, if he have a son; and if he have no son and his parents are his heirs, then **to his mother appertaineth the third**; and if he have brothers (or sisters—Ali), then to his mother appertaineth the sixth, after any legacy he may have bequeathed, or debt (hath been paid). Your parents or your children: Ye know not which of them is nearer unto you in usefulness. It is an injunction from Allah. Lo! Allah is Knower, Wise. And unto you belongeth a half of that which **your wives** leave, if they have no child; but if they have a child then unto you the fourth of that which they leave, after any legacy they may have bequeathed, or debt (they may have contracted, hath been paid). And **unto them belongeth the fourth of that which ye leave if ye have no child, but if ye have a child then the eighth of that which ye leave**, after any legacy ye may have bequeathed, or debt (ye may have contracted, hath been paid). And if a man or a woman have a distant heir (having left neither parent nor child), and he (or she) have a brother or a sister (only on the mother's side) then to each of them twain (the brother and the sister) the sixth, and if they be more than two, then they shall be sharers in the third, after any legacy that may have been bequeathed or debt (contracted) not injuring (the heirs by willing away more than a third of the heritage) hath been paid. A commandment from Allah. Allah is Knower, Indulgent.

They ask thee for a pronouncement. Say: Allah hath pronounced for you concerning distant kindred. If a man die childless and he have a sister, hers is half the heritage, and he would have inherited from her had she died childless. And **if there be two sisters, then theirs are two-thirds of the heritage**, and if they be brethren, men and women, unto the male is the equivalent of the share of two females. Allah expoundeth unto you, so that ye err not. Allah is Knower of all things (*Surah* 4:11-12,177, emp. added).

Consider how these directives actually play out in application. Suppose a man dies childless, leaving behind two or more daughters, his two parents, and his wife. According to verse 11, the daughters will receive 2/3 of the total inheritance, the parents combined will receive 1/3 (1/6 x 2), and according to verse 12, the wife will receive 1/8. But these amounts exceed the available estate. Consider another scenario: A man dies leaving only his mother, his wife, and two sisters. According to verses 11-12, the mother would receive 1/3 and the wife would receive 1/4. According to verse 177, the two sisters would receive a combined total of 2/3. But these figures again exceed the available inheritance. Such examples could be multiplied (see Katz, n.d.). These problematic verses have forced Muslim scholars to postulate tortuous explanations and, ultimately, to introduce their own rules by which to settle inheritance issues. But the rules, by definition, must simply dismiss one aspect of the Quran's directives in order to comply with another (see Rasool, et al., n.d.). In other words, the explanations and solutions offered, demonstrate that the Quran is in hopeless self-contradiction. The author of the Quran obviously felt compelled (very likely as a result of the pressure of an immediate and pressing circumstance) to venture into an area of practicality and specificity. However, in so doing, he failed to weigh the cumulative effect of his impulsive, logically inconsistent directives.

CONDEMNING FALSE GODS

The Quran frequently condemns the idolatry and polytheism of the Arabs. Next to the doctrine of hell, polytheism is undoubtedly the second most addressed subject in the Quran. Most of the utterances Muhammad directed to his contemporaries condemned their idolatry, because "they set up rivals to Allah" (*Surah* 14:30). However, in a surah devoted to vindicating the

Divine Unity, delivered in the year prior to the Hijrah, Allah
commanded Muhammad to refrain from condemning the deities to whom the pagan Arabs gave allegiance:

> Follow that which is inspired in thee from thy Lord; there
> is no God save Him; and turn away from the idolaters.
> Had Allah willed, they had not been idolatrous. We have
> not set thee as a keeper over them, nor art thou responsi-
> ble for them. **Revile not those unto whom they pray
> beside Allah** lest they wrongfully revile Allah through
> ignorance. Thus unto every nation have We made their
> deed seem fair. Then unto their Lord is their return, and
> He will tell them what they used to do (*Surah* 6:107-109,
> emp. added).

Allah's stated rationale for Muhammad refraining from speaking abusively of pagan deities is that to do so may cause them, in
their ignorance ("out of spite"–Ali), to do the same to Allah. However, this admonition stands in contradiction to Quranic revelations–revelations allegedly relayed by Muhammad to his contemporaries–that do this very thing:

> Have ye thought upon Al-Lat and Al-Uzza and Manat,
> the third, the other? Are yours the males and His the fe-
> males? That indeed were an unfair division! They are
> but names which ye have named, ye and your fathers,
> for which Allah hath revealed no warrant. They follow
> but a guess and that which (they) themselves desire (*Surah*
> 53:19-23).

> And they have plotted a mighty plot, and they have said:
> Forsake not your gods. Forsake not Wadd, nor Suw'a,
> nor Yaghuth and Ya'uq and Nasr. And they have led many
> astray, and Thou increasest the wrong-doers in naught
> save error (*Surah* 71:22-24).

These verses make direct reference to the gods of the pagan Arabs.
Muhammad, in accordance with Allah's directives–would have
delivered these declarations to his contemporaries who worshipped false gods–in direct violation of the previous surah. One
would expect this kind of inconsistency from a mere man who
was reacting orally to the circumstances he encountered, tailor-

ing his utterance to address the specific situation, but unconscious of utterances to the contrary in other settings separated by months or years.

ADULTERY, WITNESSES, AND RETRIBUTION

The reader will remember from chapter 1 the incident reported in the *Hadith* concerning rumors and gossip circulated against Muhammad's favorite wife A'ishah, regarding alleged sexual misconduct. Muhammad claimed to receive a revelation that denounced the talebearers and exonerated A'ishah. The surah, however, possesses the unmistakable indications of a humanly originated revelation that one would expect from a frustrated and resentful man who had become fed up with the gossip, and who wished to side with his wife. The indulgence of the reader is requested in giving full consideration to the following section of the Quran:

> A Sura which We have sent down and which We have ordained: in it We have sent down Clear Signs, in order that you may receive admonition. The woman and the man guilty of adultery or fornication, flog each of them with a hundred stripes: let not compassion move you in their case, in a matter prescribed by Allah, if you believe in Allah and the Last Day: and let a party of the Believers witness their punishment. Let no man guilty of adultery or fornication marry any but a woman similarly guilty, or an Unbeliever: nor let any but such a man or an Unbeliever marry such a woman: to the Believers such a thing is forbidden. And those who launch a charge against chaste women, and produce not four witnesses (to support their allegations), flog them with eighty stripes; and reject their evidence ever after: for such men are wicked transgressors; Unless they repent thereafter and mend (their conduct); for Allah is Oft-Forgiving, Most Merciful. And for those who launch a charge against their spouses, and have (in support) no evidence but their own, their solitary evidence (can be received) if they bear witness four times (with an oath) by Allah that they are solemnly

telling the truth; And the fifth (oath) (should be) that they
solemnly invoke the curse of Allah on themselves if they
tell a lie. But it would avert the punishment from the wife,
if she bears witness four times (with an oath) by Allah,
that (her husband) is telling a lie; And the fifth (oath)
should be that she solemnly invokes the wrath of Allah
on herself if (her accuser) is telling the truth. If it were not
for Allah's grace and mercy on you, and that Allah is
Oft-Returning, full of wisdom, (you would be ruined indeed) (*Surah* 24:1-10).

The surah then continues with more explicit references to the
accusations made against A'ishah.

Observe the conflicting, contradictory, and illogical admonitions embedded in this one section of the surah. First, while adul-
terers are to receive a beating of 100 stripes, false accusers are to
receive 80 (see chapter 7 for a further discussion regarding the
number). Apart from the logic behind the differing punishments,
this directive is in conflict with the Old Testament's handling of
the situation. If an accusing brother's charges were found to be
false, the false witness was to receive **the same punishment** that
he hoped to inflict on his brother (Deuteronomy 19:18-19).

Second, an adulterer may only marry another adulterer–or
an unbeliever. But this injunction clashes with the Quran's insistence that believers are not to marry unbelievers (*Surah* 2:221;
60:10). So the Quran **requires** a believing adulterer to marry an
unbeliever (or another believing adulterer), but also **forbids**
the believing adulterer to marry an **unbeliever**.

Third, four witnesses are required before charges of adultery
may be sustained (see chapter 7 for further discussion of the number). But if the husband is the accuser, four witnesses are not necessary. In fact, only **his word** (testimony) is necessary to sustain
the charge of adultery against his wife. Where is the logic in requiring **four** witnesses to sustain adultery–but **only one** if that
one is the husband?

Fourth, the testimony of a false accuser may never be accepted
again–unless he repents. But this injunction is inherently self-

contradictory and essentially meaningless. The reason given for never again accepting such a person's testimony is that he is a "wicked transgressor." But if he would lie about someone committing adultery, he would certainly lie about his repentance! The Quran is guilty of bringing up a feature and making a threat that, in practice, is superfluous and meaningless. It should have simply said that if the transgressor repents, he would be forgiven. Adding the aspect of discredited future testimony makes no sense—unless the transgressor's future testimony would be forever **rejected even if he did repent**.

Fifth, a husband may accuse his wife of infidelity with no witnesses other than his own word, and his testimony will count as the necessary four witnesses, if he will swear five oaths—four that he is telling the truth and a fifth one that the curse of Allah rests upon him if he is lying. However, his accused wife may avoid being punished even in the face of her husband's five oaths, if she also will swear the same five oaths—four that her husband is lying and a fifth oath that the curse of Allah rests upon her if he is telling the truth. But the man who would deliberately accuse his wife of adultery, knowing full well she is innocent, would certainly have no difficulty offering additional lies (five oral oaths) that he is telling the truth. And the adulterous wife would surely view her lying denial of his accusation as insignificant in comparison to the adultery she committed (and the prospect of a severe beating). The directive is meaningless, and quite obviously arose from an imperfect, uninspired author.

Additionally, notice that the Quran leaves a husband and wife who mutually accuse each other (he accusing her of adultery, she accusing him of lying) in an irresolvable stalemate. If the husband is lying, the woman avoids punishment by affirming her innocence. If the husband is telling the truth, the woman who committed adultery would have no trouble lying about it— thereby avoiding punishment. Once again, the Quranic injunction is effectively meaningless and beneath the dignity of deity— betraying its uninspired origin.

PHARAOH'S MAGICIANS: BELIEVERS OR NOT?

The reader will recall from chapter 4 that the Quran maintains that Pharaoh's magicians converted to Islam (*Surah* 7:120-122; 20:70; 26:46-48). The reader is urged to flip back to those pages and be reminded of the fact that the Quran gives explicit indication that the conversion of the wizards occurred immediately on the heels of Moses' rod swallowing up their own rods. However, a fourth recounting of the same incident contradicts this very point:

> Pharaoh said: "Bring me every sorcerer well versed." When the sorcerers came, Moses said to them: "You throw what you (wish) to throw!" When they had had their throw, Moses said: "What you have brought is sorcery: Allah will surely make it of no effect: for Allah does not prosper the work of those who make mischief. And Allah by His Words proves and establishes His Truth, however much the Sinners may hate it!" But **none believed in Moses** except some children of his People, because of the fear of Pharaoh and his chiefs, lest they should persecute them; and certainly Pharaoh was mighty on the earth and one who transgressed all bounds. Moses said: "O my People! If you do (really) believe in Allah, then in Him put your trust if you submit (your will to His)" (*Surah* 10:79-84–Ali, emp. added).

The reference to "children of his People" is an unmistakable reference to Moses' own people, i.e., the Israelites, even as subsequent verses in the context demonstrate (vss. 85ff.). This account matches fairly closely with the other three accounts in the Quran–except in the forthright declaration that "none believed." Indeed, the reason is given for this continuing unbelief–"fear of Pharaoh and his chiefs."

Another discrepancy involving the Pharaoh of Moses' day concerns his stated fate. The Quran forthrightly declares that Pharaoh and his army were drowned in the Red Sea: "And he wished to scare them from the land, but **We drowned him** and those with him, **all together**" (*Surah* 17:103, emp. added); "So

We seized him and his hosts, and **We flung them into the sea**: now behold what was the End of those who did wrong! (*Surah* 28:40–Ali, emp. added); "So, when they angered Us, We punished them and **drowned them every one**. And We made them **a thing past,** and an example for those after (them)" (*Surah* 43: 55-56, emp. added). These verses and their contexts are straightforward in affirming that the Pharaoh who Moses faced was killed by drowning. But this affirmation is in direct contradiction with another surah that claims that Pharaoh converted to Islam at the last moment and was saved:

> And We brought the Children of Israel across the sea, and Pharaoh with his hosts pursued them in rebellion and transgression, till, when the (fate of) drowning overtook him, he exclaimed: I believe that there is no God save Him in whom the Children of Israel believe, and I am of those who surrender (unto Him), What! Now! When hitherto thou hast rebelled and been of the wrongdoers? But **this day We save thee in thy body** that thou mayest be a portent for those after thee. Lo! most of mankind are heedless of Our portents (*Surah* 10:91-93, emp. added).

Observe that here the Quran not only claims that Pharaoh was saved from drowning, it even uses precision in emphasizing this rescue was "in thy body," i.e., Pharaoh was saved while in his body. The fact of this contradiction is strengthened further by the contextual parallel seen between *Surah* 10 and *Surah* 17. Both surahs allude to the circumstance of the Israelites being given the Promised Land in the verse immediately following the drowning of Pharaoh (10:94; 17:104). Such discrepancies are not infrequent in the Quran.

HISTORICAL INACCURACY

Kings and Prophets in Israel

The Quran also contains anachronisms, historical compressions, and garbled chronology. For example, observe the following allusion to the Israelites in relation to the appointment of kings:

The Jews and Christians say: We are sons of Allah and His loved ones. Say: Why then doth He chastise you for your sins? Nay, ye are but mortals of His creating. He forgiveth whom He will, and chastiseth whom He will. Allah's is the Sovereignty of the heavens and the earth and all that is between them, and unto Him is the journeying. O people of the Scripture! Now hath Our messenger come unto you to make things plain after an interval (of cessation) of the messengers, lest ye should say: There came not unto us a messenger of cheer nor any Warner. Now hath a messenger of cheer and a Warner come unto you. Allah is Able to do all things. And (remember) **when Moses said unto his people**: O my people! Remember Allah's favour unto you, how **he placed among you Prophets, and He made you kings**, and gave you that (which) He gave not to any (other) of (His) creatures. O my people! Go into the holy land which Allah hath ordained for you. Turn not in flight, for surely ye turn back as losers (*Surah* 5:18-21, emp. added).

Anyone familiar with the history of the Jews knows that their first king was Saul. But Saul was appointed king **some 500 years after Moses**! The same may be said of prophets:

And when ye said unto Moses: O Moses! We are weary of one kind of food; so call upon thy Lord for us that he bring forth for us of that which the earth groweth—of its herbs and its cucumbers and its corn and its lentils and its onions. He said: Would ye exchange that which is higher for that which is lower? Go down to settled country, thus ye shall get that which ye demand. And humiliation and wretchedness were stamped upon them and they were visited with wrath from Allah. That was because they disbelieved in Allah's revelations and **slew the prophets** wrongfully. That was for their disobedience and transgression (*Surah* 2:61, emp. added).

The Israelites slew no prophets in Moses' day. Moses was, in fact, the premiere prophet for the nation of Israel: "Above all, the creative founder of the Israelitish national religion, Moses, is a prophet in the eminent sense of the word" (Orelli, 1939, 4:2467). Muhammad had undoubtedly heard of the many kings and prophets in the Old Testament among the Israelites. But as he was dependent on oral sources and his own memory, the details of chronology would have escaped him.

Some have suggested that "making kings" does not refer to the kings who were later appointed in Israel, but rather is a reference to what God made the Israelites themselves to be, i.e., a nation of kings. But, of course, this explanation leaves the Quran in the same predicament—since God did no such thing. He made them a "kingdom of priests" (Exodus 19:6)—but not kings. The eventual appointment of kings was **foretold** in Moses' day (Deuteronomy 17:14ff.), but the monarchy was a future circumstance, and the nation itself was never a nation of kings.

Pharaoh's Advisor and the Tower

Another example pertains to the narratives concerning the Pharaoh who opposed Moses:

> And Pharaoh said: O Chiefs! I know not that ye have a god other than me, so kindle for me (a fire), O Haman, to bake the mud; and set up for me a lofty tower in order that I may survey the god of Moses; and lo! I deem him of the liars. And he and his hosts were haughty in the land without right, and deemed that they would never be brought back to Us (*Surah* 28:38-39).

> And Pharaoh said: O Haman! Build for me a tower that haply I may reach the roads, the roads of the heavens, and may look upon the God of Moses, though verily I think him a liar. Thus was the evil that he did made fairseeming unto Pharaoh, and he was debarred from the (right) way. The plot of Pharaoh ended but in ruin (*Surah* 40:36-37).

The allusion to the construction of a tower, out of baked bricks of mud, out of haughtiness, for the purpose of reaching up into the heavens, bears a striking resemblance to those very details in the biblical account of the Tower of Babel (Genesis 11:1ff.)—an event that took place centuries before the Pharaoh of Moses' day. The name "Haman," on the other hand, connects with the prominent official of the Persian King Ahasuerus (Xerxes I) many centuries after Moses (Esther 3:1ff.). The Haman of the Quran, like the biblical character, held a prominent position in the sight of his king (*Surah* 28:6,8; 40:24). With such heavy reliance on oral Jewish sources, it is easy to see how the author of the Quran could portray the Pharaoh (from Exodus) as asking Haman (from Esther) to build a tower (from Genesis). The likelihood of such happening is strengthened by the fact that the Quran associates Korah with Pharaoh and Haman (*Surah* 29:39; 40:24). And a rabbinical source that reports details pertaining to the Tower of Babel (*Sanhedrin* 109a) proceeds to relate details concerning Korah (*Sanhedrin* 110a).

CONCLUSION

Many additional internal discrepancies that riddle the Quran have been identified over the centuries. Those noted in this chapter are sufficient to establish the point: the Quran manifests characteristics that indicate its human origin.

One of the most disturbing and disconcerting literary features of the Quran is its constant piecemeal approach to subject matter. In addition to innumerable repetitions and unusually redundant exclamations, the Quran flits from one idea to another without any real connection between them. It is difficult to establish context at any given point in the narrative since, so often, there is none! Possible explanations for this characteristic is that the verses were collected after Muhammad's death and compiled together in a different form and order than originally uttered—a circumstance that has serious implications for inspiration (see chapter 6). Another explanation is that the author of the Quran was an uninspired man who was simply giving vent—off the cuff, on the spur of the moment—to his own interests, frustrations, views, and impulsive reactions to his surroundings. His own intellectual development and mental acumen prevented him from providing a cogent, coherent, logical, sustained analysis of and defense of each topic presented. If the Quran were actually inspired by God, the diligent student would be able to pin down precise meanings based on contextual features and clues embedded in the text by the divine Author (as is the case with the Bible). Instead, the thought units of the Quran are frequently disconnected, ambiguous, vague, and undecipherable. This internal attribute alone is sufficient for the unbiased reader to conclude that God is not the Author of the Quran.

Page excerpt
from the Quran

Chapter 6

TEXTUAL TRANSMISSION

If a supernatural being were to communicate information to a human being for the purpose of providing His Word to all humanity, three processes would be essential. First, the initial human recipient of the message would need to be "inspired," i.e., specially guided in his initial reception of the divine message. His oral utterances would need to be errorless. Second, his inerrant oral proclamations would need to be committed to writing in a pristine, unaltered condition—divinely guarded from the errors typical of human authors. Third, the original inerrant written production would need to be sufficiently preserved and transmitted so that succeeding generations of people would have access to the same information and be reasonably certain that the message had not been altered. On all three of these critical counts, the credibility of the Quran is called into question.

To the informed mind, it is evident that **all** documents (including the Bible and the Quran) that have been passed down through history have undergone variation. Thus, the need exists to engage in scholarly investigation in order to reconstruct the original text. This necessity should cause no great concern. The original readings of the Old and New Testaments can be, and have been, recovered through the science of textual criticism (see Appendix 1). To the Muslim mind, however, even to contemplate subjecting the Quran to textual criticism is unthinkable and blasphemous. The Muslim masses are convinced that the original text of the Quran has been preserved in a completely unchanged state. Muslim scholar Nasr articulated this virtually universal sentiment:

> For Muslims, everything about the Quran is sacred—its sounds, the very words of the Arabic language chosen by God to express His message, the letters in which it is written, and even the parchment or paper that constitutes the physical aspect of the sacred text. Muslims carry the Quran with full awareness of its sacred reality and usually **do not touch it unless they have made their ablutions and are ritually clean**. They **kiss it and pass under it when going on a journey**, and many carry a small copy of it with them at all times for protection. The Quran is that central sacred presence that determines all aspects of Muslim life and the source and fountainhead of all that can be authentically called Islamic (2003, pp. 42-43, emp. added).

Muslims, in fact, in comparing Islam with Christianity, parallel the Quran, not with the Bible, but with Christ (Nasr, 2002, p. 23). So, for the average Muslim, the issue of whether the Quran has been preserved—unchanged since its first appearance—is a nonissue. It is not even open for consideration.

DUBIOUS TRANSMISSION

It is ironic that Muslims frequently make the uninformed claim that the Bible has been corrupted through transmission over the centuries, while the Quran is exempt from such a predicament. Yet the process by which the Quranic text was crystallized, **as reported by the Islamic scholars themselves**, demonstrates that the preservation of the text of the Quran has been a precarious procedure from the beginning. Muslims universally insist that Muhammad was illiterate, i.e., he could not read or write. They maintain that he received nonliterary (i.e., unwritten) revelations from the angel Gabriel from A.D. 610 to near his death in 632, which he then **repeated orally** to his contemporaries (Nasr, 2003, p. 39). He never wrote down any of his revelations himself—a fact confirmed by the Quran itself (*Surah* 6:7; 7:158; 17:93; 25:5; 29:48,51). The text of the Quran therefore existed initially in a purely oral form as uttered by Muhammad.

The next stage in the transmission and preservation of the Quran was its retrieval from the minds and memories of its initial hearers. It was only later—at least a year after Muhammad's death—that followers began to gather their recollections of Muhammad's oral utterances that had been written on date palm leaves, camel bones, parchments, and other assorted materials. While some Muslim scholars claim that all the surahs of the Quran had been recorded in writing before Muhammad's death—"a question on which there are conflicting traditions" (Gibb, 1953, p. 33)—Pickthall admits:

> But the written surahs were **dispersed among the people**; and when, in a battle which took place during the Caliphate of Abu Bakr—that is to say, within two years of the Prophet's death—a large number of those who knew the whole Koran by heart were killed, a collection of the whole Koran was made and put in writing (p. xxviii, emp. added).

Compare this claim with a similar one offered by Muslim apologists:

> [T]he Qur'an was recited publicly in front of both the Muslim and non-Muslim communities during the life of the Prophet Muhammad. The entire Qur'an was also completely written down in lifetime of the Prophet, and numerous companions of the Prophet memorized the entire Qur'an word-for-word as it was revealed. So unlike other scriptures, the Qur'an was always in the hands of the common believers, it was always thought to be God's word and, **due to widespread memorization**, it was perfectly preserved (Masters, et al., 2003, emp. added).

Islamic apologists seem unconcerned that this process of trans-ferring the Quran from the memories of followers to written form was an **uninspired** process, i.e., with no supernatural guidance attached to it. Fallible human memory is a dubious basis on which to stake God's Word. The memories and subjective recollections of uninspired men are far more feeble and suspect than the work of translators and scribes who work from existing manuscripts. In sharp contrast, the Bible was **written down by inspiration— i.e., by divine guidance** (1 Corinthians 14:37; 2 Timothy 3:16; 2 Thessalonians 2:15). No such claim is made for the Quran. Ad-ditionally, the fragments were thrown together without regard to chronology or system, whereas the New Testament books are self-contained, with separate and identifiable themes, and pos-sess chronological correlation to the whole. Muslim scholar Mah-moud Ayoub admits that the Quran "consisted of **scattered frag-ments** either privately collected or preserved in **human mem-ory**. It was **the Muslim community** which in the end gave the Quran its final form and reduced it to a single standard version which remains unchanged to this day" (as quoted in MacRuaidh, n.d., emp. added). The "Muslim community"? Not God?

Abu Bakr, the first caliph, is credited with collecting together the written fragments, oral traditions, and memories of Muslims to produce the first official, written Quran. Rodwell recounts the traditional Muslim reports:

> The scattered fragments of the Koran were in the first in-stance collected by his immediate successor Abu Bekr, about a year after the Prophet's death, at the suggestion of Omar, who foresaw that, as the Muslim warriors, **whose memories were the sole depositaries of large por-tions of the revelations**, died off or were slain, as had been the case with many in the battle of Yamama, A.H. 12 [A.D. 634–DM], the loss of the greater part, or even of the whole, was imminent. Zaid Ibn Thabit, a native of Medina, and one of the Ansars, or helpers, who had been Muhammad's amanuensis, was the person fixed upon to carry out the task, and we are told that he "gathered together" the fragments of the Koran from every quar-

ter, "from date leaves and tablets of white stone, and **from the breasts of men**." The copy thus formed by Zaid probably remained in the possession of Abu Bekr during the remainder of his brief caliphate, who committed it to the custody of Haphsa, one of Muhammad's widows, and this text continued during the ten years of Omar's caliphate to be the standard. In the copies made from it, **various readings naturally and necessarily sprung up**; and these, under the caliphate of Othman, led to such serious disputes between the faithful, that it became necessary to interpose.... Othman determined **to establish a text which should be the sole standard**, and entrusted the redaction to the Zaid already mentioned, with whom he associated as colleagues, three, according to others, twelve of the Koreisch, in order to secure the purity of that Meccan idiom in which Muhammad had spoken, should any occasions arise in which the collators might have to decide upon **various readings**. Copies of the text formed were thus forwarded to several of the chief military stations in the new empire, and **all previously existing copies were committed to the flames** (1950, pp. 1-2, emp. added).

Two observations are noteworthy. First, the fact that Abu Bakr even felt compelled to produce a single volume of the Quran is proof that one did not exist previously. Notice the wording of the relevant *Hadith*:

Narrated Zaid bin Thabit:

SAHIH AL-BUKHARI

Abu Bakr As-Siddiq sent for me when the people of Yamama had been killed (i.e., a number of the Prophet's Companions who fought against Musailama). (I went to him) and found 'Umar bin Al-Khattab sitting with him. Abu Bakr then said (to me), "'Umar has come to me and said: 'Casualties were heavy among the Qurra' of the Qur'an (i.e., those who knew the Quran by heart) on the day of the Battle of Yamama, and I am afraid that more heavy casualties may take place among the Qurra' on other battlefields, **whereby a large part of the Qur'an may be lost**. Therefore I suggest, you (Abu Bakr) order that the Qur'an be collected.' I said to 'Umar, 'How can you do something which Allah's Apostle did not do?' 'Umar said, 'By Allah, that is a good project.' 'Umar kept on urging me to accept his proposal till Allah opened my chest for it and I began to realize the good in the idea which 'Umar had realized." Then Abu Bakr said (to me): "You are a wise young man and we do not have any suspicion about you, and you used to write the Divine Inspiration for Allah's Apostle. So you should search for (the fragmentary scripts of) the Qur'an and collect it in one book." By Allah if they had ordered me to shift one of the mountains, it would not have been heavier for me than this ordering me to collect the Qur'an. Then I said to Abu Bakr, "How will you do something which Allah's Apostle did not do?" Abu Bakr replied, "By Allah, it is a good project." Abu Bakr kept on urging me to accept his idea until Allah opened my chest for what He had opened the chests of Abu Bakr and 'Umar. So I started looking for the Qur'an and collecting it from (what was written on) palmed stalks, thin white stones **and also from the men who knew it by heart**, till I found the last Verse of Surat At-Tauba (Repentance) with Abi Khuzaima Al-Ansari (as quoted in MacRuaidh, emp. added).

If the Quran had been already committed to writing and collated, the deaths of reciters would not have been the great concern that it obviously was to Caliph Bakr. Second, with the allusions to "memories," "fragments," "date leaves," "the breasts of men," "one of Muhammad's widows," "disputes between the faithful," "three to twelve colleagues," "previously existing copies were committed to the flames"—the reader is surely surprised that the transmission of the textual integrity of the Quran was dependent upon such problematic circumstances.

Observe further that although this official action was taken in an effort to establish and finalize the text of the Quran, the matter still was not settled. The issue resurfaced years later during the caliphate of Uthman, and was of such concern that further steps had to be taken. Again, the *Hadith* report the details:

Anas ibn Malik
SAHIH AL-BUKHARI

> Hudhayfah ibn al-Yaman came to Uthman at the time
> when the people of Sham and the people of Iraq were
> waging war to conquer Armenia and Azerbaijan. Hudhay-
> fah was afraid of their (the people of Sham and Iraq) **dif-
> ferences in the recitation of the Qur'an**, so he said to
> Uthman, "O chief of the believers! Save this nation be-
> fore they differ about the Book (Qur'an) as Jews and the
> Christians did before." So Uthman sent a message to
> Hafsah saying, "Send us the manuscripts of the Qur'an
> so that we may compile the Qur'anic materials in per-
> fect copies and return the manuscripts to you." Hafsah
> sent it to Uthman. Uthman then ordered Zayd ibn Thabit,
> Abdullah ibn az-Zubayr, Sa'id ibn al-'As, and Abdur Rah-
> man ibn Harith **to rewrite the manuscripts in perfect
> copies**. Uthman said to the three Qurayshi men, "In case
> you disagree with Zayd ibn Thabit **on any point in the
> Qur'an**, then write it in the dialect of Quraysh as the
> Qur'an was revealed in their tongue." They did so, and
> when they had written many copies, Uthman returned
> the original manuscripts to Hafsah. Uthman sent to ev-
> ery Muslim province one set of what they had copied,
> and ordered that **all the other Qur'anic materials**,
> whether written in fragmentary manuscripts or whole
> copies, **be burnt** (as quoted in MacRuaidh, emp. added).

One Muslim Web site offers the following polemic rebuttal to
the charge that the transmission of the Quran in its earliest years
was precarious:

> [S]ome of the Companions **made mistakes in writing**
> or wrote down one reading instead of another…. Chris-
> tians like to hypocritically criticize the fact that Uthman
> burned copies of the Quran, etc., which is a big distor-
> tion. What he burned were **incorrect copies** of the Quran,
> which, strictly speaking, were not Qurans at all…. All of the
> Companions knew what the Quran was, so they burned
> **those with mistakes** (Squires, 2004, emp. added).

Even as the Muslim apologist offers his rebuttal, he seems oblivious to the fact that he has conceded the point: both memories

and written fragments contained mistakes! If some of the Companions of Muhammad wrote down portions of the Quran that later were deemed by other Companions to be **mistakes**, and whose transcriptions needed to be **burned**, who is to say that the former Companions were incorrect and the latter Companions were correct? Why should the memories of **some** of the Companions be preferred over the memories of the **others**? What some deemed as **mistakes**, others of equal authority, credibility, and memorization skill deemed as **accurate**.

Additionally, this means that the initial codification of the text of the Quran would date back only to the third caliphate–some twenty years after Muhammad's death (cf. Nasr, 2002, p. 24; Braswell, 1996, p. 248; Watt, 1961, p. 16), at which time the present non-chronological order of the surahs was effected, based largely on length (Rahman, 1979, p. 40).

Even if one assumes that Muhammad's original oral utterances were transferred accurately into written form, and even if Abu Bakr and Uthman managed to reconstruct the original oral utterances of Muhammad and commit them to an accurately written Quran, the third serious challenge to the Quran's authenticity–the transmission of that original writing down through the centuries to succeeding generations–remains. The science that deals with this question is known as "textual criticism." The task of the textual critic is to ascertain the original, pure form of a given document. A wealth of manuscript evidence attests to the authenticity of the New Testament (see Appendix 1). Though the Quran arose centuries **after** the appearance of New Testament revelation, the textual evidence that could authenticate the purity of the Quranic text has never been subjected to the scholastic analysis that has been so intensively applied to the Bible. An almost irrational, blind resistance even to **contemplating** the extant manuscript evidence prevails within Islam as a whole.

[NOTE: An examination of the available manuscript evidence for the Quran lies outside the purview and objective of this present study. Recommended research materials as a beginning point for the interested reader would include the following: Grohmann, 1958, pp. 213-231; Puin, 1996, pp. 107-111; "The Quranic Manuscripts"; Roper, 1992-1993; Deroche, 1992; Abbott, 1939; Arberry, 1967; Mark, 1999; Goldsack, 1906; "Textual Variants…"; Harris, 1926; Margoliouth, 1925; Gilchrist, 1986; Jeffery, 1952.]

Contrast these realizations with the Bible. The Bible teaches that once God's inspired spokesmen verbalized words, those words that God desired to be preserved for future generations necessarily had to be committed to writing by means of the same process of divine guidance. The Word from God had to be "confirmed" by the miraculous (see chapter 9). The extension and transference of inspiration from the spoken word to the written word is a critical and essential step. The Quran lacked this authentication process.

JUMBLED COLLATION

Another very serious indication of the Quran's tenuous textual transmission is the fact that individual verses, even phrases, apply to different occasions, but have been placed together as if referring to a single occasion. As Gibb explained: "[M]ost of the Medinan and many of the Meccan suras are composite, containing discourses or different periods bound up together" (1953, p. 24). Muslim translator Mohammed Pickthall admitted as much: "The arrangement is not easy to understand. Revelations of various dates and on different subjects are to be found together in one surah; verses of Madinah revelation are found in Meccan surahs; some of the Madinah surahs, though of late revelation, are placed first and the very early Meccan surahs at the end" (p. xxviii). This predicament constitutes a formidable obstacle to the effort to establish the transmission of an inerrant Quran.

Consider a few instances of the jumbled state of the Quranic text in which verses appear to be out of place. Regarding *Surah* 47, Pickthall explains: "It belongs to the first and second years after the Hijrah, **with the exception of v. 18**, which was revealed during the Hijrah" (p. 361, emp. added). In *Surah* 56–a Meccan surah–verse 40, according to Pickthall, "is said to have been revealed at Al-Madinah" (p. 385). Concerning *Surah* 61, Pickthall notes:

> In the copy of the Koran which I have followed, it is stated to have been revealed at Mecca, **though its contents evidently refer to the Madinah period**. It may have been revealed while the Prophet and his companions were encamped in the valley of Mecca during the negotiations of the Truce of Hudeybiyah, **with which some of its verses are associated by tradition** (p. 397, emp. added).

Regarding *Surah* 73, Pickthall states: "A very early Meccan revelation with the exception of the last verse, which all authorities assign to Al-Madinah" (p. 418). Concerning *Surah* 2, Pickthall notes: "The period of revelation is the years 1 and 2 A.H. **for the most part**, certain verses of legislation being considered as of later date" (p. 34, emp. added). Regarding *Surah* 6, Pickthall observes: **"With the possible exception of nine verses**, which some authorities–e.g., Ibn Salamah–ascribe to the Madinah period, the whole of this Surah belongs to the year before the Hijrah" (p. 108, emp. added). Regarding *Surah* 7: "The best authorities assign the whole of it to about the same period as Surah VI... though some consider vv. 163-167 to have been revealed at Al-Madinah" (p. 121). Concerning the 75 verses of *Surah* 8, Pickthall explains: "The date of revelation is the second year of the Hijrah **for the most part**. Some good Arabic authorities hold that vv. 30-40, or some of them, were revealed at Mecca just before the Hijrah" (p. 138, emp. added). However, he also notes that "[t]he concluding verses are of later date" (p. 137). *Surah* 10 is said to be "a late Meccan Surah, **with the exception of three verses** revealed at Al-Madinah" (p. 157, emp. added). This circumstance could be repeated many times over (cf. Pickthall, pp. 61,95,165, 182,186,195, et al.; cf. Rodwell–note #3, p. 339; notes #2 and #3, p. 325; note #1, p. 328; note #3, p. 332; note #1, p. 388).

All of these observations are uninspired speculations of mere men. That these clarifications have to be postulated is evidence that the Quran is a hodgepodge of verses and phrases precariously pieced together by unknown, uninspired redactors. Many of the original contexts have been lost, resulting in multiple potential meanings—or completely undecipherable meanings—as well as uncertain interpretations and applications. Additionally, portions of the Quran are so specific in their allusions that the original events that occasioned them are now indistinguishable. Islamic commentators themselves disagree as to their context and, hence, proper meaning (e.g., Pickthall's note #1, p. 39 on *Surah* 2:72-73).

Two related areas of concern regarding the Quran and its transmission are the matter of "abrogation" as well as the problem created by the development of diacritical marks in Arabic writing. Regarding the former question, Rodwell observed that "Muslims admit that there are 225 verses cancelled by later ones" (1950, p. 349). Regarding the latter question, Arabic scholar N.J. Dawood remarked in the introduction to his translation of the Quran: "[O]wing to the fact that the kufic script in which the Koran was originally written contained no indication of vowels or diacritical points, variant readings are recognized by Muslims as of equal authority" (1976, p. 10). The interested reader may study these issues and their impact on the Quran's credibility by consulting the extant literature (e.g., MacRuaidh; "On the Integrity…"; Geisler and Saleeb, 2002, pp. 62,98-99,201-202; Trifkovic, 2002, pp. 74-83; Noldeke, 1892; Green, 2001).

TRANSLATING THE QURAN

Muslims generally have been reluctant, even resistant, to translating the Quran into other languages—a notion known as the doctrine of the inimitability (*i'jaz*) of the Quran (Rahman, 1979, p. 40). The usual explanation for this hesitation has been that the meaning cannot be fully transferred from the Arabic into other languages. For example, Islamic scholar Seyyed Hossein Nasr referred to the Quran as "the verbatim Word of God in Islam" (2003, p. 3). Consequently, it is claimed, "no translation has been able or ever will be able to render the full meaning and 'presence' of the text" (p. 45). Pickthall announced in the preface to his translation of the Quran: "The Koran cannot be translated. That is the belief of old-fashioned Sheykhs and the view of the present writer.... It is only an attempt to present the meaning of the Koran" (p. vii). These declarations betray what J.I. Packer labeled an almost "superstitious regard" for the Quran (1958, pp. 89-90). They manifest an unjustified reverence for the Arabic language.

Of course, this claim is unfounded and indefensible—for at least two reasons. While misunderstanding and misinterpretation certainly can occur, all linguists know that the accurate transference of meaning from one language to another is achievable. Millions of people who speak differing languages are able to communicate with each other everyday. The United Nations and governments around the world regularly engage in political and economic interaction, fully capable of grasping each other's intended meanings. The fact that misunderstanding sometimes occurs does not negate the fact that correct meanings may be conferred from one language to another, and that the participants can **know** that they have understood each other correctly. Was God incapable of providing the world with His Word in such a way that its meaning can be transferred into the thousands of human languages that exist? If **we** can understand each other by overcoming language barriers—**surely the originator of human language can communicate His message through multiple human languages!** The claim that the Quran cannot be fully comprehended unless one reads it in Arabic is a claim that demonstrates ignorance of linguistics and the science of translation (see Appendix 1).

Additionally, the claim stands in conflict with the nature of God. The one true God would not insist that His Word remain in one language—let alone Arabic. He would not require the whole world to learn Arabic. In fact, this claim stands in contradiction to the Quran itself. Since it speaks favorably of the Bible (though Muslims now claim it has been corrupted), the Quran implicitly endorses the fact that God previously conveyed His will in **three** languages (i.e., Hebrew, Aramaic, and Greek). Yet, no Greek-speaking person was required to learn Hebrew or Aramaic, and no one whose native language was Hebrew was required to learn Greek. Jesus, Himself a Jew, often quoted from the Greek translation of the Old Testament. The very nature of God's communicative activities militates against the notion that He would suddenly lock His Word into one language, and then require everyone to learn how to understand and read that fourth language. In fact, the fixation—even obsession—that the Quran manifests toward "Arabic" (12:2; 13:37; 16:103; 20:113; 26:195; 39:28; 41: 3; 42:7; 43:3; 46:12; cf. 41:44) implies a human author who was overly influenced by, enamored with, and subject to his restricted, limited linguistic environment. [NOTE: Though the Quran repeatedly claims to have been given in "pure and clear" (*Surah* 16:103) **Arabic** speech—"in the perspicuous **Arabic tongue**" (*Surah* 26:195)—the fact is that it contains several foreign, **non**-Arabic words. For example, Syriac words occur in the Quran, including *masih* (Messiah) in *Surah* 3:45, *furqan* (salvation) in *Surah* 2:50, and *istabraq* (silk brocade) in *Surah* 76:21 (cf. Mingana, 1927, pp. 77-98; Margoliouth, 1939, pp. 53-61; Shorrosh, 1988, p. 199).]

CONCLUSION

Unlike the Bible, the textual integrity of the Quran lacks verification and authentication. Those who originally committed the Quran to writing were uninspired men. They depended on the fallible memories of uninspired men. The widespread Muslim attempt to wave aside the questions about the textual integrity of the Quran will not make the issue go away for those who are earnest seekers of truth. At this stage of the discussion, insufficient evidence has been forthcoming to demonstrate the accurate preservation of the Quran. Blindly dismissing the entire matter as irrelevant does not alter this fact.

Some feel that the Quran has been transferred substantially intact from its beginning to the present. Consider, for example, the following observation: "It is true that the Quran has been exceptionally well preserved and its text is very much that which was first compiled at the inception of Islam" (Gilchrist, 1986). Even if the manuscript evidence were to be forthcoming that could authenticate the textual integrity of the Quran, nevertheless, the evidence already presented in this book, and in the chapters to follow, renders the textual genuineness of the Quran essentially irrelevant. Its divine origin is called into more serious question on separate grounds.

Chapter 7

THE QURAN VS. THE NEW TESTAMENT: CONFLICTING CENTRAL DOCTRINES

Islam is ever evolving and splintering–like Christianity. Both, therefore, stand or fall, not on the basis of what adherents and practitioners say or do, but on the basis of authentication of their ultimate and final standards of authority, i.e., the Quran and the Bible. It is absolutely imperative that the reader recognizes the distinction between New Testament Christianity and the corrupt forms that developed **after** the first century, i.e., Catholicism and Protestant Denominationalism (cf. Miller, 2003b; Miller, 2003e). The same may be said of Islam. All that flies under the banner of "Islam" does not serve as an accurate manifestation of Quranic legislation.

It is equally imperative that the reader recognizes that the Quran and the Bible are in hopeless conflict and contradiction with each other. The discord and dissonance is weighty, extensive, and irresoluble. They conflict with one another on significant matters of doctrine, and they conflict with one another on scores of less-important minor details. Muslim apologists are sufficiently aware of these irreconcilable differences, to the extent that they have formulated, and vociferously defend, their official explanation—i.e., the Quran is correct and accurate, while the Bible has been hopelessly corrupted in transmission. That the original text of the Bible has been demonstrated unequivocally to be intact is given brief treatment in Appendix 1. That the Quran contains discrepancies was addressed in chapter 5. The present chapter identifies a few of the many conflicts that exist between the Quran and the Bible over major doctrinal matters.

In the first place, Christianity and Islam are in hopeless contradiction with each other regarding several significant concepts and core doctrines—contradictions that strike at the very heart of their respective approaches to religion, life, spirituality, and human existence. The most crucial contention—the greatest tension between the two religions—pertains to the person of Christ. On this solitary point, Islam and Christianity, the Bible and the Quran, can **never** agree. This disagreement is of such momentous import, and of such great magnitude, that the inexorable incompatibility is permanent.

THE PERSON OF JESUS

Jesus is alluded to in Pickthall's translation in 14 surahs. Observe a few of the Quran's declarations concerning the person of Jesus:

> Say: O People of the Scripture! [a reference to Christians—DM] Come to an agreement between us and you: that we shall worship none but Allah, and that we shall **ascribe no partner unto Him**, and that none of us shall **take others for lords beside Allah** (*Surah* 3:64, emp. added).
>
> And behold! Allah will say: "O Jesus the son of Mary! Did you say to men, 'worship me and my mother as gods in derogation of Allah'?" He will say: "Glory to You!

Never could I say what I had no right (to say). Had I said such a thing, You would indeed have known it. You know what is in my heart, though **I do not know what is in Yours.** For You know in full all that is hidden. Never said I to them anything except what You commanded me to say, to wit, 'Worship Allah, my Lord and your Lord'; And I was a witness over them whilst I dwelt amongst them; when You took me up, You were the Watcher over them, and You are a Witness to all things (*Surah* 5:116-117, Ali's translation, emp. added).

Praise be to Allah Who hath revealed the Scripture unto His slave…to give warning of stern punishment from Him…and to warn those who say: **Allah hath chosen a son,** (A thing) whereof they have no knowledge, nor (had) their fathers. **Dreadful is the word that cometh out of their mouths.** They **speak naught but a lie** (*Surah* 18:1-5, emp. added).

And they say: The Beneficent hath taken unto Himself a son. Assuredly **ye utter a disastrous thing,** whereby almost the heavens are torn, and the earth is split asunder and the mountains fall in ruins, **that ye ascribe unto the Beneficent a son,** when **it is not meet for (the Majesty of) the Beneficent that He should choose a son.** There is none in the heavens and the earth but cometh unto the Beneficient **as a slave** (*Surah* 19:88-93, emp. added).

Allah hath not chosen any son, nor is there any God along with Him; else would each God have assuredly championed that which he created, and some of them would assuredly have overcome others. Glorified be Allah above all that they allege (*Surah* 23:91, emp. added).

He unto Whom belongeth the sovereignty of the heavens and the earth, **He hath chosen no son nor hath He any partner in the sovereignty.** He hath created everything and hath meted out for it a measure (*Surah* 25:2, emp. added).

And the Jews say: Ezra is the son of Allah, and **the Christians say: The Messiah is the son of Allah.** That is their saying with their mouths. They imitate the saying of those who disbelieved of old. **Allah (Himself) fighteth against them. How perverse are they!** They have taken as lords beside Allah their rabbis and their monks and **the Messiah son of Mary,** when they were bidden to worship only One God. There is no God save Him (*Surah* 9:30-31, emp. added).

The Originator of the heavens and the earth! **How can He have a child, when there is for Him no consort,** when He created all things and is aware of all things? Such is Allah, your Lord. There is no God save Him, the Creator of all things, so worship Him (*Surah* 6:102-103, emp. added).

These references, and many others (e.g., 2:116; 6:101; 17:111; 19:35; 39:3-6; 43:14,59,81; 72:3-4; cf. 112), demonstrate that the Quran depicts Jesus as a mere man—a prophet like Muhammad—who was created by God like all other created beings: "The Messiah, son of Mary, was no other than a messenger, messengers (the like of whom) had passed away before him" (*Surah* 5:75; cf. 42:9,13,21). Indeed, when Jesus is compared to any of the prophets (listed as Abraham, Ishmael, Isaac, and Jacob), Allah is represented as stating: "We make no distinction between any of them" (*Surah* 2:136; 3:84). Though the Quran seems to accept the notion of the virgin conception (*Surah* 21:91), to attribute divinity to Jesus, or to assign to Jesus equal rank with God, is to utter a "dreadful" and "disastrous" thing of such proportions as nearly to tear the Universe apart. It is to formulate "nothing but a lie" (cf. *Surah* 16:51)! The Quran portrays Jesus as specifically **denying** any sonship. He is depicted in the same category with all who approach God—not as a son, but merely as a slave. In fact, the Quran declares that Jesus was created just like Adam: "Lo! the likeness of Jesus with Allah is as the likeness of Adam. He created him of dust, then He said unto him: Be! and he is" (*Surah* 3:59). Further, if Allah had so chosen, **He could destroy the Messiah** along with all other created things:

They indeed have disbelieved who say: Lo! Allah is the Messiah, son of Mary. Say: Who then can do aught against Allah, **if He had willed to destroy the Messiah son of**

Mary, and his mother and everyone on earth? Allah's is the Sovereignty of the heavens and the earth and all that is between them. He created what He will. And Allah is Able to do all things (*Surah* 5:17, emp. added).

Here, indeed, is **the number one conflict** between Islam and Christianity: the deity and person of Christ. If Christ is Who the Bible represents Him to be, then Islam and the Quran are completely fictitious. If Jesus Christ is Who the Quran represents Him to be, then Christianity is baseless and blasphemous. On this point alone, these two religions can **never** achieve harmony. To the Muslim, it is blasphemy to attribute divinity to Muhammad; to the Christian, it is blasphemy **not** to attribute divinity to Christ. The New Testament is very, very clear: the heart, core, and soul of the Christian religion is **allegiance to Jesus Christ as God, Lord, and Savior**.

To exhaust what the New Testament has to say on this subject would require volumes (cf. John 21:25). However, it only takes a few verses to establish the clarity with which the New Testament affirms the divine nature of Jesus. The entire book of John is devoted to defending the divine identity of Christ, articulated in its thematic statement: "And truly Jesus did many other signs in the presence of His disciples, which are not written in this book; but these are written that you may believe that **Jesus is the Christ, the Son of God,** and that believing you may have life in **His** name (John 20:30-31, emp. added). The book of John pinpoints seven "signs," i.e., miraculous acts, performed by Jesus while He was on Earth that **proved** His divine personhood—beginning with the very first verse that forthrightly affirms: "In the beginning was the Word, and the Word was with God, and **the Word was God**. He was in the beginning with God. **All things were made through Him**, and without Him nothing was made that was made. In Him was life, and the life was the light of men" (John 1:1-4, emp. added). The "Word" is Jesus (1:14). If "without Him nothing was made that was made," then Jesus Himself was not made. He is not a created being. He partakes of divinity, and shares status as Creator. This thesis reaches its climactic pinnacle when Thomas was forced to arrive at the only possible conclusion regarding the person of Jesus, when he exclaimed: "My Lord and My God!" (John 20:28). To the Muslim and the Quran, such a declaration is preposterous, horrifying, blasphemous, and absolutely unacceptable. But it is the unmistakable teaching of the New Testament.

In the Old Testament, when Moses encountered God at the burning bush, he asked God to clarify His name so that he would be able to respond appropriately to the Israelites when he went to them in Egypt on God's mission. God answered: "'I AM WHO I AM.' And He said, 'Thus you shall say to the children of Israel, 'I AM has sent me to you'" (Exodus 3:14). "I Am" is a reference to the eternality of God. Being God, He is eternal—with no beginning and no end. He is self-existent, and has always existed. Yet in the book of John, Jesus repeatedly identified His own person with this same appellation (John 4:26; 8:24,28,58; 13:19). For example, when Jesus explained to the hostile Jews that Abraham had rejoiced to see His day, they responded, "You are not yet fifty years old, and have You seen Abraham?" Jesus retorted: "Most assuredly, I say to you, before Abraham was, I AM" (John 8:58). The Jews unquestionably understood Jesus' remark to be a claim to divinity, and promptly took up stones to execute Him for blasphemy (vs. 59).

Another Bible text where the deity of Jesus is set forth in precise terms is the book of Colossians. Paul forcefully affirmed regarding Jesus: "He is the image of the invisible God, the firstborn over all creation. For **by Him all things were created** that are in heaven and that are on earth, visible and invisible, whether thrones or dominions or principalities or powers. All things were created through Him and for Him. And **He is before all things**, and in Him all things consist" (1:15-17, emp. added); "For **in Him dwells all the fullness of the Godhead bodily**" (2:9, emp. added).

Such depictions of Jesus are frequent in the New Testament. Jesus was certainly a prophet, as the Quran itself affirms (*Surah* 4:163); but Jesus was not **just** a prophet. He was God in the flesh.

In fact, oral confession of the **deity** of Christ is prerequisite to becoming a Christian (Romans 10:9-10). This singular point makes Christianity and Islam forever incompatible. One must be a **Christian** to be saved (John 14:6; Acts 4:12; 26:28; 1 Peter 4:16), and yet one cannot be a Christian without believing in and verbally confessing the **deity** of Christ. One cannot even pray to God, let alone have sins remitted by Him, without approaching Him through Jesus (John 14:6,13; 15:16; 16:23-24; Romans 5:2; Ephesians 2:18). The Bible declares that Jesus was the final revelation of God to man (Hebrews 1:1-3). There have been no others.

Observe the following juxtaposition of passages from the Quran and the New Testament:

> *Surah* 23:91–"**Allah hath not chosen any son**, nor is there any God along with Him."
> Matthew 17:5–"This is **My beloved Son**, in whom I am well pleased. Hear Him!"

> *Surah* 18:4-5–"those who say: Allah hath chosen a son... speak naught **but a lie**."
> 1 John 2:22-23–"**Who is a liar** but he who denies that Jesus is the Christ? He is antichrist who denies the Father **and the Son. Whoever denies the Son does not have the Father either**; he who acknowledges the Son has the Father also."

> *Surah* 19:92–"It is not meet for (the Majesty of) the Beneficent **that He should choose a son**."
> John 5:23–"All should **honor the Son just as they honor the Father**. He who does not honor the Son does not honor the Father who sent Him."
> 1 John 4:15–"Whoever confesses that **Jesus is the Son of God**, God abides in him, and he in God."
> 1 John 5:10-12–"He who believes in the Son of God has the witness in himself; he who does not believe God has made Him a liar, because he has not believed the testimony that **God has given of His Son**. And this is the testimony: that God has given us eternal life, and **this life is in His Son**. He who has the Son has life; **he who does not have the Son of God does not have life**."

THE DEATH AND RESURRECTION OF JESUS: ATONEMENT, SIN, AND REDEMPTION

Another very significant clash between the Quran and the Bible, intimately aligned with the person and deity of Jesus, is His redemptive role. The death, burial, and resurrection of Jesus Christ are showcased in the New Testament as the central platform of Christianity (cf. 1 Corinthians 15:1-4; cf. Acts 2:22-36; 3:13-18; 4:2,10,25-28; 5:30-31; 17:31; et al.). The primary reason Jesus came into the world was to carry out the absolutely necessary plan of salvation, the means of atonement that makes it possible for God to forgive sin (Isaiah 53:10-11; Mark 10:45; Luke 19:10; 2 Corinthians 5:19; Philippians 2:5-8; 1 Timothy 2:5-6). It is only through Christ that forgiveness of sin can occur (Acts 4:12; 13:38; Ephesians 2:18). And it is only through Christ's shed **blood** that this remission could be achieved (Hebrews 9:11-10:4,19; 2:14; Colossians 1:14,20; 1 Peter 1:18-21; Revelation 1:5). Christ's crucifixion (necessarily followed by His resurrection) is unequivocally the supreme feature of the Christian religion. Without that unique and singular event, propitiation would be **impossible** (Romans 3:25; Hebrews 2:17; 1 John 2:2). Atonement for sin is a mandatory, indispensable necessity—intimately linked with the very nature of deity. God cannot remain just, while simply overlooking or dismissing human sin (Romans 3:25).

But the Quran, in conspicuous contradistinction, shows abject ignorance of the notion of atonement. It, in fact, denies the historicity of the crucifixion of Christ. In a passage that recounts the frequent disobedience of the Jews, the point is made:

> And because of their saying: We slew the Messiah Jesus son of Mary, Allah's messenger—**They slew him not nor crucified, but it appeared so unto them**; and lo! those who disagree concerning it are in doubt thereof; they have no knowledge thereof save pursuit of a conjecture; **they slew him not for certain**, but Allah took him up unto Himself. Allah was ever Mighty, Wise (*Surah* 4:157-158, emp. added).

Since Jesus (allegedly) was not actually crucified, it follows that
He likewise was not resurrected from the dead:

> (And remember) when Allah said: O Jesus! Lo! **I am
> gathering thee and causing thee to ascend unto Me**,
> and am cleansing thee of those who disbelieve and am
> setting those who follow thee above those who disbe-
> lieve until the Day of Resurrection. Then unto Me ye
> will (all) return, and I shall judge between you as to that
> wherein ye used to differ (*Surah* 3:55, emp. added).

In sharp contrast, the New Testament places the resurrection
as the platform on which the rest of the Christian system rests. If
Jesus was not crucified and subsequently resurrected from the
dead, then Christianity is a sham and completely indefensible.
As Paul declared:

> Now if Christ is preached that He has been raised from
> the dead, how do some among you say that there is no
> resurrection of the dead? But if there is no resurrection
> of the dead, then Christ is not risen. And **if Christ is not
> risen, then our preaching is empty and your faith is
> also empty**. Yes, and **we are found false witnesses of
> God**, because we have testified of God that He raised up
> Christ, whom He did not raise up—if in fact the dead do
> not rise. For if the dead do not rise, then Christ is not
> risen. And **if Christ is not risen, your faith is futile;
> you are still in your sins!** Then also those who have
> fallen asleep in Christ have perished. If in this life only
> we have hope in Christ, we are of all men the most piti-
> able (1 Corinthians 15:12-19, emp. added).

The author of the Quran appears oblivious to this deficiency.
He endorses Christianity (as long as Christians will acknowl-
edge God as singular), but denies the resurrection. Yet the Christian religion itself admits that if the resurrection did not take place,
it is a false religion. In fact, the very name "Christian" would be a
blasphemous term if Christ is not to be worshipped as God and
Savior. To identify oneself, or others, as "Christians" in an approving manner should be as unacceptable and repugnant to Islam as the identification of Muslims as "Mohammedans." Yet
the Quran frequently lends dignity to the term "Christian" in an
approving manner (*Surah* 2:62,111,113,120; 5:51,69,82; 22:17).

The Means of Forgiveness

Rejecting the crucial role occupied by the death and resurrection of Jesus, the Quran of necessity must leave the impression that God can simply forgive people if they will repent and submit (i.e., become Muslims). To "believe" means to accept Allah as the one and only God, and to accept Muhammad as Allah's ultimate and final messenger. Resignation and submission of one's will to this foundational principle (the *shahadas*), accompanied by good deeds in life, **is the means** of forgiveness in the Quran. Consider the following passages:

> And as for those who **believe and do good works,** He will pay them their wages in full (*Surah* 3:57, emp. added).

> Then, as for those who **believed and did good works,** unto them will He pay their wages in full, adding unto them of His bounty; and as for those who were scornful and proud, them will He punish with a painful doom (*Surah* 4:173, emp. added).

> O ye who believe! If ye keep your duty to Allah, He will give you discrimination (between right and wrong) and **will rid you of your evil thoughts and deeds, and will forgive you**. Allah is of infinite bounty (*Surah* 8:29, emp. added).

> And those who **believed and did good works** are made to enter the Gardens underneath which rivers flow, therein abiding by permission of their Lord, their greeting therein: Peace! (*Surah* 14:23, emp. added).

> Say: O My slaves who have been prodigal to their own hurt! Despair not of the mercy of Allah, Who forgiveth all sins. Lo! He is the Forgiving, the Merciful. **Turn unto Him repentant, and surrender unto Him,** before there come unto you the doom, when ye cannot be helped (*Surah* 39:53-54, emp. added).

These verses spotlight the Quran's formula for salvation. Turning from unbelief to Allah is the specific grounds upon which Allah can forgive past sin and extend continuing forgiveness to the believer (cf. *Surah* 11:3; 26:51; 45:30; 46:31). Not only does the Quran nowhere offer a deeper explanation by which forgiveness may be divinely bestowed (i.e., blood atonement), it states explicitly that it is genuine (i.e., non-hypocritical) belief and good deeds that rectify sin:

And **those who believe and do good works** and believe in that which is revealed unto Muhammad–and it is the truth from their Lord–**He riddeth them of their ill-deeds** and improveth their state (*Surah* 47:2, emp. added).

And whosoever striveth, striveth only for himself, for lo! Allah is altogether Independent of (His) creatures. And as **for those who believe and do good works, We shall remit from them their evil deeds** and shall repay them the best that they did.... And as for those who believe and do good works, We verily shall make them enter in among the righteous (*Surah* 29:6-7,9, emp. added).

Compare Ali's translation of these same verses:

And if any strive (with might and main), **they do so for their own souls**: for Allah is free of all needs from all creation. Those who believe and work righteous deeds, from them **We shall blot out all evil (that may be) in them**, and We shall reward them according to the best of their deeds.... And those who believe and work righteous deeds, them We shall admit to the company of the Righteous (emp. added).

Another example is seen in the following Quranic utterance:

Thou seest the wrong-doers fearful of **that which they have earned**, and it will surely befall them; while those who **believe and do good works** (will be) in flowering meadows of the Gardens, having what they wish from their Lord. This is the great preferment. This it is which Allah announceth unto His bondmen who **believe and do good works**. Say (O Muhammad, unto mankind): I ask of you no fee therefore, save lovingkindness among kinsfolk. And whoso **scoreth a good deed** We add unto its good for him. Lo! Allah is Forgiving, Responsive. Or say they: He hath invented a lie concerning Allah? If Allah willed, He could have sealed thy heart (against them). And Allah will wipe out the lie and will vindicate the truth by His words. Lo! He is aware of what is hidden in the breasts (of men). And He it is Who **accepteth repentance** from his bondmen, **and pardoneth the evil deeds,** and knoweth what ye do. And **accepteth those who do good works,** and giveth increase unto them of His bounty. And as for disbelievers, theirs will be an awful doom (*Surah* 42:22-26, emp. added).

Where Pickthall has "whoso **scoreth a good deed,**" Ali renders it: "**if any one earns any good** We shall give him an increase of good in respect thereof" (vs. 23). The Quran explains that when Allah's warnings and signs eventually come to pass, "no good will it do to a soul to believe in them then, if it believed not before nor **earned righteousness through its faith**....He that does good shall have ten times as much to his credit" (Ali's translation of *Surah* 6:159,161, emp. added). Such verses underscore the fact that **the means** by which Allah can forgive sins is the Muslim's commission of good deeds (cf. *Surah* 25:70; 39:35; 64:9).

In fact, the good deeds must outweigh the bad deeds on the Day of Judgment: "Then, he whose balance (of good deeds) will be (found) heavy, will be in a Life of good pleasure and satisfaction. But he whose balance (of good deeds) will be (found) light, will have his home in a (bottomless) Pit. And what will explain to you what this is? (It is) a Fire blazing fiercely!" (*Surah* 101:6-11, Ali's translation). The Quran even states explicitly that **good deeds drive away evil deeds**:

> And lo! unto each thy Lord will verily repay his works in full. Lo! He is informed of what they do. So tread thou the straight path as thou art commanded, and those who turn (unto Allah) with thee, and transgress not. Lo! He is Seer of what ye do.... Establish worship at the two ends of the day and in some watches of the night. Lo! **good deeds annul ill deeds**. This is a reminder for the mindful. And have patience, (O Muhammad), for lo! Allah loseth not the wages of the good (*Surah* 11:111-112,114-115, emp. added).

Allah will, in fact, simply overlook the evil deeds of those who become Muslims: "Those are they from whom We accept the best of what they do, and **overlook their evil deeds**. (They are) among the owners of the Garden. This is the true promise which they were promised (in the world)" (*Surah* 46:16, emp. added). Ali renders "overlook" as "pass by." So according to the Quran, forgiveness from Allah is grounded in and dependent upon the act of becoming a Muslim and maintaining that status with good deeds. No wonder the September 11, 2001 Islamic terrorists could visit a strip bar just prior to their suicidal mission (Farrington, 2001). They understood the Quran's teaching that good deeds enable God to overlook the bad.

In contrast, the Bible certainly teaches that good deeds are necessary to salvation (Acts 10:35; Romans 2:6). In fact, faith itself is a "work"–a **deed** that the individual must **do** (John 6:29). Repentance, confession of the deity of Jesus with the mouth, and water baptism are likewise all necessary prerequisites to the reception of forgiveness from God (Acts 2:38; 17:30; Romans 10: 9-10). However, the New Testament teaches that obedience to divinely specified deeds does not make those deeds meritorious, i.e., they do not **earn** salvation for the individual. They are **conditions** of salvation–but not the **grounds** of salvation. They do not erase or rectify past sin. **Atonement** must still be made for all sins previously committed (Isaiah 59:1-2).

Much of Christendom has gone awry on this point. Especially since the Protestant Reformation, the pendulum shifted to the extreme, unbiblical contention that all one need do is "believe," what Martin Luther labeled "faith alone" (*sola fide*) (cf. Lewis, 1991, pp. 353-358; Butt, 2004). The Quran advocates the equally incorrect opposite extreme of earning forgiveness by human works of merit. The New Testament actually steers a middle course between these two extremes by insisting that no sin can be forgiven without the shed blood of Jesus. Here is the grace of Christianity–God doing for humanity what humanity is powerless to do for itself, i.e., atone for its own sin. This gracious act of God is unmerited, undeserved, and unearned (Ephesians 2:8-9). Nothing humans **do** can repay God for this indescribable gift (2 Corinthians 9:15). Nevertheless, in order for the alien sinner to access the rich blessing of forgiveness based on the blood of Christ, he or

she must render obedience to the Gospel of Christ (Romans 6:
16-17; 2 Thessalonians 1:8; Hebrews 5:9) through faith, repentance, confession, and baptism (Hebrews 11:6; Luke 13:3; Romans
10:9-10; 1 Peter 3:21). This obedient response to Christ does not
earn forgiveness for the sinner, or **counteract** past misdeeds.
Rather, it represents compliance with the divinely (not humanly)
mandated prerequisites by which one **receives and accepts**
the gift of salvation that God offers to those who will respond appropriately. [NOTE: The New Testament term that is translated
"Gospel," meaning "good news" (Bruce, 1977, pp. 1ff.), refers
specifically to the sacrifice of Christ on the cross as the sole means
by which sin may be forgiven. Incredibly, the Quran is silent on
the need for atonement and Christ's death on the cross, and yet
it speaks approvingly of "*Injil*" (or "*Injeel*"), i.e., the Gospel, apparently referring to the revelation that Muhammad thought
was revealed to Jesus.]

Animal Sacrifice

Another feature of the Quran related to atonement is the in-
clusion of animal sacrifice. The reader will remember that Muhammad himself sacrificed animals. For example, on his farewell pilgrimage to Mecca, animals were sacrificed at Aqabah
(Lings, 1983, p. 334; cf. p. 323). In a surah labeled "The Hajj" (or
Pilgrimage), the Quran describes the ritualistic sacrifice of animals in connection with the Ka'bah:

> Behold! We gave the site, to Abraham, of the (Sacred)
> House (saying): "Do not associate anything (in worship)
> with Me; and sanctify My House for those who compass
> it round, or stand up, or bow, or prostrate themselves
> (therein in prayer). And proclaim the Pilgrimage among
> men...that they may witness the benefits (provided) for
> them, and celebrate the name of Allah, through the Days
> appointed, over the cattle which He has provided for
> them (for sacrifice): then you eat thereof and feed the
> distressed ones in want. Then let them complete the
> rites prescribed for them, perform their vows, and (again)
> circumambulate the Ancient House." Such (is the Pil-

grimage): whoever honors the sacred rites of Allah, for him it is good in the sight of his Lord. Lawful to you (for food in Pilgrimage) are cattle, except those mentioned to you (as exceptions)...and **whoever holds in honor the Symbols of Allah (in the sacrifice of animals)**, such (honor) should come truly from piety of heart. In them you have benefits for a term appointed: in the end **their place of sacrifice** is near the Ancient House. To every people **We appointed rites (of sacrifice), that they might celebrate the name of Allah** over the sustenance He gave them from animals (fit for food). But your God is One God (Allah): submit then your wills to Him (in Islam): and you give the good news to those who humble themselves, to those whose hearts, when Allah is mentioned, are filled with fear, who show patient perseverance over their afflictions, keep up regular prayer, and spend (in charity) out of what We have bestowed upon them. The **sacrificial camels** We have made for you as among the Symbols from Allah: in them is (much) good for you: then pronounce the name of Allah over them **as they line up (for sacrifice)**: when they are down on their sides (after slaughter), you eat thereof, and feed such as (beg not but) live in contentment and such as beg with due humility: thus have We made animals subject to you, that you may be grateful. It is not their meat nor their blood, that reaches Allah: it is your piety that reaches Him: He has thus made them subject to you, that you may glorify Allah for His guidance to you: and proclaim the Good News to all who do right (*Surah* 22:26-37, Ali's translation, emp. added).

Of course, the Muslim rejoinder to this point is that animal sacrifice is not for atonement, as Muslim scholar Mohammed Pickthall explains:

> The slaughter of animals for food for the poor which is one of the ceremonies of the Muslim pilgrimage is not a propitiatory sacrifice, but is in commemoration of the sacrifice of Abraham which marked the end of human sacrifices for the Semitic race, and which made it clear that the only sacrifice which God requires of man is the surrender of his will and purpose—i.e., Al-Islam (p. 244).

While it is true that the Quran appears to associate animal sacrifice with thanksgiving to Allah for blessings, rather than as a means of atonement, Pickthall's explanation nevertheless confirms the fact that the Quran enjoins a **religious** ritual sacrifice of animals. If the sacrifice were merely for food or to give to the poor, is no food eaten or no poor folk assisted the rest of the year? The fact remains that in New Testament Christianity no provision whatsoever is made for ritual "ceremonies" involving the slaughter of animals. God never authorized **human** sacrifice in the first place—a thought that was deplorable to God (Jeremiah 7:31; 32:35), but was actually practiced by some Israelites long after Abraham (2 Kings 16:3; 17:17; 21:6). **Animal** sacrifice belonged to the "shadows" of a spiritually primitive, pre-Christian period that was completely set aside in Christ (Hebrews 10:1). The sacrifice of animals is one of many **external** rituals associated with Islam and the Quran that is conspicuously absent in the New Testament, and that is incompatible with Christianity.

JESUS' PERSONAL CONDUCT

The Quran's confusion regarding the person of Jesus manifests itself repeatedly—a confusion that reflects the misconceptions and misrepresentations of the New Testament that were prevalent within Christendom in the sixth and seventh centuries, which, in turn, were mistakenly accepted into the Quran. For example, consider the Quran's report of Allah's communication with Mary regarding Jesus:

> (And remember) when the angels said: O Mary! Lo! Allah giveth thee glad tidings of a word from Him, whose name is the Messiah, Jesus, son of Mary, illustrious in the world and the Hereafter, and one of those brought near (unto Allah). **He will speak unto mankind in his cradle** and in his manhood, and he is of the righteous. She said: My Lord! How can I have a child when no mortal hath touched me? He said: So (it will be). Allah createth what He will. If He decreeth a thing, He saith unto it only: Be! and it is. And He will teach him the Scripture and wisdom, and the Torah and the Gospel. And will

make him a messenger unto the children of Israel, (saying): Lo! I come unto you with a sign from your Lord. Lo! **I fashion for you out of clay the likeness of a bird, and I breathe into it and it is a bird, by Allah's leave.** I heal him who was born blind, and the leper, and I raise the dead, by Allah's leave. And I announce unto you what ye eat and what ye store up in your houses. Lo! herein verily is a portent for you, if ye are to be believers (*Surah* 3:45-49, emp. added).

A parallel passage is found in *Surah* 5:

When Allah saith: O Jesus, son of Mary! Remember My favour unto thee and unto thy mother; how I strengthened thee with the holy Spirit, so that **thou spakest unto mankind in the cradle** as in maturity; and how I taught thee the Scripture and Wisdom and the Torah and the Gospel; and how **thou didst shape of clay as it were the likeness of a bird by My permission, and didst blow upon it and it was a bird by My permission**, and thou didst heal him who was born blind and the leper by My permission; and how thou didst raise the dead, by My permission; and how I restrained the Children of Israel from (harming) thee when thou camest unto them with clear proofs, and those of them who disbelieved exclaimed: This is naught else than mere magic (5:110, emp. added).

Even the casual reader of the New Testament is familiar with Jesus healing the blind and lepers, and raising the dead. But the New Testament is conspicuously silent about Jesus creating birds or speaking from the cradle, even as it is silent on nearly all details of Jesus' childhood. That is because the Quran's allusion to Jesus fashioning birds out of clay, which then came to life, was a fanciful Christian fable with a wide circulation. It is found, for example, in the *Arabic Gospel of the Infancy of the Savior* (15:1-6) that dates from the second century (Hutchison, 1939, 1:199)— four hundred years before Muhammad's birth:

And when the Lord Jesus was seven years of age, he was on a certain day with other boys his companions about the same age. Who when they were at play made clay into several shapes, namely asses, oxen, birds, and other figures, each boasting of his work, and endeavouring to exceed the rest. Then the Lord Jesus said to the boys, I will command these figures which I have made to walk. And immediately they moved, and when he commanded them to return, they returned. He had also made the figures of birds and sparrows, which, when he commanded to fly, did fly, and when he commanded to stand still, did stand still (*The Lost Books...*, 1979, pp. 52-53).

A similar legend is found in the *Gospel of Thomas* (1:4-9) that likewise predates (Cullmann, 1991, 1:442) the production of the Quran:

Then he took from the bank of the stream some soft clay, and formed out of it twelve sparrows; and there were other boys playing with him.... Then Jesus clapping together the palms of his hands, called to the sparrows, and said to them: Go, fly away; and while ye live remember me. So the sparrows fled away, making a noise (*The Lost Books...*, p. 60).

Observe also in the above Quranic passage the allusion to Jesus speaking while yet in His cradle. This point is elaborated more fully in *Surah* 19 where, after giving birth to Jesus beside the trunk of a palm tree in a remote location, Mary returned to her people carrying the child in her arms and received the following reaction:

Then she brought him to her own folk, carrying him. They said: O Mary! Thou hast come with an amazing thing. Oh sister of Aaron! Thy father was not a wicked man nor was thy mother a harlot. Then she pointed to him. They said: How can we talk to one who is in the cradle, a young boy? He spake: Lo! I am the slave of Allah. He hath given me the Scripture and hath appointed me a Prophet, and hath made me blessed wheresoever I may be, and hath enjoined upon me prayer and alms-giving so long as I remain alive, and (hath made me) dutiful toward her who bore me, and hath not made me arrogant, unblest. Peace on me the day I was born, and the day I die, and the day I shall be raised alive! Such was Jesus, son of Mary: (this is) a statement of the truth concerning which they doubt (*Surah* 19:27-34).

The idea that Jesus spoke while yet in the cradle preceded the Quran, having been given in the *Arabic Gospel of the Infancy of the Savior* (1:2-3): "Jesus spoke, and, indeed when He was lying in His cradle said to Mary his mother: I am Jesus, the Son of God, the Logos, whom thou hast brought forth, as the Angel Gabriel announced to thee; and my Father has sent me for the salvation of the world" (Roberts and Donaldson, 1951, 8:405). These mythical accounts are contrary to the Bible's depiction of the Christ. Yet the legendary folklore extant in the centuries immediately following the production of the New Testament is replete with such absurdities, which obviously were so commonplace that the author of the Quran mistook them as authentic and legitimate representations of the New Testament.

THE DOCTRINE OF GOD:
ALLAH VS. THE GOD OF THE BIBLE

When reading the Quran, one is surprised time and time again with the fact that the Allah of the Quran conducts himself quite differently from the God of the Bible. Of course, "Allah" is simply the Arabic word for "God," like its equivalent Old Testament Hebrew term *elohim*–a general term for deity that was used by the Jews to refer both to the one true God, as well as to the false deities of their pagan neighbors (e.g., Genesis 35:2; Deuteronomy 29:18; Daniel 3:25). So the term "God" in whatever language (English, Arabic, or Hebrew) is a generic term to refer to deity. Muslims claim that the Allah they worship is the same God that Abraham and the Jews worshipped. Nevertheless, it is possible for one to pay lip service to following the God of the Bible, and yet so recast Him that He ceases to be the same Being about which one reads on the pages of the Bible. The meaning and identity that each culture or religion attaches to the word may differ radically.

Many current Christian authors do this very thing when they claim to be writing about the Jesus of the New Testament. They misrepresent Jesus, recasting and refashioning the Jesus of the

Bible into essentially a different Being than the One depicted on the pages of the New Testament—one who is unconcerned about obedience, and whose grace forgives just about everybody **unconditionally** (e.g. Lucado, 1996). But that is not the Jesus of the New Testament. They have so misrepresented the person, nature, and conduct of Jesus that for all practical purposes, their writings depict a **different** Jesus.

In like fashion, the Quran has Allah saying and doing things that the God of the Bible simply would not say or do. Actions and attitudes are attributed to Allah that stand in stark contradistinction to the character of the God of the Bible. Though Allah is claimed by Muslims to be the same God as the God of the Old Testament, the Quran's depiction of deity is nevertheless sufficiently **redefined** as to make Allah distinct from the God of the Bible. This stark contrast is particularly evident in the biblical doctrine of the Trinity.

Trinity

The Bible depicts deity as singular, i.e., there is one and only one divine essence or Being (Deuteronomy 6:4; Isaiah 45:5; 1 Corinthians 8:6; 1 Timothy 2:5; James 2:19). However, the Bible also clearly depicts God as a triune Being—three distinct persons within the one essence—with a triune nature. For example, during the Creation week, God stated: "Let **us**..." (Genesis 1:26, emp. added). Both the Holy Spirit (Genesis 1:2) and Christ (John 1:1-3) were present and active at the Creation with God the Father. The New Testament alludes to the "Godhead" (Acts 17:29; Romans 1:20; Colossians 2:9). At the baptism of Jesus while He was in human form, the Father spoke audibly from heaven, and the Holy Spirit descended on Jesus (Matthew 3:16-17). All three are sometimes noted together (Matthew 28:19; 2 Corinthians 13:14). Each person of the Godhead is fully God, fully deity, fully divine. Jesus is repeatedly referred to as God (Matthew 1:22-23; John 1:1-3,14; 8:58; 20:28; Micah 5:2). The Holy Spirit is also divine (John 14:26; 15:26; Romans 15:19; 1 Corinthians 2:10-11; Ephesians 4:4; Hebrews 9:14).

In contrast to the biblical portrait, the Quran goes out of its way to denounce the notion of Trinity:

> O People of the Scripture! Do not exaggerate in your religion nor utter aught concerning Allah save the truth. The Messiah, Jesus son of Mary, was only a messenger of Allah, and His word which He conveyed unto Mary, and a spirit from Him. So believe in Allah and His messengers, **and say not "Three"–Cease! (it is) better for you!–Allah is only One God. Far is it removed from His transcendant majesty that he should have a son.** His is all that is in the heavens and all that is in the earth. And Allah is sufficient as Defender. The Messiah will never scorn to be a slave unto Allah, nor will the favoured angels. Whoso scorneth His service and is proud, all such will He assemble unto Him (*Surah* 4:171-172, emp. added).

> They surely disbelieve who say: Lo! Allah is the Messiah, son of Mary. The Messiah (himself) said: O Children of Israel, worship Allah, my Lord and your Lord. Lo! whoso ascribeth partners unto Allah, for him Allah hath forbidden Paradise. His abode is the Fire. For evil-doers there will be no helpers. **They surely disbelieve who say: Lo! Allah is the third of three**; when there is no God save the One God. If they desist not from so saying a **painful doom** will fall on those of them who disbelieve. Will they not rather turn unto Allah and seek forgiveness of Him? For Allah is Forgiving, Merciful (*Surah* 5:72-74, emp. added).

The Christian is surely startled to read such forthright denunciations on those who believe in the Godhead as depicted in the Bible. The Quran declares in unmistakable terms that those who do believe in the Trinity will be excluded from paradise, and will experience a "painful doom" by burning in the fire of hell.

Regarding the third person of the Godhead, Muslims insist that the Quran knows nothing of the Holy Spirit–all seeming references simply being, in the words of Muslim scholar Mohammed Pickthall, "a term for the angel of Revelation, Gabriel (on whom be peace)" (Pickthall, p. 40). Thus the Quran denies the person of the Holy Spirit, acknowledges the existence of Jesus while denying His divinity, and insists that the person of Allah is singular in nature. The Quran and the Bible are in dire contradiction with each other on the doctrine of the Trinity.

Attributes/Actions Contrary to the God of The Bible

In addition to the clash between the Bible and the Quran in terms of how to conceptualize God, the Quran also depicts the **behavior** of deity very differently from the Bible. Allah says and does things that the God of the Bible did not and would not say or do. The Quran's representation of the sovereignty of God (like Calvinism) contradicts the character of God by attributing actions to Him that are unlike deity.

For example, the Quran repeatedly represents God, on the occasion of the creation of Adam, requiring the angels/djinn to bow down and worship this first human. All did so with the exception of Iblis (i.e., Satan), who refused to do so on the ground that Adam was a mere mortal:

> Verily We created man of potter's clay of black mud altered, and the Jinn did We create aforetime of essential fire. And (remember) when thy Lord said unto the angels: Lo! I am creating a mortal out of potter's clay of black mud altered, so, when I have made him and have breathed into him of My spirit, **do ye fall down, prostrating yourselves unto him**. So the angels fell prostrate, all of them together save Iblis. He refused to be among the prostrate. He said: O Iblis! What aileth thee that thou art not among the prostrate? He said: Why should I prostrate myself unto a mortal whom Thou hast created out of potter's clay of black mud altered? He said: Then go thou forth from hence, for verily thou art outcast. And lo! the curse shall be upon thee till the Day of Judgement (*Surah* 15:26-35, emp. added; cf. 2:34; 7:11-12; 17:61; 18:51; 20:116; 38:72-78).

This characterization of deity is completely untenable. This one incident by itself illustrates that Allah is not the God of the Bible, and the Quran is not the Word of God. The God of the Bible simply would not do what the Quran says He did. Numerous Bible verses convey the complete impropriety—even blasphemy—that the worship of a mere human constitutes. Humans are forbidden to worship other humans (Acts 10:25-26; 14:14-15). Humans are forbidden to worship angels (Colossians 2:18; Revelation 19:10; 22:8-9). And, most certainly, angels are not to worship mere humans. The Law of Moses declared that worship is to be directed to God (Deuteronomy 6:13; 10:20). When Satan tempted Jesus, and Satan urged Jesus to worship him, Jesus quoted this Deuteronomic declaration from the Law of Moses, and then added His own divine commentary: "and **Him only** you shall serve" (Matthew 4:10, emp. added). No one and no thing is the rightful object of worship—except deity!

Interestingly enough, Satan's reasoning in the Quran was actually biblical and right! Not only should angels not worship humans, but Satan recognized that, as an angelic being, Adam occupied a status that was beneath his own accelerated, celestial existence—a fact affirmed by the Bible: "What is man that You are mindful of him, and the son of man that You visit him? For You have made him **a little lower than the angels**, and You have crowned him with glory and honor" (Psalm 8:4-5, emp. added; cf. Hebrews 2:9). The Quranic depiction of God ordering Iblis/Satan to worship Adam is a serious breach of divine propriety, and a further indication of the Quran's conflict with the Bible. [Once again, the Quran appears to have been influenced by Jewish sources, since the Talmudists also represent the angels as bestowing special attention and honor on Adam (*Sanhedrin* 29; *Midrash Rabbah* on Gen. par. 8).]

Another example of conduct that is unbecoming of deity is the Quran's repeated declaration that God **causes** some people to err or lack understanding:

> Allah confirmeth those who believe by a firm saying in the life of the world and in the Hereafter, and **Allah**

sendeth wrong-doers astray. And Allah doeth what He will (*Surah* 14:27, emp. added); Such is Allah's guidance, wherewith He guideth whom He will. And him **whom Allah sendeth astray**, for him there is no guide.... Will not Allah defend His slave? Yet they would frighten thee with those beside Him. He **whom Allah sendeth astray**, for him there is no guide. And he whom Allah guideth, for him there can be no misleader (*Surah* 39:23, 36-37, emp. added); He **whom Allah sendeth** astray, for him there is no protecting friend after Him. And thou (Muhammad) wilt see the evil-doers when they see the doom, (how) they say: Is there any way of return?.... And they will have no protecting friends to help them instead of Allah. He **whom Allah sendeth astray**, for him there is no road (*Surah* 42:44,46, emp. added; cf. 2: 6-7; 6:25,39,111,126; 7:178,186; 13:27,33; 35:8).

The Quran leaves one with the idea that since God is God, He can do whatever He chooses. But this notion is false. If God is perfect and infinite in all of His attributes, then He cannot and will not do anything that is out of harmony with His nature and character (e.g., Titus 1:2; cf. Miller, 2003d). The Bible teaches that God wants all people to do right and to be saved (1 Timothy 2:4). It is not His will that any should perish eternally (2 Peter 3: 9). Consequently, God would not **cause** anyone to do evil. He may accommodate a person's decision to reject Him (e.g., Matthew 13:13), but the God of the Bible does not lead people astray or cause their unbelief [NOTE: for further analysis of this claim, see Butt and Miller, 2003; Lyons, 2003b).] Nor does He deliberately try to trick people or cause them to stumble (James 1:13). But the Quran states that Allah places wicked leaders in every town in order for them to plot wicked behavior: "And thus have We made in every city great ones of its wicked ones, that they should plot therein. They do but plot against themselves, though they perceive it not" (*Surah* 6:124).

In its zest to denounce the paganism that characterized seventh century Arabs, the Quran also goes so far as to declare that **Allah does not love prodigals**:

They are losers who besottedly have slain their children without knowledge, and have forbidden that which Allah bestowed upon them, inventing a lie against Allah. They indeed have gone astray and are not guided. He it is Who produceth gardens trellised and untrellised, and the date-palm, and crops of divers flavour, and the olive and the pomegranate, like and unlike. Eat ye of the fruit thereof when it fruiteth, and pay the due thereof upon the harvest day, and be no prodigal. Lo! **Allah loveth not the prodigals** (*Surah* 6:141-142, emp. added; cf. 7:31).

Ali translates "prodigals" as "wasters," i.e., those who waste the crops—a rendering which makes no sense in view of the fact that the admonition refers to the failure to pay the required dues—not the wasting of produce. In either case, Allah is represented as **not loving** such individuals.

Consider another passage from the Quran on the same subject (translated by Ali): "Those who reject Faith will suffer from that rejection: and those who work righteousness will spread their couch (of repose) for themselves (in heaven): that He may reward those who believe and work righteous deeds, out of His Bounty. For **He does not love those who reject Faith**" (*Surah* 30:44-45, emp. added; cf. 3:32,57,140; 40:35). Further, Allah "loveth not the impious and guilty" (*Surah* 2:276).

What a contrast with the God of the Bible! He hates sin and sinful actions (Proverbs 6:16-19; Romans 12:9; cf. Jackson, 2003a; Jackson, 2003b), but **loves the sinner** and sent His Son to die on behalf of the sinner (John 3:16; Romans 5:8; 1 Timothy 2:6; Hebrews 2:9; 1 John 2:2). He decidedly wants **all** men to be saved, and **none** to perish (1 Timothy 2:4; 2 Peter 3:9). The loss of souls gives Him absolutely no pleasure (Ezekiel 18:23,32; 33:11), and He brings just punishment only reluctantly (Lamentations 3:33).

CONCLUSION

Many additional conflicts exist between the Quran and the New Testament on matters of doctrine. Those addressed in this chapter are sufficient to illustrate the incompatibility of Islam and Christianity. In the next chapter, attention is directed to additional conflicts—those that demonstrate the chasm that exists between the Quran and the New Testament regarding ethics.

Chapter 8

THE QURAN VS. THE NEW TESTAMENT: CONFLICTING ETHICS

Anyone who has read both the Quran and the New Testament cannot help but be struck by the glaring disparity that exists between the two in their respective treatments of ethical matters. Two such matters are addressed in this chapter: polygamy and armed conflict.

POLYGAMY

Those who have modeled their thinking after New Testament Christianity are, to say the least, a bit surprised, if not shocked and appalled, that Islam countenances polygamy. In fact, this feature of the Quran is a source of embarrassment to Muslim apologists, as evinced by the excuses they offer to soften its glaring presence (e.g., Rahman, 1979, p. 38). But the Christian mind must realize that Muhammad's Islam arose out of Arabia in the sixth and seventh centuries A.D. The Arab culture was well known for the practice of polygamy, in which men were allowed as many wives as they chose. The Quran addressed this social circumstance by placing a limitation on the number of wives a man is permitted. The wording of the pronouncement comes in a surah titled "Women": "And if ye fear that ye will not deal fairly by the orphans, marry of the women, who seem good to you, two or three or four; and if ye fear that ye cannot do justice (to so many) then one (only) or (the captives) that your right hands possess" (*Surah* 4:3; cf. 4:24-25,129; 23:6; 30:21; 70:30).

To appreciate the full extent of the Quran's endorsement of polygamy, as well as to preserve context, the reader is asked to exercise the necessary patience to read two lengthy passages. The first is a transparent sanction of Muhammad's own polygamous practices:

> O Prophet! Lo! We have made lawful unto thee thy wives unto whom thou hast paid their dowries, and those whom thy right hand possesseth of those whom Allah hath given thee as spoils of war, and the daughters of thine uncle on the father's side and the daughters of thine aunts on the father's side, and the daughters of thine uncles on the mother's side and the daughters of thine aunts on the mother's side who emigrated with thee, and a believing woman if she give herself unto the Prophet and the Prophet desire to ask her in marriage—a privilege for thee only, not for the (rest of) believers—We are aware of that which We enjoined upon them concerning their wives and, those whom their right hands possess—that thou mayst be free from blame, for Allah is Forgiving, Merciful. Thou canst defer whom thou wilt of them and receive unto thee whom thou wilt, and whomsoever thou desirest of those whom thou hast set aside (temporarily), it is no sin for thee (to receive her again); that is better; that they may be comforted and not grieve and may all be pleased with what thou givest them, Allah knoweth what is in your hearts (O men) and Allah is Forgiving, Clement. It is not allowed thee to take (other) women henceforth, nor that thou shouldst change them for other wives even though their beauty pleased thee save those whom thy right hand possesseth. And Allah is Watcher over all things. O ye

who believe!.... And when ye ask of them (the wives of the Prophet) anything, ask it of them from behind a curtain. That is purer for your hearts and for their hearts. And it is not for you to cause annoyance to the messenger of Allah nor that ye should ever marry his wives after him. Lo! that in Allah's sight would be an enormity (*Surah* 33:50-53).

These admonitions bear a remarkable resemblance to Mormon Joseph Smith's own advocacy of plural marriages and the revelation allegedly received from God admonishing his own wife, Emma Smith, to be receptive to his polygamy:

Verily, I say unto you: A commandment I give unto mine handmaid, Emma Smith, your wife, whom I have given unto you, that she stay herself and partake not of that which I commanded you to offer unto her; for I did it, saith the Lord, to prove you all, as I did Abraham, and that I might require an offering at your hand, by covenant and sacrifice. And let mine handmaid, Emma Smith, receive all those that have been given unto my servant Joseph, and who are virtuous and pure before me; and those who are not pure, and have said they were pure shall be destroyed, saith the Lord God. For I am the Lord thy God, and ye shall obey my voice; and I give unto my servant Joseph that he shall be made ruler over many things; for he hath been faithful over a few things, and from henceforth I will strengthen him. And I command mine handmaid, Emma Smith, to abide and cleave unto my servant Joseph, and to none else. But if she will not abide this commandment she shall be destroyed, saith the Lord; for I am the Lord thy God, and will destroy her if she abide not in my law. But if she will not abide this commandment, then shall my servant Joseph do all things for her, even as he hath said; and I will bless him and multiply him and give unto him an hundredfold in this world, of fathers and mothers, brothers and sisters, houses and lands, wives and children, and crowns of eternal lives in the eternal worlds. And again, verily I say, let mine handmaid forgive my servant Joseph his trespasses; and then shall she be forgiven her trespasses, wherein she has trespassed against Me; and

I, the Lord thy God, will bless her, and multiply her, and make her heart to rejoice (*Doctrine and Covenants,* 1981, 132:51-56).

One would fully expect uninspired men to manifest the same *modus operandi* and concern for the same issues—especially as they reflect upon their own human desires (i.e., lusts) and preferences.

The second Quranic passage that acquaints the reader with the extent to which polygamy is not only permitted or tolerated, but also **advocated and encouraged**, is one titled "Banning." The *Hadith* offer three traditions that provide the background details that help to make sense of the surah. The one generally preferred by Muslim commentators speaks of Hafsah finding the Prophet in her room with Mariyah—the Coptic girl given to Muhammad by the ruler of Egypt, who became the mother of his only son, Ibrahim—on a day that, according to his customary rotation among his wives, was assigned to A'ishah. The distress that Hafsah manifested was so disturbing to the Prophet that he vowed with an oath that he would have no more to do with Mariyah, and requested that Hafsah say nothing to A'ishah. But Hafsah, who was not nearly as distressed as she made out, with devilish glee, promptly informed A'ishah, bragging about how easily she had achieved the ejection of Mariyah—an accomplishment that pleased the other wives as well (see Pickthall, n.d., pp. 404-405; Lings, 1983, pp. 276-279). With these background details in mind, the reader is invited to read the surah that was elicited by the situation:

> In the name of Allah, the Beneficent, the Merciful. O Prophet! Why bannest thou that which Allah hath made lawful for thee, seeking to please thy wives? And Allah is Forgiving, Merciful. Allah hath made lawful for you (Muslims) absolution from your oaths (of such a kind), and Allah is your Protector. He is the Knower, the Wise. When the Prophet confided a fact unto one of his wives and when she afterward divulged it and Allah apprised him thereof, he made known (to her) part thereof and passed over part. And when he told it her she said: Who hath

told thee? He said: The Knower, the Aware hath told me. If ye twain turn unto Allah repentant, (ye have cause to do so) for your hearts desired (the ban); and if ye aid one another against him (Muhammad) then lo! Allah, even He, is his protecting Friend, and Gabriel and the righteous among the believers; and furthermore the angels are his helpers. It may happen that his Lord, if he divorce you, will give him in your stead wives better than you, submissive (to Allah), believing, pious, penitent, inclined to fasting, widows and maids. O ye who believe! Ward off from yourselves and your families a Fire whereof the fuel is men and stones, over which are set angels strong, severe, who resist not Allah in that which He commandeth them, but do that which they are commanded. (Then it will be said): O ye who disbelieve! Make no excuses for yourselves this day. Ye are only being paid for what ye used to do. O ye who believe! Turn unto Allah in sincere repentance! It may be that your Lord will remit from you your evil deeds and bring you into Gardens underneath which rivers flow, on the day when Allah will not abase the Prophet and those who believe with him. Their light will run before them and on their right hands: they will say: Our Lord! Perfect our light for us, and forgive us! Lo! Thou art Able to do all things. O Prophet! Strive against the disbelievers and the hypocrites, and be stern with them. Hell will be their home, a hapless journey's end. Allah citeth an example for those who disbelieve: the wife of Noah and the wife of Lot, who were under two of our righteous slaves yet betrayed them so that they (the husbands) availed them naught against Allah and it was said (unto them): Enter the Fire along with those who enter. And Allah citeth an example for those who believe: the wife of Pharaoh when she said: My Lord! Build for me a home with thee in the Garden, and deliver me from Pharaoh and his work, and deliver me from evildoing folk; And Mary, daughter of 'Imran, whose body was chaste, therefore We breathed therein something of Our Spirit. And she put faith in the words of her Lord and His Scriptures, and was of the obedient (*Surah* 66).

Observe that the surah is complete with threats of the fire of hell, as well as the allusion to the wives of Noah and Lot as examples of disobedient wives who went to hell. Can there be any doubt that the Quran approves of and encourages polygamy?

Setting aside the issue of why Muhammad was exempt from this limitation (*Surah* 33:50–see chapter 3), the divine origin of the Quran is discredited on the basis of its stance on polygamy. In the first place, for all practical purposes the Quran authorizes a man to have as many wives as he chooses, since its teaching on divorce contradicts its teaching on marriage. Unlike the New Testament, which confines permission to divorce on the sole ground of sexual unfaithfulness (Matthew 19:9), the Quran authorizes divorce for any reason (e.g., *Surah* 2:226-232,241; 33:4, 49; 58:2-4; 65:1-7). If a man can divorce his wife for any reason, then the limitation that confines a man to four wives is effectively meaningless—merely restricting a man to four legal wives **at a time**. Theoretically, in his lifetime, a man could have an **unlimited** number of wives—all with the approval of God!

In the second place, Jesus declared in no uncertain terms: "Whoever divorces his wife, **except for sexual immorality**, and marries another, commits adultery; and whoever marries her who is divorced commits adultery" (Matthew 19:9, emp. added). Jesus gave one, and only one, reason for divorce in God's sight. In fact, even the Old Testament affirmed that God "hates divorce" (Malachi 2:16). The teaching of the Bible on divorce is a higher, stricter, nobler standard than the one advocated by the Quran. The two books, in fact, **contradict each other** on this point.

In the third place, why does the Quran stipulate the number "four"? Why not three or five wives? The number four would appear to be an arbitrary number with no significance—at least, none is given. Though the passage in question indicates the criterion of a man's ability to do justice to those he marries, there is no reason to specify the number four, since men would vary a great deal in the number of women that they would have the ability to manage fairly.

The answer may be seen in the influence of the contemporaneous Jewish population of Arabia. Sixth-century Arabia was a tribal-oriented society that relied heavily on oral communication in social interactions. As noted in chapter 4, Muhammad would have been the recipient of considerable information conveyed orally by his Jewish, and even Christian, contemporaries. Many tales, fables, and rabbinical traditions undoubtedly circulated among the Jewish tribes of Arabia. The Jews themselves likely were lacking in much book-learning, having been separated from the mainstream of Jewish thought and intellectual development in their migration to the Arabian peninsula. The evidence demonstrates that the author of the Quran borrowed extensively from Jewish and other sources. The ancient Talmudic record (*Arbah Turim, Ev. Hazaer* 1) stated: "A man may marry many wives, for Rabba saith it is lawful to do so, if he can provide for them. Nevertheless, the wise men have given good advice, that a man should **not marry more than four wives**" (as quoted in Rodwell, 1950, p. 411, emp. added; Tisdall, 1905, pp. 129-130). The similarity with the wording of the Quran is too striking to be coincidental. It can be argued quite convincingly that the magic number of four was drawn from currently circulating Jewish teaching.

In the fourth place, the polygamy countenanced by the Quran on Earth will be extended into the heavenly realm (*Surah* 13:23; 36:55; 40:8; 43:70). Of course, this viewpoint was explicitly contradicted by Jesus Christ (Matthew 22:30–see chapter 9).

Islam and the Quran have a great many features that the Christian mind (i.e., one guided by the New Testament) finds ethically objectionable. Polygamy is simply one among many such ethical "difficulties." The Bible and the Quran are in significant conflict on this subject.

ARMED CONFLICT, VIOLENCE, WAR, AND BLOODSHED

One would expect an uninspired book to contradict itself or speak ambiguously on various subjects, at times appearing both to endorse and condemn a practice. So it is with physical violence in the Quran. However, despite the occasional puzzling remark that may seem to imply the reverse, the Quran is replete with explicit and implicit sanction and promotion of armed conflict, violence, and bloodshed by Muslims. For example, within months of the Hijrah, Muhammad claimed to receive a revelation that clarified the issue:

> Now when ye **meet in battle** those who disbelieve, then it is **smiting of the necks** until, when ye have routed them, then making fast of bonds; and afterward either grace or ransom till the **war** lay down its burdens. That (is the ordinance). And if Allah willed He could have punished them (without you) but (thus it is ordained) that He may try some of you by means of others. And **those who are slain** in the way of Allah, He rendereth not their actions vain (*Surah* 47:4, emp. added).

> **Fight in the way of Allah against those who fight against you**, but begin not hostilities. Lo! Allah loveth not aggressors. And **slay them wherever ye find them**, and drive them out of the places whence they drove you out, for **persecution is worse than slaughter**. And fight not with them at the Inviolable Place of Worship until they first attack you there, but if they attack you (there) **then slay them**. Such is the reward of disbelievers. But if they desist, then lo! Allah is Forgiving, Merciful. And **fight them** until persecution is no more, and religion is for Allah. But if they desist, then let there be no hostility except against wrongdoers. The forbidden month for the forbidden month, and forbidden things in **retaliation**. And **one who attacketh you, attack him in like manner as he attacked you**. Observe your duty to Allah, and know that Allah is with those who ward off (evil) (*Surah* 2:190-194, emp. added).

> **Warfare is ordained for you**, though it is hateful unto you; but it may happen that ye hate a thing which is good for you, and it may happen that ye love a thing which is bad for you. Allah knoweth, ye know not. They question thee (O Muhammad) with regard to warfare in the sacred month. Say: Warfare therein is a great (transgres-

sion), but to turn (men) from the way of Allah, and to disbelieve in Him and in the Inviolable Place of Worship,
and to expel his people thence, is a greater with Allah;
for **persecution is worse that killing**. And they will
not cease from fighting against you till they have made
you renegades from your religion, if they can (*Surah* 2:
216-217, emp. added).

Muhammad was informed that **warfare was prescribed for
him**! Though he may have hated warfare, it was actually good
for him, and what he loved, i.e., non-warfare, was actually bad
for him! And though under normal circumstances, fighting is
not appropriate during sacred months, killing was warranted
against those who sought to prevent Muslims from practicing their
religion. **Killing is better than being persecuted!** A similar
injunction states: "**Sanction is given unto those who fight** because they have been wronged; and Allah is indeed Able to give
them victory" (*Surah* 22:39, emp. added). In fact, "Allah **loveth
those who battle** for His cause in ranks, as if they were a solid
structure" (*Surah* 61:4, emp. added).

In a surah titled "Repentance" that issues stern measures to
be taken against idolaters, the requirement to engage in carnal
warfare is apparent:

> Freedom from obligation (is proclaimed) from Allah and
> His messenger toward those of the idolaters with whom
> ye made a treaty: Travel freely in the land four months,
> and know that ye cannot escape Allah and that Allah
> will confound the disbelievers (in His guidance). And a
> proclamation from Allah and His messenger to all men
> on the day of the Greater Pilgrimage that Allah is free
> from obligation to the idolaters, and (so is) His messen-
> ger. So, if ye repent, it will be better for you; but if ye are
> averse, then know that ye cannot escape Allah. Give tid-
> ings (O Muhammad) of a painful doom to those who
> disbelieve. Excepting those of the idolaters with whom
> ye (Muslims) have a treaty, and who have since abated
> nothing of your right nor have supported anyone against
> you. (As for these), fulfill their treaty to them till their
> term. Lo! Allah loveth those who keep their duty (unto

Him). Then, when the sacred months have passed, **slay the idolaters wherever ye find them**, and take them (captive), and besiege them, and prepare for them each ambush. But if they repent and establish worship and pay the poor-due, then leave their way free. Lo! Allah is Forgiving, Merciful (*Surah* 9:1-5, emp. added).

The ancient Muslim histories elaborate on the occasion of these admonitions: "[T]he idolaters were given four months' respite to come and go as they pleased in safety, but after that God and His Messenger would be free from any obligation towards them. War was declared upon them, and they were to be slain or taken captive wherever they were found" (Lings, 1983, p. 323).

Later in the same surah, "**Fight against** such of those who have been given the Scripture as believe not in Allah nor the Last Day, and forbid not that which Allah hath forbidden by His messenger, and follow not the religion of truth, until they pay the tribute readily, **being brought low**" (*Surah* 9:29, emp. added). "Those who have been given the Scripture" is a reference to Jews and Christians. The surah advocates coercion against Jews and Christians in order to physically force them to pay the *jizyah*—a special religious tax imposed on religious minorities (see Nasr, 2002, p. 166). Pickthall explains the historical setting of this Quranic utterance: "It signified the end of idolatry in Arabia. The Christian Byzantine Empire had begun to move against the growing Muslim power, and this surah contains mention of a greater war to come, and instructions with regard to it" (p. 145). Indeed, the final verse of *Surah* 2 calls upon Allah to give Muslims "victory over the disbelieving folk" (vs. 286), rendered by Rodwell: "give us victory therefore over the infidel nations." That this stance by the Quran was to be expected is evident from the formulation of the Second Pledge of Aqabah, in which the men pledged their loyalty and their commitment to protecting Muhammad from all opponents. This pledge included duties of war, and was taken only by the males. Consequently, the First Aqabah pact, which contained no mention of war, became known as the "pledge of the women" (Lings, p. 112).

Additional allusions to warfare in the Quran are seen in the surah, "The Spoils," dated in the second year of the Hijrah (A.D. 623), within a month after the Battle of Badr:

> And **fight them** until persecution is no more, and religion is all for Allah.... If thou comest on them in the war, deal with them so as to **strike fear** in those who are behind them.... And let not those who disbelieve suppose that they can outstrip (Allah's purpose). Lo! **they cannot escape**. Make ready for them all thou canst **of (armed) force and of horses** tethered, that thereby ye may dismay the enemy of Allah and your enemy, and others beside them whom ye know not.... O Prophet! **Exhort the believers to fight**. If there be of you twenty stedfast they shall overcome two hundred, and if there be of you a hundred stedfast they shall overcome a thousand of those who disbelieve, because they (the disbelievers) are a folk without intelligence.... It is not for any Prophet to have captives **until he hath made slaughter in the land**. Ye desire the lure of this world and Allah desireth (for you) the Hereafter, and Allah is Mighty, Wise. Had it not been for an ordinance of Allah which had gone before, an awful doom had come upon you on account of what ye took. Now enjoy what ye have won, as lawful and good, and keep your duty to Allah. Lo! Allah is Forgiving, Merciful (*Surah* 8:39,57,59-60,65,67-69, emp. added; cf. 33:26).

Muslim scholar Pickthall readily concedes the context of these verses:

> vv. 67-69 were revealed when the Prophet had decided to spare the lives of the prisoners taken at Badr and hold them to ransom, against the wish of Omar, who would have executed them for their past crimes. The Prophet took the verses as a reproof, and they are generally understood to mean that no quarter ought to have been given in that first battle (p. 144).

So the Quran indicates that at the Battle of Badr, no captives should have been taken. The enemy should have been completely slaughtered, with no quarter given. This very fate awaited the Jewish Bani Qurayzah, when some 700 men were beheaded by the Muslims with Muhammad's approval (Lings, p. 232). Likewise, members of a clan of the Bani Nadir were executed in Khaybar for concealing their treasure rather than forfeiting it to the Muslims (Lings, p. 267).

Another surah describes how allowances respecting the daily prayers were to be made for Muhammad's Muslim warriors when engaged in military action:

> And when ye go forth in the land, it is no sin for you to curtail (your) worship if ye fear that those who disbelieve may attack you. In truth the disbelievers are an open enemy to you. And when thou (O Muhammad) art among them and arrangest (their) worship for them, let only a party of them stand with thee (to worship) and **let them take their arms**. Then when they have performed their prostrations let them fall to the rear and let another party come that hath not worshipped and let them worship with thee, and **let them take their precaution and their arms**. Those who disbelieve long for you to neglect your arms and your baggage that they may attack you once for all. It is no sin for you to lay aside your arms, if rain impedeth you or ye are sick. But take your precaution. Lo! Allah prepareth for the disbelievers shameful punishment. When ye have performed the act of worship, remember Allah, standing, sitting and reclining. And when ye are in safety, observe proper worship. Worship at fixed hours hath been enjoined on the believers. **Relent not in pursuit of the enemy** (*Surah* 4:101-104, emp. added; cf. 73:20).

These verses show that the Quran implicitly endorses armed conflict and war to advance Islam.

Muslim historical sources themselves report the background details of those armed conflicts that have characterized Islam from its inception—including Muhammad's own warring tendencies involving personal participation in and endorsement of military campaigns (cf. Lings, pp. 86,111). Muslim scholar Pickthall's own summary of Muhammad's war record is an eye-opener: "The number of the campaigns which he led in person during the last ten years of his life is twenty-seven, in nine of which there was hard fighting. The number of the expeditions which he planned and sent out under other leaders is thirty-eight" (n.d., p. xxvi).

What a contrast with Jesus–Who never once took up the sword or encouraged anyone else to do so! The one time that one of His close followers took it upon himself to do so, the disciple was soundly reprimanded and ordered to put the sword away, with the added warning: "all who take the sword will perish by the sword" (Matthew 26:52). Indeed, when Pilate quizzed Jesus regarding His intentions, He responded: "My kingdom is not of this world. If My kingdom were of this world, **My servants would fight**, so that I should not be delivered to the Jews; but now My kingdom is not from here" (John 18:36, emp. added)–the very opposite of the Aqabah pact. And whereas the Quran boldly declares, "And **one who attacks you, attack him in like manner as he attacked you**" (*Surah* 2:194; cf. 22:60), Jesus counters, "But whoever slaps you on your right cheek, turn the other to him also" and "love your enemies" (Matthew 5:39,44). The New Testament record presents a far higher, more noble and godly ethic on the matter of violence and armed conflict. In fact, the following verses demonstrate how irrevocably deep the chasm is between the Quran and the New Testament on this point:

> [L]ove your enemies, bless those who curse you, do good to those who hate you, and pray for those who spitefully use you and persecute you, that you may be sons of your Father in heaven; for He makes His sun rise on the evil and on the good, and sends rain on the just and on the unjust. For if you love those who love you, what reward have you? (Matthew 5:44-46).

> But I say to you who hear: **Love your enemies, do good to those who hate you, bless those who curse you, and pray for those who spitefully use you**. To him who strikes you on the one cheek, **offer the other also**. And from him who takes away your cloak, do not withhold your tunic either. Give to everyone who asks of you. And from him who takes away your goods do

not ask them back. And just as you want men to do to you, you also do to them likewise. But if you love those who love you, what credit is that to you? For even sinners love those who love them. And if you do good to those who do good to you, what credit is that to you? For even sinners do the same. And if you lend to those from whom you hope to receive back, what credit is that to you? For even sinners lend to sinners to receive as much back. **But love your enemies, do good, and lend, hoping for nothing in return**; and your reward will be great, and you will be sons of the Most High. For He is kind to the unthankful and evil. Therefore be merciful, just as your Father also is merciful (Luke 6:27-36, emp. added).

What an amazing contrast! The New Testament says to love, bless, do good to, and pray for those who persecute you. The Quran says "persecution is worse than killing" (*Surah* 2:217)–i.e., it is better to kill your persecutors than to endure their persecutions!

The standard Muslim attempt to justify the Quran's endorsement of violence is that such violence was undertaken in self-defense (e.g., *Surah* 42:41). Consider the following Muslim explanation:

At the time when this surah (*Surah* 2–DM) was revealed at Al-Madinah, the Prophet's own tribe, the pagan Qureysh at Mecca, were preparing to attack the Muslims in their place of refuge. Cruel persecution was the lot of Muslims who had stayed in Meccan territory or who journeyed thither, and Muslims were being prevented from performing the pilgrimage. The possible necessity of fighting had been foreseen in the terms of the oath, taken at Al-Aqabah by the Muslims of Yathrib before the Flight, to defend the Prophet as they would their own wives and children, and **the first commandment to fight** was revealed to the Prophet before his flight from Mecca; but there was no actual fighting by the Muslims until the battle of Badr. Many of them were reluctant, having before been subject to a rule of strict non-violence. It was with difficulty that they could **accept the idea of fighting** even in **self-defence** [sic].... (Pickthall, p. 33, emp. added).

Apart from the fact that the claim that Muhammad's advocacy of fighting was justifiable on the ground of self-defense is contrary to the historical facts (since the wars waged by Muhammad and the territorial expansion of Islam achieved by his subsequent followers cannot **all** be dismissed as defensive), this explanation fails to come to grips with the propriety of shedding of blood and inflicting violence–**regardless of the reason**. Muslim scholar Seyyed Nasr seems unconscious of the inherent self-contradiction apparent in his own remark:

> The spread of Islam occurred in waves. In less than a century after the establishment of the first Islamic society in Medina by the Prophet, **Arab armies had conquered** a land stretching from the Indus River to France and brought with them Islam, which, contrary to popular Western conceptions, **was not, however, forced on the people by the sword** (2003, p. 17, emp. added).

In other words, Muslim armies physically conquered–by military force and bloodshed–various nations, forcing the population to submit to Muslim **rule**, but did not require them to become Muslims! One suspects that, at the time, the technical distinction escaped the citizens of those conquered countries, even as it surely does the reader.

The Quran appears to have been somewhat influenced by the law of Moses in this regard. For example, the Quran states: "If ye punish, then punish with the like of that wherewith ye were afflicted" (*Surah* 16:126). Similarly, "O ye who believe! Retaliation is prescribed for you in the matter of the murdered; the freeman for the freeman, and the slave for the slave, and the female for the female.... And there is life for you in retaliation, O men of understanding, that ye may ward off (evil)" (*Surah* 2:178-179). One is reminded of the *lex talionis* [literally "law as (or of) retaliation"] of the law of Moses. However, whereas the Quran appears to enjoin retaliation, the *lex talionis* were not intended to promote retaliation. Enjoining retaliation would be in direct conflict with the nature of God. God is never vindictive. The New Testament law does not differ with the Old Testament in the areas of proper values, ethics, mercy, and justice. The "eye for an eye" injunctions of the Old Testament were designed to be **prohibitive** in their thrust, i.e., they humanely **limited and restricted** legal punishment to a degree in keeping with the crime. That is, they prevented dispensers of justice from punishing too harshly or too much. They were intended to inculcate into Israelite society the principle of confining retribution to appropriate parameters.

The fact that the author of the Quran failed to grasp this feature of God's laws is evident in various Quranic injunctions: "As for the thief, both male and female, **cut off their hands**. It is the reward of their own deeds, an exemplary punishment from Allah. Allah is Mighty, Wise" (*Surah* 5:38, emp. added).

> The adulterer and the adulteress, scourge ye each one of them (with) **a hundred stripes**. And let not pity for the twain withhold you from obedience to Allah, if ye believe in Allah and the Last Day. And let a party of believers witness their punishment.... And those who accuse honourable women but bring not **four** witnesses, **scourge them (with) eighty stripes** and never (afterward) accept their testimony—They indeed are evildoers (*Surah* 24:2,4, emp. added).

These latter verses conflict with Mosaic injunction on two significant points. First, on the one hand, it **doubles** the more reasonable and appropriate forty stripes (Deuteronomy 25:3)—a number that the Jews were so concerned not to exceed that they counted thirty-nine and stopped to allow for accidental miscount (2 Corinthians 11:24). On the other hand, this eighty increases to one hundred for adultery. Second, the requirement of four witnesses is an unreasonable number. The two or three witnesses of the Bible (Deuteronomy 17:6; 19:15; Matthew 18:16; 2 Corinthians 13:1; 1 Timothy 5:19) strikes a logical medium between the precariousness of only a single witness on the one hand, and the excessive and unlikely availability of the four witnesses required by the Quran.

It is true that the God of the Bible enjoined violent, armed conflict for the Israelites in the Old Testament. He did so in order to eliminate the morally corrupt Canaanite civilizations who lived in Palestine prior to the Israelite occupation of the land (Deuteronomy 9:4; 18:9-12; Leviticus 18:24-25,27-28). There simply was no viable solution to their condition except extermination. Their moral depravity was "full" (Genesis 15:16). They had slumped to such an immoral, depraved state, with no hope of recovery, that their existence on this Earth had to be ended— just like in Noah's day when God waited while Noah preached for years but was unable to turn the world's population from its wickedness (Genesis 6:3,5-7; 1 Peter 3:20; 2 Peter 3:5-9).

Additionally, since the nation of Israel was also a civil entity in its own right, the government was also charged with implementing civil retribution upon lawbreakers. However, with the arrival of New Testament Christianity—an international religion intended for all persons without regard to ethnicity or nationality—God has assigned to **civil government** (not the church or the individual) the responsibility of regulating secular behavior. God's people who live posterior to the cross of Christ (i.e., Christians) are not charged by God with the responsibility of inflicting physical punishment on the evildoer. Rather, civil government is charged with the responsibility of maintaining order and punishing lawbreakers (Romans 13:1-7; Titus 3:1; 1 Peter 2:13-14). Observe Paul's explanation of this dichotomy:

> Let every soul be subject to the governing authorities. For there is no authority except from God, and the authorities that exist are appointed by God. Therefore whoever resists the authority resists the ordinance of God, and those who resist will bring judgment on themselves. For rulers are not a terror to good works, but to evil. Do you want to be unafraid of the authority? Do what is good, and you will have praise from the same. For he is God's minister to you for good. But if you do evil, be afraid; for he does not bear the sword in vain; for he is God's minister, **an avenger to execute wrath** on him who practices evil. Therefore you must be subject, not only because of wrath but also for conscience' sake. For because of this you also pay taxes, for they are God's ministers attending continually to this very thing. Render therefore

to all their due: taxes to whom taxes are due, customs to
whom customs, fear to whom fear, honor to whom honor
(Romans 13:1-7, NKJV, emp. added).

One translation (NIV) renders the boldface type in the above
quote "an agent of wrath to bring punishment." But this assign-
ment of judicial and penal retribution to the government is a
contrast in Paul's discussion with what he wrote in the three verses
prior to this quotation:

> Beloved, **do not avenge yourselves**, but rather **give
> place to wrath**; for it is written, "Vengeance is Mine, I will
> repay," says the Lord. Therefore "If your enemy is hun-
> gry, feed him; If he is thirsty, give him a drink; For in so
> doing you will heap coals of fire on his head." Do not be
> overcome by evil, but overcome evil with good (Romans
> 12:19-21, NKJV, emp. added).

Notice that the very responsibility that is **enjoined** on the government, i.e., "an avenger to execute wrath" by use of the sword
in 13:4, is **strictly forbidden** to the individual Christian in 12:
19, i.e., "do **not** avenge yourselves, but rather **give place** to wrath."
To "give place to wrath" means to allow God's wrath to show itself in His own appointed way that, according to the next few
verses, is by means of the civil government.

True Christianity (i.e., that which is based strictly on the New
Testament) dictates peace and non-retaliatory promotion of itself. The "absolute imperative" (Rahman, 1979, p. 22) of Islam is
the **submission/conversion** of the whole world. In stark contrast, the absolute imperative of New Testament Christianity is
the **evangelism** of the whole world, i.e., the **dissemination** of
the message of salvation—whether people embrace it or not (Matthew 28:18-20; Mark 16:15-16; Luke 24:46-47). Absolutely no
coercion is admissible from the Christian (i.e., New Testament)
viewpoint. The Crusades, the Spanish Inquisition, and all other
violent activities undertaken in the name of Christ and Christianity have been in complete conflict with the teaching of the
New Testament. The perpetrators acted without the authority
and sanction of Christ.

Islam seeks to bring the entire world into submission to Allah and the Quran—even using *jihad*, coercion, and force; Christianity seeks to go into all the world and to announce the "good news" that God loves every individual, that Jesus Christ died for the sins of everyone, and that He offers salvation, forgiveness, and reconciliation. **BUT**, each person has free choice to accept or reject without any retaliation by Christians against those who choose to reject. Jesus taught His disciples, when faced with opposition and resistance, simply to walk away: "And whoever will not receive you nor hear your words, when you depart from that house or city, shake off the dust from your feet" (Matthew 10:14). In fact, on one occasion when a Samaritan village was particularly nonreceptive, some of Jesus' disciples wished to command fire to come down from heaven to consume them! But Jesus rebuked them and said, "'You do not know what manner of spirit you are of. For the Son of Man did not come to destroy men's lives but to save them.' And they went to another village" (Luke 9:55). Muhammad and the Quran stand in diametrical opposition to Jesus and the New Testament.

If the majority of Muslims were violent, that would not prove that Islam is a religion of violence. The vast majority of those who claim to be "Christian" are practicing a corrupted form of the Christian faith. So the validity of any religion is determined ultimately not by the imperfect, inaccurate practice of the religion by even a majority of its adherents, but by the official authority or standard upon which it is based, i.e., its Scriptures. The present discussion in the world regarding whether or not *jihad* includes physical force in the advancement of Islam is ultimately irrelevant (cf. Nasr, 2002, pp. 256-266). The Quran unquestionably endorses violence, war, and armed conflict. No wonder a substantial number of Muslims manifest a maniacal, reckless abandon in their willingness to die by sacrificing their lives in order to kill as many "infidels" (especially Israelis and Americans) as possible. They have read the following:

> Now when ye meet in battle those who disbelieve, then it is smiting of the necks.... And **those who are slain in**

the way of Allah, He rendereth not their actions vain. He will guide them and improve their state, and **bring them in unto the Garden** [Paradise—DM] which He hath made known to them (*Surah* 47:4-6, emp. added).

O ye who believe! Be not as those who disbelieved and said of their brethren who went abroad in the land or were **fighting in the field**: If they had been (here) with us they would not have died or been killed.... And what **though ye be slain in Allah's way** or die therein? Surely pardon from Allah and mercy are better than all that they amass. What **though ye be slain** or die, when unto Allah ye are gathered?.... So those who...**fought and were slain,** verily **I shall remit their evil deeds** from them and verily I shall **bring them into Gardens** underneath which rivers flow—a reward from Allah (*Surah* 3:156-158,195, emp. added).

Even if the vast majority of Muslims in the world reject violence and refrain from terrorist activity (which would appear to be the case), it is still a fact that the Quran (as well as the example of Muhammad himself) endorses the advancement of Islam through physical force. While Muslim apologist Seyyed Hossein Nasr insists that "the traditional norms based on peace and openness to others" characterize true Islam and the majority of Muslims, in contradistinction, he freely admits that at times Islam "has been forced to take recourse to physical action in the form of defense" (Nasr, 2002, pp. 112,110). This concession cannot be successfully denied in view of the Quran's own declarations. Hence, the Muslim is forced to maintain the self-contradictory position that, yes, there have been times that Islam has been properly violent and, yes, the Quran does endorse violence, but, no, most Muslims are not violent, and then only in self-defense. As reprehensible and cowardly as Islamic terrorists have shown themselves to be in recent years, an honest reading of the Quran leads one to believe that they, at least, are more consistent with, and true to, their own Scriptures.

CONCLUSION

While the Quran contains some commendable ethical regulations, it simply does not come up to the moral heights of the Bible. It approves various moral and social evils like polygamy, bloodshed, and slavery (e.g., 4:3,25,36,92; 5:89; 16:71; 23:6; 24:32-33,58; 30:28; 33:50-55; 58:3; 70:30; 90:13; cf. Philemon 16). It assigns to women an inferior status—even allowing beatings from husbands:

> Men are in charge of women, because Allah hath made the one of them to excel the other, and because they spend of their property (for the support of women). So good women are the obedient, guarding in secret that which Allah hath guarded. As for those from whom ye fear rebellion, admonish them and banish them to beds apart, and scourge them. Then if they obey you, seek not a way against them. Lo! Allah is ever High Exalted, Great (*Surah* 4:34; cf. 4:11; 2:223,228,282; 38:45; 16:58-59; see also Brooks, 1995; Trifkovic, 2002, pp. 153-167; Lull, n.d.).

The conflicting ethics advocated in the Quran are further proof of the Quran's human origin.

Prophet Muhammad appearing at the Ka'bah to rid the populace of an unwanted dragon
Nakkas Osman, 1595.
Hazine 1222, folio 123a
Credit: TOPKAPI PALACE MUSEUM

Chapter 9

THE QURAN VS. THE NEW TESTAMENT: ADDITIONAL CONFLICTS

In addition to the conflicts between the Quran and the New Testament over central doctrines and ethical issues, the two also clash on a variety of miscellaneous matters. This chapter discusses the Quran's treatment of the afterlife (including the concepts of heaven, paradise, and hell), the role of miracles, the place of rituals, and the Quran's failure to distinguish between New Testament Christianity and the corrupt forms extant in Muhammad's day.

AFTERLIFE

The Quran's portrayal of afterlife and the spirit realm is a confused hodgepodge of borrowed ideas from a variety of sources, as well as the author's own misconceptions. While the Bible does not clarify every aspect of life beyond the grave, nor answer every question that one might raise about that realm, it nevertheless affords a consistent, cohesive, definitive treatment of the subject that contrasts sharply with the Quran.

Seven Heavens?

The Quran makes repeated reference to the existence of seven heavens. Consider the following allusions: "He it is Who created for you all that is in the earth. Then turned He to the heaven, and fashioned it as **seven heavens**. And He is Knower of all things" (*Surah* 2:29, emp. added); "Say: Who is Lord of **the seven heavens**, and Lord of the Tremendous Throne? They will say: Unto Allah (all that belongeth). Say: Will ye not then keep duty (unto Him)?" (*Surah* 23:86-87, emp. added); "The **seven heavens** and the earth and all that is therein praise Him" (*Surah* 17:44, emp. added). Speaking of the creation of the Universe, the Quran states: "Then He ordained them **seven heavens** in two Days and inspired in each heaven its mandate; and we decked the nether heaven with lamps, and rendered it inviolable" (*Surah* 41:12, emp. added). Noah's admonitions to his contemporaries included reminders of Allah's creative activities: "See ye not how Allah hath created **seven heavens** in harmony, and hath made the moon a light therein, and made the sun a lamp?" (*Surah* 71:15-16, emp. added; see also 23:17; 65:12; 67:3; 78:12).

In sharp contrast to the Quran's "seven" heavens, the Bible speaks of only three. The "first heaven" is the Earth's atmosphere—the "sky"–where the birds fly (Genesis 1:20; 8:2; Isaiah 55:10; Luke 13:19). The "second heaven" is "outer space"–where the Sun, Moon, and stars are situated (Genesis 15:5; 22:17; Deuteronomy 4:19; Nahum 3:16). These two heavens together are referred to in the first verse of the Bible: "In the beginning, God created the **heavens** (plural–DM) and the earth" (Genesis 1:1, emp. added). The "third heaven" in biblical thought is the spirit realm beyond the physical realm where God and other celestial beings reside (Deuteronomy 10:14; 26:15; 1 Kings 8:27,30). It often is referred to as the "heaven of heavens"–a Semitism wherein the genitive is used for the superlative degree—meaning the highest or ultimate heaven (cf. "Song of songs," "King of kings," "Lord of lords"). While the Bible uses the number seven frequently, it **never** mentions anything about any so-called "seven heavens"—even in the apocalyptic book of Revelation where the number seven is used figuratively and prominently (54 times). The Quran's allusions cannot be rationalized as poetic or figurative, since none of the Quranic citations gives any indication of a **figurative** use.

Where did the Quran get its notion of seven heavens? Once again, uninspired sources clarify the circumstance. Jewish rabbis frequently spoke of seven heavens (Ginzberg, 1909, 1:9; 1910, 2:260,313; 1911, 3:96; 1925, 5:9-11,23,30). They also spoke of seven gates to hell (Ginzberg, 5:19,267; 1928, 6:438), another feature copied into the Quran that is in conflict with the Bible: "And lo! for all such, hell will be the promised place. It hath seven gates, and each gate hath an appointed portion" (*Surah* 15:43-44). Additionally, the Quran's use of the phrase "the seven paths" (*Surah* 23:17) is a Talmudic expression (Rodwell, 1950, p. 145).

Paradise

The term "paradise" is of Persian derivation, and referred to "a grand enclosure or preserve, hunting-ground, park, shady and well-watered" (Thayer, 1901, p. 480). The Jews used the term as "a garden, pleasure-ground, grove, park," and came to apply it to that portion of hades that was thought "to be the abode of the souls of the pious until the resurrection" (p. 480). With this linguistic background, the word is used in three senses in the Bible: (1) it is used in the Septuagint (Genesis 2:8,9,10,15,16; 3:2,3, 4,9,11,24,25), the Greek translation of the Old Testament, to refer to the literal Garden of Eden on Earth where Adam and Eve lived (*Septuagint...*, 1970, pp. 3-5). It normally is translated "garden" in English versions; (2) it is used one time, in a highly figurative New Testament book, to refer to the final abode of the saved, i.e., heaven (Revelation 2:7); and (3) it is used in connection with the hadean realm. The Hebrew Old Testament term for this waiting place is *sheol*, and the New Testament term is *hades*.

The Quran shows no awareness of these biblical distinctions. Instead, it advocates the existence of seven heavens (as noted), paradise (which apparently is among the seven heavens), and hell—an evident reflection of the uninspired influence of both Jewish and Persian sources of the sixth and seventh centuries.

According to the Bible, hades is a broad term that designates the receptacle of disembodied spirits where all humans who die await the Lord's return (Luke 23:43; Luke 16:19-31; 2 Corinthians 12:4) prior to the resurrection (1 Corinthians 15:35-54), the Judgment, and the final disposition of all humans to one of two ultimate eternal realms, i.e., heaven or hell. This realm encompasses two "compartments": one for the deceased righteous, and one for the deceased wicked. The area inhabited by the righteous is "paradise," while the area for the wicked is "tartarus." Very little information is actually given in the Bible in the way of description regarding hades. In fact, the **only** descriptive detail provided (Luke 16:19-31) indicates that within hades, (1) paradise is described as a place where one is "comforted" (vs. 25), and (2) it is separated from tartarus by "a great gulf" (vs. 26). That's it! Absolutely no additional elaboration is given regarding paradise—no couches, no maidens, no rivers of water, no gold goblets. Hades, within which are paradise and tartarus, is, in fact, a **temporary** realm that will be terminated at the Judgment (Revelation 20:13-14). From that point forward, only two eternal realms will exist: heaven and hell.

The only detailed description given of heaven in the Bible is in the book of Revelation—a self-declared **apocalypse** (*apocalupsis*–"revelation"–1:1), i.e., a symbolic, figurative depiction that is not to be understood literally (see Swete, 1911, pp. xxii-xxxii; Gasque, 1975, 1:200-204; Thomson, 1939, 1:162-163). Hence, the "street of gold" (21:21), "pure river of water of life" (22:1), "tree of life" (22:2), and cube-shaped, walled city situated on twelve foundations of precious stones with pearl gates (21:19-21) are explicitly stated to be strictly figurative ("signified"–1:1). The Bible seems to go out of its way to avoid attempting to describe a nonphysical, spiritual, eternal realm to humans who live in a physical, finite realm. It says just enough to "whet the appetite" of an honest seeker of truth, without succumbing to the mistake of overwhelming the reader with a **wholly carnal impression of heaven**. The Quran commits precisely this blunder. Paradise is repeatedly represented in literal, materialistic terms:

> Therefore Allah hath warded off from them the evil of that day, and hath made them find brightness and joy; And hath awarded them for all that they endured, a Garden and **silk attire**; Reclining therein upon **couches**, they will find there neither (heat of) a sun nor bitter cold. The **shade** thereof is close upon them and the **clustered fruits** thereof bow down. **Goblets of silver** are brought round for them, and **beakers (as) of glass (bright as) glass but (made) of silver**, which they (themselves) have measured to the measure (of their deeds). There are they watered with a cup whereof the mixture is of Zanjabil, **the water of a spring** therein, named Salsabil. There serve them **youths of everlasting youth**, whom, when thou seest, thou wouldst take for scattered pearls. When thou seest, thou wilt see there bliss and high estate. Their **raiment will be fine green silk and gold embroidery. Bracelets of silver** will they wear. Their Lord will slake their thirst with a pure drink. (And it will be said unto them): Lo! this is a reward for you. Your endeavour (upon earth) hath found acceptance (*Surah* 76:11-22, emp. added).

> But for him who feareth the standing before his Lord there are **two gardens**. Which is it, of the favours of your Lord, that ye deny? Of **spreading branches**, Which is it, of the favours of your Lord, that ye deny? Wherein are **two fountains flowing**. Which is it, of the favours of your Lord, that ye deny? Wherein is **every kind of fruit** in pairs. Which is it, of the favours of your Lord, that ye deny? Reclining upon **couches lined with silk brocade**, the **fruit** of both gardens near to hand. Which is it, of the favours of your Lord, that ye deny? Therein are **those of modest gaze**, whom neither man nor jinni will have touched before them, Which is it, of the favours of your Lord, that ye deny? (In beauty) like the jacynth and

the coral-stone. Which is it, of the favours of your Lord that ye deny? Is the reward of goodness aught save goodness? Which is it, of the favours of your Lord, that ye deny? And beside them are **two other gardens,** Which is it, of the favours of your Lord, that ye deny? **Dark green with foliage.** Which is it, of the favours of your Lord, that ye deny? Wherein are **two abundant springs.** Which is it, of the favours of your Lord, that ye deny? Wherein is fruit, **the date-palm and pomegranate.** Which is it, of the favours of your Lord, that ye deny? Wherein (are found) the good and beautiful–Which is it, of the favours of your Lord, that ye deny?–**Fair ones,** close-guarded in pavilions–Which is it, of the favours of your Lord, that ye deny? Whom neither man nor jinni will have touched before them–Which is it, of the favours of your Lord, that ye deny? **Reclining on green cushions and fair carpets.** Which is it, of the favours of your Lord, that ye deny? Blessed be the name of thy Lord, Mighty and Glorious! (*Surah* 55:46-78, emp. added).

In addition to the multiple gardens or paradises (55:46,62; cf. 83:18-19; Lings, pp. 95,202) with couches, green cushions, carpets, silk attire, silver bracelets, goblets and beakers of silver, shade, branches and foliage, fountains and springs, dates and pomegranates, youthful servants of everlasting youth and fair virgins, paradise also will include golden trays or dishes (43:71), flowering meadows (42:22), a pure wine (non-intoxicating–56:19) sealed with musk and mixed with water from the heavenly spring of Tasnim (83:25-28), multiple storied halls or mansions (29:58; 34:37; 39:20), fowl flesh (56:21), thornless lote-trees (56:28), and clustered plantains (56:29). The references to paradise in such materialistic terms go on and on in the Quran (cf. 15:45-47; 18:32; 22:23; 35:33; 37:41-49; 38:51-53; 44:51-55; 47:15; 52:17-28; 88:8-16; et al.). The contexts in which they occur discount the standard Muslim explanation that they are "figurative." In fact, one verse even equates the fruit on Earth with the fruit in paradise: "And give glad tidings (O Muhammad) unto those who believe and do good works; that theirs are Gardens underneath which rivers flow; as often as they are regaled with food of the fruit thereof, they say: **This is what was given us aforetime**; and it is given to them in resemblance" (*Surah* 2:25, emp. added).

One would think that Muslim women would feel short-changed in the afterlife. Paradise for men will include access to maidens: "pure companions" (2:25; 3:15; 4:57), "fair ones with wide, lovely eyes" (44:54; 52:20–or "beautiful, big and lustrous eyes"–Ali; cf. 55:72) like "hidden eggs (of the ostrich)" and "hidden pearls" (37:49; 56:23), "those of modest gaze" (37:48; 38:53–or "chaste women restraining their glances, [companions] of equal age"–Ali; cf. 55:56; 78:33), who are "good and beautiful" (55:70), "virgins" (56:36), "whom neither man nor jinni will have touched before them" (55:56,74). Such lascivious, lustful appeals to sensual and sexual passions are transparent–and typical of male authors unguided by a higher power.

Additionally, the Quran and the Bible conflict with one another on the matter of marriage in the afterlife. The Quran unquestionably indicates that marriage will persist in paradise (*Surah* 13:23; 36:55; 40:8; 43:70). In fact, God Himself will perform the ceremonies: "Lo! those who kept their duty will be in a place secure amid gardens and water-springs, attired in silk and silk embroidery, facing one another. Even so (it will be). And **We shall wed them** unto fair ones with wide, lovely eyes" (44:54, emp. added; cf. 52:20). But Jesus soundly refuted this notion in His interchange with the Sadducees: "For in the resurrection they neither marry nor are given in marriage, but are like angels of God in heaven" (Matthew 22:30).

The emphasis on food, drink, and physical pleasures in the Quranic depictions of afterlife reflect a perspective that one would anticipate from a desert-bound Arab Bedouin. This preoccupation with carnal things and material comforts exposes the description as uninspired, and stands in stark contrast with the Bible's handling of the subject. So also with the redundancy of repetitious phrases: "gardens underneath which rivers flow" (used 32 times in Pickthall–see Al-nasir).

Hell

The classic Christian doctrine of hell receives a most interesting treatment in the Quran, providing a number of fanciful particulars and whimsical embellishments. On the Day of Judgment, unbelievers will be "dragged into the Fire upon their faces" (*Surah* 54:48) "by their scalps" (*Surah* 70:16, Dawood, Sale, Rodwell translations). Their faces will be "blackened" (*Surah* 39:60). They will have manacles, chains, and yokes placed upon them (*Surah* 34:33; 40:71; 76:4), and be subjected to "hooked rods of iron" (*Surah* 22:21). One surah even declares that the wife of Abu Lahab (one of Muhammad's bitter opponents) "will have upon her neck a halter of palm-fibre" (*Surah* 111:5)–apparently **fireproof** palm fiber!

According to the Quran, hell is a place of raging, fiercely blazing fire (*Surah* 73:12; 92:14; 101:11) with leaping, piercing, burning flames (*Surah* 4:10; 17:97; 25:11; 37:10; 48:13; 77:30-31; 85:10; 104:6-7), in which people "neither die nor live" (*Surah* 87:12-13). In addition to flames, hell also contains scorching winds, black smoke (*Surah* 56:42-43), and boiling hot water through which the disbelievers will be dragged (*Surah* 40:71-72; 55:44). In fact, unbelievers will both **drink** and **be drenched with** boiling water:

> Lo! We have prepared for disbelievers Fire. Its tent encloseth them. If they ask for showers, they will be **showered with water like to molten lead** which burneth the faces. **Calamitous the drink** and ill the resting-place! (*Surah* 18:30, emp. added).

> These twain (the believers and the disbelievers) are two opponents who contend concerning their Lord. But as for those who disbelieve, garments of fire will be cut out for them; **boiling fluid will be poured down on their heads.** Whereby **that which is in their bellies, and their skins too, will be melted**; And for them are **hooked rods of iron.** Whenever, in their anguish, they would go forth from thence they are driven back therein and (it is said unto them): Taste the doom of burning (*Surah* 22:19-22, emp. added; cf. 6:70; 10:5; 37:67; 44:48; 56:54,93)

The ingested boiling water will cut and tear the bowels (*Surah* 47:15). Yet the drinking of boiling water apparently will be accompanied by an occasional **cold** drink: "Hell, where they will burn, an evil resting place. Here is **a boiling and an ice-cold draught**, so let them taste it, and other (torment) of the kind in pairs (the two extremes)!" (*Surah* 38:57-59, emp. added; cf. 78: 24-25). Ali renders the phrase: "a boiling fluid, and a fluid dark, murky, intensely cold!"

In addition to liquid, the diet of the unbeliever will include some solid food: "On that day (many) faces will be downcast, toiling, weary, scorched by burning fire, drinking from a boiling spring, no food for them **save bitter thorn-fruit** which doth not nourish nor release from hunger" (*Surah* 88:2-7, emp. added). The Quran alleges the existence of a specific tree from which hell's occupants will eat:

> Is this better as a welcome, or the tree of Zaqqum? Lo! We have appointed it a torment for wrong-doers. Lo! it is a tree that springeth in the heart of hell. Its crop is as it were the heads of devils. And lo! they verily must eat thereof, and fill (their) bellies therewith. And afterward, lo! thereupon they have a drink of boiling water (*Surah* 37:62-67).

> All will certainly be gathered together for the meeting appointed for a Day well-known. Then will you truly— O you that go wrong, and treat (Truth) as Falsehood!— you will surely taste of the Tree of Zaqqum. Then will you fill your insides therewith, and drink Boiling Water on top of it: Indeed you shall drink like diseased camels raging with thirst! Such will be their entertainment on the Day of Requital! (*Surah* 56:50-56, Ali).

> Lo! the tree of Zaqqum, the food of the sinner! Like molten brass, it seetheth in their bellies as the seething of boiling water (*Surah* 44:43-46).

Uninspired Jewish folklore postulated the same tree (cf. *Sukkah* 32).

The Quran also claims that hell possesses "keepers" or "guardians" (*Surah* 40:49; 96:18). Malik is the primary angel in charge of hell who presides over the torments inflicted on unbelievers:

"The sinners will be in the punishment of Hell, to dwell therein (forever).... They will cry: 'O Malik! Would that your Lord put an end to us!' He will say, 'Nay, but you shall abide!'" (*Surah* 43: 74,77, Ali). Of course, the Bible says nothing of any so-called guardians of hell. In fact, the Bible teaches that even Satan is not presently in hell. Rather, "our adversary the devil walks about like a roaring lion, seeking whom he may devour" (1 Peter 5:8; cf. Job 1:7; 2:2). It is true that, according to the Bible, some angels are being confined as they await the Judgment: "And the angels who did not keep their proper domain, but left their own abode, He has reserved in everlasting chains under darkness for the judgment of the great day" (Jude 6). But their location is tartarus within the hadean realm (2 Peter 2:4). In the meantime, Satan and his angels will be thrown into the lake of fire at the end of time (Matthew 25:41; Revelation 20:10).

Additional allusions in the Quran to unbiblical (and outlandish) concepts regarding hell (also borrowed from uninspired ancient rabbinical literature) include: (1) a veil between hell and Paradise (*Surah* 7:46), drawn from the legend recorded in the Midrash on Ecclesiastes 7:14 (cf. Tisdall, 1905, p. 124), as well as a place between the two that enables a "crier" to communicate with both sides (*Surah* 7:44); and (2) the report of angels who eavesdrop on God (*Surah* 15:18; 37:8; 67:5; cf. *Hagigah* 6.1).

Even giving the Quran allowance for the difficulty of representing a nonphysical, eternal realm in language that enables humans to derive a sufficient understanding of the horror of hell, the Quran makes the mistake of depicting hell materialistically as a place for physical bodies. It offers an abundance of detail that removes the impression of hell being a spiritual realm. It shows no understanding or awareness of eternity involving a spiritual, nonmaterial realm where human spirits will be clothed with new, spiritual bodies. The Bible, on the other hand, provides clarification on just such matters, giving just enough information for the honest, objective reader to grasp this very point, i.e., that it will be a nonphysical realm, but will entail unending pain and suffering for the spiritual body (Matthew 25:31-46; Luke

12:4-5; John 5:28; 1 Corinthians 15:35-55). The Bible is sufficiently generic to be credible. The Quran suffers from the embellishment that one would expect from an uninspired, human author. Its myriad of detail on this subject cannot be dismissed as merely figurative.

Next to the doctrine of monotheism, the doctrine of hell and punishment receives more attention than any other doctrine in the Quran—maybe even more than monotheism. In fact, to the unbiased reader, the Quran is positively top heavy—completely unbalanced—in its almost constant emphasis on fire, torment, and eternal punishment. Keeping in mind there are 114 surahs in the Quran, observe that the word "hell" occurs 102 times in Pickthall's translation (95 in Ali) in 54 surahs. "Fire" occurs 161 times (203 in Ali) in 65 surahs. "Punish/punishment" occurs 115 times (169 in Ali) in 43 surahs. "Doom" occurs 215 times in 62 surahs. This means that the Quran refers to hell, fire, doom, and punishment in **92 of its 114 surahs**—which is **80 percent** of the Quran! In sharp contrast, the New Testament—which approximates the Quran in length—uses the word "hell" (*gehenna*) **only 12 times** (Matthew 5:22,29,30; 10:28; 18:9; 23:15,33; Mark 9:43,45,47; Luke 12:5; James 3:6). While the Bible most definitely emphasizes the certainty and inevitability of eternal punishment, it places the subject in proper perspective and provides a divinely balanced treatment. The Quran, on the other hand, is thoroughly preoccupied with incessant threats of punishment *ad infinitum.* Its inordinate fixation on hell, fire, torment, and punishment is another proof of its human origin.

PERFORMANCE AND ROLE OF MIRACLES/SIGNS

Muhammad never claimed (as the Quran verifies) to be able to work miracles (though subsequent Muslim tradition so claims). The Quran justifies this absence of the miraculous by claiming that (1) the miracles performed and revelations given by prophets who preceded Muhammad, and (2) the visible aspects of nature, and the physical blessings of God, were sufficient signs to establish the Prophet's credibility. The Quran indicates repeatedly that Muhammad's appearance as a prophet of Allah, and the revelations he uttered, were sufficient justification for his hearers to accept him (cf. Gibb, 1953, p. 28). In fact, the Quran challenged Muhammad's critics to see if they could produce revelations that rivaled the ones he offered (the same challenge issued in defense of the *Book of Mormon* [see "The Challenge...," 1990]): "And if ye are in doubt concerning that which We reveal unto Our slave (Muhammad), then produce a surah of the like thereof, and call your witnesses beside Allah if ye are truthful" (*Surah* 2: 23; cf. 10:39; 11:12; 17:88). In contrast, the Bible does not issue such a challenge, for the simple reason that other remarkable documents that claim to be of divine origin have been produced through the centuries. Their claim of inspiration cannot be verified on the basis of such ambiguous, disputable criteria as the perceived talent of the human author or the length of time needed to produce the writing. Rather, as the Bible logically maintains, the spoken word must be confirmed or authenticated by the miraculous: supernatural acts performed by the spokesman himself.

Indeed, the New Testament declares that miracles served the singular function of **confirmation**. When an inspired speaker stepped forward to declare God's Word, God **validated** or **endorsed** the speaker's remarks by empowering the speaker to perform a miracle. Many New Testament passages articulate this fact quite plainly. For example, the apostles "went forth, and preached everywhere, the Lord working with them, and **confirming** the word by the **signs** that followed" (Mark 16:20, emp. added). The Hebrews writer asked: "[H]ow shall we escape, if we neglect so great a salvation; which having at the first been **spoken** through the Lord, was **confirmed** unto us by them that heard; God also **bearing witness** with them, both by **signs and wonders**, and by manifold powers, and by gifts of the Holy Spirit" (Hebrews 2:3-4, emp. added). Referring to the initial proclamation of the Gospel to the Samaritans, Luke stated: "[A]nd the multitudes gave heed with one accord unto **the things that were spoken** by Philip, when they heard, and saw the **signs** which he did" (Acts 8:6, emp. added).

These passages, and many others (e.g., Acts 4:29-30; 13:12; 14:3; 15:12; Romans 15:18-19; 1 Corinthians 2:4; 1 Thessalonians 1:5; cf. Exodus 4:30), show that the purpose of miracles was to **authenticate** the oral/spoken word as God's Word. Miracles **legitimized** and **verified** the teaching of God's messengers, as over against the many false teachers (like Simon in Acts 8:9, or Pharaoh's magicians in Exodus 7:11) who attempted to mislead the people. In the late nineteenth century, Greek lexicographer Joseph Thayer worded this point well when he noted that "sign" (*semeion*) was used in the New Testament "of miracles and wonders by which God authenticates the men sent by him, or by which men prove that the cause they are pleading is God's" (1901, p. 573). Even the miracles that Jesus performed were designed to back up His claim (i.e., spoken words) to be deity (John 3:2; 14:10-11)–a pattern that is repeated in the New Testament many times over (e.g., John 2:23; 5:36; 6:14; 7:31; 10:37-38,41-42; 20:30-31; Acts 2:22). In other words, Jesus performed signs and miracles to prove His divine identity and thereby authenticate His message. His message, in turn, generated faith in those who chose to believe His teachings (cf. Romans 10:17). Here is the consistent sequence presented in Scripture: **Signs➔Word➔Faith**. (1) Signs confirmed the Word; (2) the Word was presented to hearers; and (3) faith was created (by the Word) in those who received it.

The God of the Bible never expected nor required anyone to accept His Word without adequate proof. He empowered His spokesmen on Earth to verify their verbal pronouncements by performing accompanying supernatural acts (Mark 16:20; Hebrews 2:3-4). The book of John spotlights this feature repeatedly. When Nicodemus, a Pharisee and ruler of the Jews, approached Jesus one night, he stated: "Rabbi, we **know** that You are a teacher come from God; for **no one can do these signs** that You do **unless God is with him**" (John 3:2, emp. added). Nicodemus was a rational man who saw evidence that pointed to the obvious conclusion that Jesus was of divine origin.

Responding to critical Jews, Jesus defended His divine identity by directing their attention to the works (i.e., supernatural actions) He performed: "[T]he very works that I do bear witness of Me, that the Father has sent Me" (John 5:36). He made the same point to His apostles on another occasion:

> Do you not believe that I am in the Father, and the Father in Me? The words that I speak to you I do not speak on My own authority; but the Father who dwells in Me does the works. Believe Me that I am in the Father and the Father in Me, **or else believe Me for the sake of the works themselves** (John 14:10-11, emp. added).

Later, Jesus noted that when people refused to believe in Him as the Son of God, they were without excuse, since the evidence of His divine identity had been amply demonstrated: "If I had not done among them **the works which no one else did**, they would have no sin; but now they have seen and also hated both Me and My Father" (John 15:24, emp. added). So their lack of faith could not be attributed to their inability to **know the truth** regarding the person of Jesus (cf. John 8:32).

If it is the case that God does not expect a person to believe in Him **unless** adequate evidence has been made available to warrant that conclusion, then we ought to expect to see Jesus urging people **not to believe** Him **unless** He provided proof for His claims. Do we find Jesus doing so while He was on Earth? Absolutely! This fact is particularly pungent in Jesus' response to the tirade launched against Him by hard-hearted Jews who refused to face the reality of Christ's divinity. He reiterated: "The works that I do in My Father's name, they bear witness of Me" (John 10:25). His subsequent explicit declaration of His deity incited angry preparations to stone Him. He boldly challenged them: "If I do not do the works of My Father, **do not believe Me**; but if I do, though you do not believe Me, believe the works, that you may know and believe that the Father is in Me, and I in Him" (John 10:37-38, emp. added).

Since Jesus came to the planet to urge people to render obedient submission to Him (John 3:16; 8:24), it is difficult to envision Him telling people **not** to believe Him. Muhammad certainly never did so. But that is precisely what Jesus did! He has provided the world with adequate evidence for people to distinguish truth from falsehood. We can **know** that God exists, that Jesus is His Son, and that the Bible is the Word of God. If the evidence did not exist to prove these matters, God would not expect anyone to believe; nor would He condemn anyone for failing to believe—since He is fair and just (Acts 10:34-35; Romans 2:11; 2 Peter 3:9). He would not expect people to distinguish between true prophets and false prophets (cf. 2 Peter 2:1-2; 1 John 4:1) without providing the means to make the distinction.

The conclusion is obvious: If Muhammad were a prophet of God, he would have had the ability to authenticate the divine origin of his words by performing accompanying supernatural acts. Instead, **the Quran repeatedly makes excuses for Muhammad's inability to provide miraculous signs**, insisting that his hearers ought simply to accept his utterances as revelations from God. The most prominent excuse offered is that the ordinary blessings of life visible in the created order are sufficient "signs" ("portents" and "tokens") to justify Muhammad's insistence on the submission of his hearers:

> He it is Who sendeth down water from the sky, and therewith We bring forth buds of every kind; We bring forth the green blade from which we bring forth the thick-clustered grain; and from the date-palm, from the pollen thereof, spring pendant bunches; and (We bring forth) gardens of grapes, and the olive and the pomegranate, alike and unlike. Look upon the fruit thereof, when they bear fruit, and upon its ripening. Lo! **herein verily are portents** for a people who believe (*Surah* 6:100, emp. added).

> Allah created the heavens and the earth with truth. Lo! **therein is indeed a portent** for believers (*Surah* 29:44, emp. added; cf. 12:105; 42:29).

> And **of His signs is this**: He created you of dust, and behold you human beings, ranging widely! And **of His signs is this**: He created for you helpmeets from yourselves that ye might find rest in them, and He ordained

between you love and mercy. Lo, **herein indeed are portents** for folk who reflect. And **of His signs is the creation of the heavens and the earth**, and the difference of your languages and colours. Lo! **herein indeed are portents** for men of knowledge. And **of His signs** is your slumber by night and by day, and your seeking of His bounty. Lo! **herein indeed are portents** for folk who heed. And **of His signs is this**: He showeth you the lightning for a fear and for a hope, and sendeth down water from the sky, and thereby quickeneth the earth after her death. Lo! **herein indeed are portents** for folk who understand. And **of His signs is this**: The heavens and the earth stand fast by His command, and afterward, when He calleth you, lo! from the earth ye will emerge (*Surah* 30:20-25, emp. added).

Additional physical blessings to which the Quran alludes as sufficient evidence for accepting the word of Muhammad include having cattle for food and transportation (*Surah* 40:79-81), the night, day, Sun, and Moon (*Surah* 10:6-7,68; 31:29; 41:37), rain (*Surah* 7:57-58; 41:39), ships gliding on the sea (*Surah* 31:31), man created out of dust (*Surah* 30:20), providing men with wives (*Surah* 30:21), the wind (*Surah* 30:46), provisions (*Surah* 39:52; 40:13), and firm hills and flowing streams (*Surah* 13:2-4). Of course, the physical phenomena of the Universe certainly do constitute evidence of an all-powerful Supreme Being, i.e., the God of the Bible (Psalm 19:1-6; Acts 14:17; Romans 1:19-20). But they certainly do not provide proof that Muhammad or the Quran are from God. Any person on the planet could point to the wonders of nature and claim that they authenticate his or her own religious pronouncements. But the conclusion would not follow from the premise.

Another attempt to sidestep Muhammad's failure to authenticate his claims with miracles is the Quran's insistence that the stories recorded in previous Scripture ought to be sufficient (*Surah* 7:64; 12:7; 20:133; 26:190; 29:15,24,51; 34:19; 40:34). The claim is further bolstered by an appeal to the Jews of the day for verification from their own scriptures that miracles had taken place in the past (*Surah* 17:101; 26:197). Of course, if the Quran's claim were true, there would have been no need for the Quran. Muhammad could have simply restated the previous revelations. Observe the Quran's representation of God's comments to Muhammad: "Is it not enough for them that We have sent down unto thee (Muhammad–DM) the Scripture (the Quran–DM) which is read unto them? Lo! herein verily is mercy, and a reminder for folk who believe" (*Surah* 29:51). So the Quran claims that the Quran, itself, should be sufficient to convince people of its divine origin. This contention contrasts sharply with the Bible's confirmation-of-revelation principle (Hebrews 2:3-4).

On several occasions, Muhammad was asked directly why he was unable to perform a miracle to back up his claims. Muhammad had three scattered responses to this challenge:

> They say: Why hath no portent been sent down upon him from his Lord? Say: Lo! **Allah is Able to send down a portent**. But most of them know not (*Surah* 6:37, emp. added).

> And they swear a solemn oath by Allah that if there come unto them a portent they will believe therein. Say: **Portents are with Allah** (*Surah* 6:110, emp. added).

> [T]hey say: Why hath not a treasure been sent down for him, or an angel come from him? **Thou art but a warner**, and **Allah is in charge** of all things (*Surah* 11:12, emp. added).

> And they say: Why are not portents sent down upon him from his Lord? Say: Portents are with Allah only, and **I am but a plain warner** (*Surah* 29:50, emp. added; cf. 6:48; 7:184; 13:7; 35:23-24; 46:9).

> Verily We sent messengers before thee, among them those of whom We have told thee, and some of whom We have not told thee; and **it was not given to any messenger that he should bring a portent save by Allah's leave**" (*Surah* 40:78, emp. added; cf. 14:11; 13:38).

> And they will say: If only a portent were sent down upon him from his Lord! Then say (O Muhammad): **The Unseen belongeth to Allah**. So wait! Lo, **I am waiting with you** (*Surah* 10:21, emp. added).

> Those who disbelieve say: If only a portent were sent down upon him from his Lord! Say: Lo! **Allah sendeth whom He will astray**, and **guideth unto Himself all who turn** (unto Him) (*Surah* 13:27, emp. added).

> Say: For myself **I have no power to benefit, nor power to hurt**, save that which Allah willeth. Had I knowledge of the Unseen, I should have abundance of wealth, and adversity would not touch me. **I am but a warner**, and a bearer of good tidings unto folk who believe (*Surah* 8: 188, emp. added).

Observe that the Quran's multi-faceted explanation as to why Muhammad performed no miracles is that: (1) Allah could do so if He chose to, but He is in charge and signs are up to Him; (2) Muhammad is just a spokesman, like past prophets, a "mortal messenger" (*Surah* 17:93) sent to warn—nothing more; and (3) Allah sends some astray and guides others. So Muhammad was given no power to offer signs as confirmations of his messages. Instead, he, like they, must simply wait on Allah (6:57,159). Of course, many religious conmen in history have offered the same dodge. The ability to confirm one's oral proclamations with supernatural acts is what sets the genuine apart from the counterfeit.

One excellent demonstration of this fact is Luke's report of the conversion of the Roman proconsul, Sergius Paulus. Elymas the sorcerer attempted to thwart Paul's effort to teach Sergius the Gospel. So Paul performed a miracle by striking Elymas blind. Luke next recorded: "Then the proconsul, when he saw what was done, believed, being astonished at the teaching of the Lord" (Acts 13:12). The miracle that Paul performed captured Sergius' attention by providing evidence by which he could recognize the divine origin of Paul's Gospel message. Over and over again in the New Testament, a close correlation is seen between the performance of miracles and the preaching of the Word of God (cf. Mark 6:12-13; Luke 9:2,6). This feature is lacking in the Quran.

The Quran further implies that Muhammad was justified in performing no miracles since, if he were to do so, the recipients of the signs would still refuse to believe: "Say: Portents are with

Allah and (so is) that which telleth you that **if such came unto them they would not believe**" (*Surah* 6:110, emp. added; cf. vs. 25; 14:9).

On one occasion, when Muhammad's credibility was questioned (as the Quran shows that it frequently was) by his opponents, who insisted that he was nothing more than a mere mortal like themselves, they intimated that they would be more inclined to believe if the messenger was an angel. The Quran reports that Muhammad responded: "If there were settled on earth, angels walking about in peace and quiet, We should certainly have sent them down from the heavens an angel for a Messenger" (*Surah* 17:94, Ali; cf. 6:8-9). But, of course, this line of reasoning is erroneous. God **did** send angels (in addition to human prophets) as messengers (e.g., Luke 1:11-20,26-38)—a truth which the Quran, itself, confirms (*Surah* 3:39,42,45; 15:8; 19:17; 22:75). In fact, the Quran contradicts itself on this point since it claims that Gabriel was the angel of revelation who revealed God's words to Muhammad, and that "Allah chooses Messengers from angels and from men for Allah is He Who hears and sees (all things)" (*Surah* 22:75, Ali). "What's good for the goose, is good for the gander!"

On another occasion, after ridiculing Muhammad's revelations as "fables," his opponents called on Allah to rain down stones upon them if, in fact, Muhammad's words were of divine origin. Observe the official response to this challenge: "But Allah would not punish them while thou wast with them, nor will He punish them while they seek forgiveness" (*Surah* 8:33). In other words, if Allah were to send some punishment on Muhammad's adversaries, (1) He might accidentally hit Muhammad as well, and (2) they need to be given more time to repent. Yet, on other occasions, Muhammad assures his opponents that Allah could very well bring some calamity from the Earth or sky upon them—and this mere possibility is a sign that should cause them to repent (*Surah* 34:9).

In 1831, William Paley summarized the stance of the Quran regarding miracles:

Mahomet did not found his pretensions upon miracles, properly so called; that is, upon proofs of supernatural agency, capable of being known and attested by others. Christians are warranted in this assertion by the evidence of the Koran, in which Mahomet not only does not affect the power of working miracles, but expressly disclaims it (pp. 363-364).

Indeed, the Quran's confused and inadequate treatment of the role of the miraculous is another proof of its uninspired status.

RITUALISM

As noted in chapter 3, the *Hadith* manifest a heavy Islamic emphasis on "holy sites" and ritualistic traditions. The Quran reflects this same inclination.

Mecca

Mecca is depicted as the spatial center of the Islamic world. In view of the way Jews and Christians have shown attachment to Jerusalem over the centuries, a Muslim may well conclude that the Bible assigns a comparable significance to Jerusalem as the Quran does Mecca. However, such an assessment would be incorrect. As noted in chapter 3 in the discussion of the *Hadith*, no **biblical** significance is attached to Jerusalem or any other "holy site" or "sacred shrine." It is true that Old Testament Judaism centered **coincidentally** on the city of Jerusalem. However, the location was tied totally to the sacrificial system of the Israelite economy, and in no way conveyed the concept that Jerusalem was to be revered or honored as holy above any other location. Judaism was specifically tied to Jerusalem simply because it was part of the land mass given to the Jews in fulfillment of the promise to Abraham (Genesis 12:1; 26:3). However, the city of Jerusalem was actually selected by David, not God, to serve as his capital after he consolidated the kingdom and expelled the Jebusites—seven-and-a-half years after coming to the throne (2 Samuel 5:5-7).

Specifically, New Testament Christianity rejects the notion of "holy sites," and makes no provision whatsoever for the establishment of any earthly locations as worthy of commemoration, veneration, or visitation. Jesus spoke decisively on the matter in His remarks directed to the Samaritan woman (John 4:19-24). Even if He had specified a holy site, no biblical reason exists for pinpointing Mecca as the appropriate site. [NOTE: The claim that Psalm 84:5-6 refers to Mecca is an erroneous claim. The "Valley of Baca" was a place in Palestine through which Jewish pilgrims passed on their way to worship at Jerusalem (Gesenius, 1847, p. 119; McClintock and Strong, 1867, 1:606)]. Hence, though many alleged "Christians" have done so, the Bible itself assigns no "sacred" significance to one location on the planet over any other.

The Quran, on the other hand, makes the mistake of referring to Mecca as the "mother-town," or "Mother of Cities," or "Mother of Villages" (*Surah* 6:93; 42:7). Doing so implies the Quran's author to be biased and limited by his own human perceptions of his Arab environment. Selecting a single location militates against the idea that Islam was intended to be a universal religion without respect to nationality or physical location (cf. *Surah* 2:125-127,144-150). Inherently ethnic in its orientation, Judaism possessed this feature. However, as a divinely intended universal religion, Christianity absolutely does not. Humans are impressed by, interested in, and devoted to such material, temporal places–but the God of the Bible countenances no such sentimentality.

The Quran even represents Allah as assuring Muhammad that though he was "debarred" from entering the Ka'bah on one occasion, he would again be allowed to do so (*Surah* 48:24-27). Muhammad was so fixated on being allowed to go to the physical location of the Ka'bah that he agreed to the Truce of Hudaybiyah, which prevented Muslims from making the rounds that year in order to be allowed to do so the next (Lings, 1983, pp. 252ff.). Would **God** make such compromises with humans? Certainly not. But a man who had struggled long and hard to get his way would do so, especially when he was so close to achieving his objective, and making the concession would guarantee "victory" the next year.

The Ka'bah

The Quran represents the Ka'bah as the most sacred place on Earth. Rodwell offers the following description of this imposing, mystifying structure:

Muhammad at the Ka'bah
Istanbul, 1595.
Hazine 1222, folio 151b
Credit: TOPKAPI PALACE MUSEUM

> The Caaba is an oblong massive structure 55 ft. in length, 45 in breadth, and the height somewhat greater than the length. At the S.E. corner is the famous Hajar El-Aswad, or Black Stone.... The Caaba stands in an open parallelogram of about 500 ft. by 530 ft. and is surrounded by colonnades, the pillars of which, made of various marbles, some Egyptian but mostly Meccan, stand in a quadruple row on the east side, and three deep on the other sides, and amount to 554. It has been rebuilt several times, but has not been materially altered since A.H. 1040 (1950, p. 497).

The degree of significance assigned by the Quran to the Ka'bah (and Mecca) as a sacred physical site is surprising–calling into question the inspiration of its author. It is the direction toward which prayers are to be uttered. Ritualistic encircling of the Ka'bah is enjoined (*Surah* 2:125,144,149,150,158,191,196,217; 3:96; 5:2, 95,97; 8:34-35; 9:7,17-19,28; 14:37; 17:1; 22:25ff.; 28:57; 29:67; 48:25,27; 52:4). To think that God would require humans (with various exceptions) to **view** a specific geographical location as superior to other locations on Earth, let alone **visit** such a place, is a ludicrous notion that betrays a materialistic understanding of religion.

Other instances of ritualism, and the veneration of sacred sites in the Quran, include Muhammad's purported trip through the seven heavens to the very presence of God (*Surah* 17:1) and the mountains of As-Safa and Al-Marwah (*Surah* 2:158). The Quran also alludes to the ritualistic "call to prayer" (*Surah* 62:9), which occurs five times each day, as well as the associated ritual ablutions:

O ye who believe! When ye rise up for prayer, wash your faces, and your hands up to the elbows, and lightly rub your heads and (wash) your feet up to the ankles. And if ye are unclean, purify yourselves. And if ye are sick or on a journey, or one of you cometh from the closet, or ye have had contact with women, and ye find not water, then go to clean, high ground and rub your faces and your hands with some of it. Allah would not place a burden on you, but He would purify you and would perfect His grace upon you, that ye may give thanks (*Surah* 5:6; cf. 4:43).

Such rituals remind one of the Catholics' hand motions of the sign of the cross over the chest, Catholic prayer beads (which parallel the 99 names of Allah in the Islamic rosary [Nasr, 2003, p. 61]), the Catholics' ritualistic utterance of "hail Marys," and the parallel between Muhammad's purported trip to heaven (*Surah* 17:1; 53:13-18) and the Catholic doctrine of Mary's bodily assumption (cf. Lings, 1983, pp. 101ff.)–all characteristics of extrabiblical religion. The New Testament knows of no such practices.

The Quran designates four months each year as sacred: "Lo! the number of the months with Allah is twelve months by Allah's ordinance in the day that He created the heavens and the earth. Four of them are sacred: that is right religion. So wrong not yourselves in them" (*Surah* 9:36). The sacred month of Ramadan and the accompanying fasting are mentioned as well (2:185; 5:97). Pilgrimage rituals even include the cutting of hair and nails to "make an end of their unkemptness" (*Surah* 22:29), as well as "offerings and garlands" (*Surah* 5:2,97). The religious rejection of certain foods (e.g., *Surah* 5:3), however, is a concept specifically repudiated by New Testament Christianity (Romans 14:3, 17; 1 Corinthians 8:8; 10:23-26,31; Colossians 2:16).

In stark contrast to the Quran, the Bible teaches that location and such humanly invented rituals have nothing to do with acceptable worship. Regard for any particular location on Earth is misplaced devotion. Devotion to shrines and ritualism characterizes corrupt religion of human origin—one that appeals to the flesh. Rituals and sacred places appeal to humans, and serve as a distraction from, and substitute for, genuine obedience to spiritual standards. Such human inventions fail to grasp the very nature and character of Deity.

MISTAKEN EQUATIONS

As noted earlier, both Muhammad and the Quran show a failure to grasp the difference between New Testament Christianity and the corrupted Christianity practiced by those who professed to be Christians in the Arabian peninsula of the sixth and seventh centuries. The fact that the Quran reflects this failure shows that its author(s) did not have divine guidance, even as it failed to detect the Jewish misrepresentations of the Old Testament as projected by the rabbinic folklore of the day (see chapter 4). The form of Christianity reflected prominently in the Quran is Catholicism (e.g., *Surah* 57:27–monasticism; *Surah* 17:56–saint worship). Anyone familiar with the first five centuries of church history is well aware of the extent to which the Christian religion was perverted and distorted. These perversions did not escape the attention of the author of the Quran. However, even when an appropriate criticism is leveled against a doctrine with which Muhammad disagreed, the criticism often will contain an implicit approval of another element that is contrary to New Testament teaching. For example, the Quran refers to Jesus as "son of Mary" 22 times. Most of these allusions are uttered by Allah Himself (*Surah* 2:87,253; 3:45; 4:171; 5:17,46,75,78,110,114,116; 9:31; 19:34; 23:50; 33:7; 43:57; 57:27; 61:6,14). Yet this phrase occurs in the New Testament **only one time**–and only then is used by certain unnamed townspeople whose use of the term shows they knew of Him only in terms of His earthly relationships, i.e., the son of Mary, and as a carpenter who had brothers and sisters (Mark 6:3). The Quran places an undue and unbiblical emphasis on Mary, thereby reflecting the Catholic notion that characterized the time (cf. *Surah* 5:116). The overwhelming emphasis in the New Testament is on Jesus being the "Son of God" (Mark 1:1; Luke 1:35; John 1:34; 3:18; 5:25; 10:36; 11:4; Acts 9:20;

Romans 1:4; 2 Corinthians 1:19; Hebrews 4:14; 7:3; 10:29; 1 John 3:8; 4:15; 5:10,13,20; et al.)—an acknowledgment made even by Satan and the demons (Luke 4:3,9,41; 8:28). [NOTE: The notion of Mary as intercessor on behalf of those still on Earth (Abbott, 1966, pp. 96,630) is reflected in the comparable role assigned to Muhammad by Muslims (Geisler and Saleeb, 2002, pp. 85ff.)].

The author of the Quran unquestionably had heard the squabbles between Christians and Jews (*Surah* 2:113). Mistakenly assuming they were supposed to follow the same book, the Quran demonstrates a lack of understanding regarding the distinction between the Old Testament and the New Testament, as well as the relationship sustained between Judaism and Christianity. This surface misconception undoubtedly contributed to the uninformed conclusion that the Bible is corrupt, and is unable to transmit God's will accurately.

ADDITIONAL CONFLICTS WITH THE BIBLE

Noah's Son

The Quran offers conflicting details regarding the global Flood of Noah's day. For example, it states that Noah and his household were saved from the Flood: "And Noah, when he cried of old, We heard his prayer and saved him **and his household** from the great affliction" (*Surah* 21:76, emp. added); "And Noah verily prayed unto Us, and gracious was the Hearer of his prayer and we saved him **and his household** from the great distress, and **made his seed the survivors**.... Then we did drown the others" (*Surah* 37:75-82, emp. added). Yet, elsewhere the Quran states that, as a matter of fact, one of Noah's sons died in the Flood. Speaking of the ark, the Quran states:

> And it sailed with them amid waves like mountains, and Noah cried unto his son—and he was standing aloof—O my son! Come ride with us, and be not with the disbelievers. He said: I shall betake me to some mountain that will save me from the water. (Noah) said: This day there

is none that saveth from the commandment of Allah save
him on whom He hath had mercy. And the wave came
in between them, so **he was among the drowned** (*Surah*
11:41-43, emp. added).

In addition to conflicting with itself on whether any of Noah's
family was lost in the Flood, the Quran conflicts with the biblical
depictions, since the Bible consistently represents Noah's entire
family—consisting of his wife, his only three sons, and his sons'
wives—as boarding the ark and surviving the Flood (Genesis 6:
10; 7:1,7,13; 8:16,18; 9:18ff.; 1 Peter 3:20). Additionally, the Quran's description of an alleged conversation between Noah and
his doomed son even as the Flood waters were swelling "like
mountains," contradicts the Bible's claim that God closed the
door of the ark, preventing any others from entering.

The Quran also conflicts with the Bible on the age of Noah
prior to the Flood—950 years versus 600 (*Surah* 29:14). The figure used by the Quran was actually the length of Noah's entire
life, which included 350 years of life **after** the Flood. Likewise,
the Quran claims Noah's wife was a disbeliever who has been
consigned to hell (*Surah* 66:10).

Water from the Rock

Another example of the Quran's confusion regarding historical events is seen in its report of the famous episode wherein Moses brought forth water from a rock: "And when Moses asked for
water for his people, We said: Smite with thy staff the rock. And
there gushed out therefrom twelve springs (so that) each tribe
knew their drinking-place. Eat and drink of that which Allah
hath provided, and do not act corruptly, making mischief in the
earth" (*Surah* 2:60, emp. added; cf. 7:160). Anyone familiar with
the biblical account is aware that the Bible reports two separate
incidents involving water from a rock—one occurring shortly after the Israelites left Egypt (Exodus 17:1-7), and another occurring almost forty years later during the period of desert wandering (Numbers 20:1-13). On the first occasion, Moses was told to

strike the rock; on the subsequent occasion, he was told to speak to the rock. The Quran refers to the first occurrence.

However, the Bible says nothing of twelve springs gushing forth from the rock. But it does say something about the Israelites and twelve springs. Three days after their departure from Egypt, but prior to the first water-from-the-rock incident, the Israelites "came to Elim, where there were twelve wells of water and seventy palm trees; so they camped there by the waters" (Exodus 15:27). One cannot help but be suspicious that the author of the Quran had heard the oral recounting of these moments in Jewish history, and compressed them into a single incident.

The Creation of the Universe

Seven verses in the Quran speak of Allah's creation of the heavens and the earth in six days: "Allah it is Who created the heavens and the earth, and that which is between them, in six Days. Then He mounted the throne" (*Surah* 32:4; cf. 7:54; 10:3; 11:7; 25:59; 50:38; 57:4). However, the Quran contains other verses that conflict with this straightforward declaration:

> Say (O Muhammad, unto the idolaters): Disbelieve ye verily in Him Who created **the earth in two Days**, and ascribe ye unto Him rivals? He (and none else) is the Lord of the Worlds. He placed therein firm hills rising above it, and blessed it and measured therein its sustenance **in four Days**, alike for (all) who ask; **then turned He to the heaven** when it was smoke, and said unto it and unto the earth: Come both of you, willingly or loth. They said: We come, obedient. Then He ordained them **seven heavens in two Days** and inspired in each heaven its mandate; and we decked the nether heaven with lamps, and rendered it inviolable (*Surah* 41:9-12).

One can accept as figurative the discourse between Allah and inanimate matter. However, the handling of numbers is clearly literal. A simple reading of these verses indicates that the Earth was created in two days, with Allah taking an additional four days to fashion hills and attend to other earthly matters. That makes six days. Then Allah turned His attention to the heavens, completing seven of them (and equipping them with lights) in two days. Two plus four plus two equals eight days.

Closely related to this discrepancy is the fact that the Quran offers conflicting comparisons regarding how Allah reckons time. In one surah, we are informed that "a Day with Allah is as a thousand years of what ye reckon" (*Surah* 22:47). This comparison is acceptable by itself, and harmonizes with the Bible. It affirms that God, being eternal, is **above** time and unaffected by time like humans (Psalm 90:4; 2 Peter 3:8). The comparison does not mean that a one-thousand-year period for humans is equivalent to a 24-hour period for God. As Lenski observed:

> With the Lord a single day is "as a thousand years," and vice versa. Let us not overlook the "as." Peter does not say: "A single day **is** a thousand years, and a thousand years **are** a day...." Whether it be a day or a thousand years as we count time, both are really the same with the Lord; neither hampers nor helps him (1966, p. 345, emp. in orig.).

But notice how the Quran ends up misconstruing this concept: "Allah it is Who created the heavens and the earth, and that which is between them, in six Days. Then He mounted the throne.... He directeth the ordinance from the heaven unto the earth; then it ascendeth unto Him in a Day, whereof the measure is a thousand years of that ye reckon" (*Surah* 32:4-5). Compare Ali's translation of verse 5 to see the point even clearer: "He rules (all) affairs from the heavens to the earth: in the end (all affairs) will go up to Him, on a Day, the space whereof will be (as) a thousand years of your reckoning." The Quran literalizes the concept—even as the Babylonian Talmudists were prone to do (e.g., *Sanhedrin* 97a). Further confirmation of this point is seen in yet another surah: "A questioner questioned concerning the doom about to fall upon the disbelievers, which none can repel, from Allah, Lord of the Ascending Stairways (whereby) the angels and the Spirit ascend unto Him in a Day whereof the span is fifty thousand years" (*Surah* 70:1-4). For "span," Ali has "measure."

A literal reference is obviously intended. Not only does this use conflict with the previous Quranic use of one thousand years, but the Universe is not even fifty thousand years old! (cf. Thompson, 1999).

Additionally, observe the sequence of the creation of the Universe as portrayed by the Quran. The impression is given that attention was given first to fashioning the Earth, followed by the seven heavens. Not only does the Bible contradict the notion of "seven heavens" (as noted earlier in this chapter), it represents the heavens and Earth being created together on the first day of Creation week. Attention then was directed on days one through three to sorting out the Earth itself, including vegetation. On day four, the Sun, Moon, and stars were placed in position in outer space. Then attention returns to the Earth and the creation of both animal and human life on days five and six (Genesis 1).

The Quran also affirms the existence of seven Earths. In a short surah on the subject of divorce, the final verses warn hearers to obey the messenger and the message from Allah, and then conclude with a typical exaltation of Allah: "Allah it is who hath created seven heavens, and of the earth the like thereof" (*Surah* 65:12). Ali's rendering is similar: "Allah is He Who created seven Firmaments and of the earth a similar number." Dawood has: "It is Allah who has created seven heavens, and earths as many." Such allusions betray the influence by the beliefs and superstitions of the people of the day.

The Creation of Man

The Quran offers a variety of conflicting concepts concerning the creation of the first human being. It claims that Allah created man from a clot (*Surah* 96:2; cf. "of congealed blood"–Ali), as well as a "drop of thickened fluid" (*Surah* 16:4; 75:37; 76:2; cf. "sperm drop"–Ali; also Pickthall's "a drop (of seed)"–53:46; 80:19). But it also claims that man was created from dust (*Surah* 3:59; 30:20; 35:11), mud (*Surah* 7:12), the earth (*Surah* 11:61), "potter's clay of black mud altered" (*Surah* 15:26,28; cf. 6:2; 32:7), and "sticky clay" (*Surah* 37:11; cf. "plastic clay"–Pickthall). And it further says that Allah "created man from water" (*Surah* 25:54; cf. 21:30; 24:45). But then it forthrightly affirms that man was created out of nothing (*Surah* 52:35). On first consideration, it is difficult to see how such diverse statements might be reconciled.

At second glance, the Quran would seem to offer resolution to the disparity of thought by proposing a **sequential** creation in four surahs:

> What aileth you that ye hope not toward Allah for dignity when **He created you by (divers) stages**? (*Surah* 71:13-14, emp. added).

> Allah created you from dust, then from a little fluid, then He made you pairs (the male and female) (*Surah* 35:11).

> Was he not a drop of fluid which gushed forth? Then he became a clot; then (Allah) shaped and fashioned and made of him a pair, the male and female (*Surah* 75:37-39).

> He it is Who created you from dust, then from a drop (of seed) then from a clot, then bringeth you forth as a child (*Surah* 40:67).

> We have created you from dust, then from a drop of seed, then from a clot, then from a little lump of flesh shapely and shapeless, that We may make (it) clear for you. And We cause what We will to remain in the wombs for an appointed time, and afterward We bring you forth as infants, then (give you growth) that ye attain your full strength (*Surah* 22:5).

These verses would appear to offer possible clarification of the situation. Allah created man **in stages**, beginning with dust, which he then transformed into fluid (sperm), which then became a clot of blood, from which Allah then shaped and fashioned the first pair. But this clarification still leaves the creation of man a confused mix. Moving from dust to fluid to a clot is a nonsensical concept. Likewise, the stipulated sequence is incoherent. "Dust," "mud," "black mud altered," and "sticky clay" are not technically the same. The ludicrous picture given is that Allah labored over a concoction of mud and clay, working and kneading the mixture to shape a human body. The female is depicted as being created in the same fashion as the male.

Pakistani Muslim Moiz Amjad makes a valiant attempt to harmonize this confused depiction (1998). First, he claims that "clot of blood" is from an Arabic word that means "anything that sticks or hangs" together, and that Muslim translators incorrectly assumed a clot of blood was intended (which he concedes is a scientifically inaccurate concept). In so doing, he pits himself against Muslim translators, the likes of which include Pickthall and Ali. Second, he claims that all verses in the Quran (e.g., *Surah* 16:4; 75:37; 96:1-2) that refer to *alaq* and *nutfah* (a drop of sperm) are referring exclusively to the ongoing procreation of humans–not the original creation of Adam–an argument that he bases on *Surah* 32:7-8: "Who made all things good which He created, and He began the creation of man from clay; then He made his seed from a draught of despised fluid." Amjad notes that the creation from clay refers to Adam, while "his seed" refers to Adam's descendants. Observe, however, that this explanation does not account adequately for the wording of the Quranic text that, admittedly, appears to blur the distinction between the original creation of man and the ongoing reproduction process by which humans now come into existence (cf. *Surah* 56:58; 86:6-7).

The sharp distinction for which Amjad contends in *Surah* 32:7-8 does not hold true for other verses. Look again at the wording of the last five verses of *Surah* 75 (vss. 36-40): "Thinketh man that he is to be left aimless? Was he not a drop of fluid which gushed forth? Then he became a clot; then (Allah) shaped and fashioned and made of him a pair, the male and female. Is not He (who doeth so) able to bring the dead to life?" Allah shaping and fashioning and making man a pair, fits only the original creation of man. But the drop of fluid that gushes forth fits only the male implantation of sperm into the woman. Compare *Surah* 35:11–"Allah created you from dust, then from a little fluid, then He made you pairs (the male and female). No female beareth or bringeth forth save with His knowledge. And no one groweth old who groweth old, nor is aught lessened of his life, but it is recorded in a Book." Making the pair (male and female) must refer to the original Creation, which then enabled females since to bear children. Yet this creation **follows** the "little fluid" of the verse. The point is even clearer in *Surah* 75:37-39–"Was he not a drop of fluid which gushed forth? Then he became a clot; then (Allah) shaped and fashioned and made of him a pair, the male and female." Allah shaping and fashioning man into a pair is an unmistakable reference to the original Creation–unless the Muslim wishes to contend that such verses refer to the development of twins in the womb! If so, why always "male and female" twins? At the very least, the verses are discordant and incoherent.

Observe also that all references to the creation of man in the Quran are conspicuously devoid of any reference to the role played by the female in reproduction. Modern genetics has determined that the female makes an equal contribution with the male in the formation of a human being–a fact recognized by the Bible (Genesis 3:15).

In contrast, the Bible gives a cohesive description of the creation of Adam, avoiding the mistakes made by the Quran. It consistently refers to the first man as having been made from dust (Genesis 2:7; 3:19; Psalm 103:14; 1 Corinthians 15:47-49). The first woman was made from a portion of the man's body (Genesis 2:21-23; 1 Corinthians 11:8; 1 Timothy 2:13). No mud, clots, drops of fluid, or water.

CONCLUSION

Islam and Christianity contradict one another. They differ in significant doctrines–including the person, role and conduct of Jesus, the nature of Deity, the attributes and actions of God (chapter 7), what constitutes appropriate ethical behavior (chapter 8), the afterlife, and how God's Word was communicated and confirmed. The more thorough one's acquaintance is with **both** the Bible and the Quran, the more obvious is the Bible's superiority over the Quran. The Bible is profound, incomparable in its spiritual depth, and possesses divine content far superior to the Quran, both in substance and treatment.

The central message of the Bible from beginning to end is the scheme of redemption–the ongoing outworking of God's plan to redeem lost humanity. It stands in stark contrast with the Quran's piecemeal, incomplete, hodgepodge mixture, with a few central concepts that lack development and cohesion. The Bible is the only book that gives a self-consistent, cohesive, plausible, rational, satisfying, accurate view of spiritual reality. Fundamental, foundational differences exist that make the Quran and the Bible irrevocably **incompatible.**

Chapter 10

"HONESTLY, NOW, WHAT WOULD ONE EXPECT?"

In an honest effort to examine any religion's claim to divine authenticity, one cannot help but observe features and characteristics of the religion that contradict its claim. It is not enough merely to **claim** divine authenticity. Anyone can do that. Nor is it enough to have acquired large numbers of adherents. Many in the course of human history have arisen at opportune moments in time, and have managed to gather a following—from Siddhartha Gautama (the Indian mystic and founder of Buddhism) and Joseph Smith (founder of Mormonism), to Adolf Hitler (whose Third Reich drew virtually the entire human race into world war) and Vladimir Lenin (communist leader of the Russian Revolution). Think of the great civilizations of ancient history that exerted widespread influence—even forcible subjugation—on large segments of the world's population, including the Assyrian, Babylonian, Macedonian (viz., Alexander the Great), and Roman Empires. The sheer number of people who embrace a philosophy, a religion, or a culture does not prove its legitimacy.

One must ask oneself, what if, indeed, Muhammad was **not** inspired of God? What if he was not given revelations from Allah through the angel Gabriel as he claimed? What if he was simply one more person in the course of human history who managed to advance the cause he promoted, convincing many people to follow him, but who was not in reality a prophet of the one true God? If Muhammad was not inspired, but merely a man who was making it up as he went along, using his own imagination and contemporaneous sources with which he was familiar, what would one expect to observe? Please give consideration to the following four general observations that demonstrate the very expectations that further undermine the Quran's claim to divine authenticity due to its endorsement of the fallacies made by its author.

INORDINATE PREOCCUPATION
WITH HIMSELF

If the Quran was from an uninspired human source, we would expect it to exceed reasonable limits in characterizing its author as genuinely guided by God. The Quran fulfills this expectation. Granted, any truly inspired book would allude to its own inspiration. But in the Quran, the focus is on Muhammad—to an excessive degree—as if the author is a typical human who is fighting hard to establish his own credibility. If Muhammad had been able to perform miracles to authenticate his claims (as the Bible teaches that we should expect of one sent from God), then he would not have had to pound the point over and over again *ad infinitum*. If God were really providing Muhammad with his revelations, there would not have been such an overemphasis on defending his prophethood. Yet that is precisely what we find in the Quran. Consider the following six manifestations of what one would expect to encounter if the author of the Quran was not supernaturally guided.

First, as expected, he defends the source of his revelations and his prophethood to an immoderate degree:

Or **would ye question your messenger** as Moses was questioned aforetime?... And those who have no knowledge say: **Why doth not Allah speak unto us,** or some sign come unto us? Even thus, as they now speak, spake those (who were) before them. Their hearts are all alike. We have made clear the revelations for people who are sure. ...Even as **We have sent unto you a messenger from among you,** who reciteth unto you Our revelations and causeth you to grow, and teacheth you the Scripture and wisdom, and teacheth you that which ye knew not. Therefore remember Me, I will remember you (*Surah* 2:108,118,151-152, emp. added; cf. vs. 129)

Of them there are **some who (pretend to) listen to you;** but We have thrown veils on their hearts, so they do not understand it, and deafness in their ears; if they saw every one of the Signs, they will not believe in them; in so much that **when they come to you, they (but) dispute with you;** the Unbelievers say: "These are nothing but tales of the ancients" (*Surah* 6:25, emp. added—Ali).

Allah coineth a similitude: a township that dwelt secure and well content, its provision coming to it in abundance from every side, but it disbelieved in Allah's favours, so Allah made it experience the garb of dearth and fear because of what they used to do. And verily there had come unto them **a messenger from among them,** but **they had denied him,** and so the torment seized them while they were wrong-doers (*Surah* 16:112-113, emp. added).

He it is Who hath sent among the unlettered ones **a messenger of their own,** to recite unto them His revelations and to make them grow, and to teach them the Scripture and Wisdom, though heretofore they were indeed in error manifest (*Surah* 62:2, emp. added).

Allah conferred a great favor on the Believers when He sent among them **a Messenger from among themselves,** rehearsing unto them the Signs of Allah, sanctifying them, and instructing them in Scripture and Wisdom, while, before that, they had been in manifest error (*Surah* 3:164—Ali, emp. added).

We know indeed that they say, "**It is a man that teaches him.**" The tongue of him they wickedly point to is notably foreign, while this is Arabic, pure and clear (*Surah* 16:103, emp. added; 40:56,69-70; et al.).

Second, as expected, this frequent defense of himself includes repetitive badgering of his hearers, insisting that they listen to and obey—not just Allah—**but him**:

O ye who believe! Obey Allah, and **obey the messenger** and those of you who are in authority; and if ye have a dispute concerning any matter, refer it to Allah **and the messenger** if ye are (in truth) believers in Allah and the Last Day.... We sent no messenger save that **he should be obeyed** by Allah's leave. And if, when they had wronged themselves, they had but come unto thee and asked forgiveness of Allah, and **asked forgiveness of the messenger**, they would have found Allah Forgiving, Merciful.... Whoso obeyeth Allah **and the messenger**, they are with those unto whom Allah hath shown favour, of the Prophets and the saints and the martyrs and the righteous. The best of company are they!.... **Whoso obeyeth the messenger obeyeth Allah**.... O ye who believe! Believe in Allah **and His messenger and the Scripture which He hath revealed unto His messenger**.... Whoso disbelieveth in Allah...and His messengers and the Last Day, he verily hath wandered astray.... Lo! those who disbelieve in Allah and His messengers, and **seek to make distinction between Allah and His messengers**, and say: We believe in some and disbelieve in others, and seek to choose a way in between; Such are disbelievers in truth; and for disbelievers We prepare a shameful doom. But those who believe in Allah and His messengers and **make no distinction between any of them**, unto them Allah will give their wages.... O mankind! **The messenger hath come unto you** with the truth from your Lord. Therefore believe (*Surah* 4:59,64,69,80,136,150-152,170, emp. added).

And it becometh not a believing man or a believing woman, when Allah **and His messenger** have decided an affair (for them), that they should (after that) claim any say in their affair; and whoso is rebellious to Allah **and His messenger**, he verily goeth astray in error manifest (*Surah* 33:36, emp. added; cf. vss. 29,31,71; 24:52, 54,62).

Say, (O Muhammad, to mankind): If ye love Allah, **follow me**; Allah will love you and forgive you your sins. Allah is Forgiving, Merciful. Say: Obey Allah **and the messenger**. But if they turn away, lo! Allah loveth not the disbelievers (in His guidance) (*Surah* 3:31-32, emp. added).

Those who oppose Allah **and His messenger** will be abased even as those before them were abased; and We have sent down clear tokens, and for disbelievers is a shameful doom (*Surah* 58:5, emp. added).

Not surprising, in addition to the explicit wording using the term "obey" with regard to Allah and the messenger (some 15 times), the Quran (Pickthall's translation) repeatedly harps on the need to accept Allah's messenger by using the phrase "the messenger" 62 times, "his messenger" 81 times, and "Allah and his messenger" 58 times.

Third, as expected, he **continually threatens his hearers with punishment** if they refuse to comply with his bidding:

Lo! those who malign Allah **and His messenger**, Allah hath **cursed them in the world and the Hereafter**, and hath **prepared for them the doom** of the disdained…. On the day when **their faces are turned over in the fire**, they say: Oh, would that we had obeyed Allah and had **obeyed His messenger**! (*Surah* 33:57, 66, emp. added).

These are the limits (imposed by) Allah. Whoso obeyeth Allah **and His messenger**, He will make him enter Gardens underneath which rivers flow, where such will dwell for ever. That will be the great success. And whoso disobeyeth Allah **and His messenger** and transgresseth His limits, **He will make him enter Fire, where such will dwell for ever; his will be a shameful doom** (*Surah* 4:13-14, emp. added).

Those who resist Allah **and His messenger** will be **humbled to dust,** as were those before them (*Surah* 58:5, emp. added; cf. 40:69ff.; 65:8; et al.).

Those who oppose Muhammad are "liars" who "invent lies" (*Surah* 2:10,61,75,78; 5:103; 6:21,24,28,94,139,141,145,149; 7:37,96,152; 9:42-43; 10:18,60,70; 11:18; 16:39,62,86,105,116; 18:5,15; 23:90; 24:13; 25:19; 26:223; 29:12,68; 34:8,43; 37:152; 39:3,32; 45:7; 46:28; 58:2,18; 59:11; 61:7; 68:44; 72:4; 95:7). The Meccans are admonished to consider the doom that came upon their predecessors when they rejected the apostles that were sent to them (e.g., *Surah* 10:14ff.,48; 40:5,21ff.,82-83). Indeed, Allah supposedly destroyed other generations for turning away from his messengers (e.g., *Surah* 6:4-6,34-42; 34:38; 35:37,44-45; 46:26ff.).

Fourth, as expected, he whines incessantly about the resistance and opposition of his hearers, complaining about their unwillingness to accept his claim to be a prophet (e.g., *Surah* 8:31; 21:36,41,45,109; 23:69ff.; 25:30ff.,41-42,77; 26:1-6; 34:34ff.,43ff.; 38; 43:30ff.; 67:9,18,26ff.). As if consoling himself and coping with rejection, he denies the charges of insanity and imbecility (*Surah* 7:66-67,184; 34:8,46), and rejects the characterization of himself as an imposter (*Surah* 35:4,23-25). He resents their frequent labeling of his messages as "fables of the men of old" (*Surah* 6:25; 8:31; 16:24; 23:83; 25:5; 27:68; 46:17; 68:15; 83:13; cf. "tales of the ancients"—Ali), and "mere magic" that he has "invented" (*Surah* 6:7; 10:16-18,38-39,77; 11:7,13,35; 12:111; 21:3,5; 23:38; 25:4; 32:3; 34:8,43; 37:15; 42:24; 43:30; 46:7-8; 52:15,33; 69:44; 74:24-25). He complains that his fellow Arabs dismiss his words as unoriginal and borrowed: "And We know well that they say: Only a man teacheth him. The speech of him at whom they falsely hint is outlandish, and this is clear Arabic speech. Lo! those who disbelieve the revelations of Allah, Allah guideth them not and theirs will be a painful doom" (*Surah* 16:103-104). These defensive reactions against the charge of fabrication are so repetitious (implying that he was frequently so accused) that the objective reader cannot help but suspect the truthfulness of the accusation—"me thinks he doth protest too much." He was also frequently dismissed as just a man—a mere "mortal" (*Surah* 17:94; 21:3; 23:24,33-34; 26:154,186; 54:24; 74:25; cf. 11:27).

The Jews (and to a lesser extent Christians) are depicted as particularly resistive and disrespectful to Muhammad: "And the Jews will not be pleased with thee, nor will the Christians, till thou follow their creed. Say: Lo! the guidance of Allah (Himself) is Guidance. And if thou shouldst follow their desires after the knowledge which hath come unto thee, then wouldst thou have from Allah no protecting friend nor helper" (*Surah* 2:120; cf. vss. 91ff.,104ff.,135; 3:98-99,110; 4:153; 5:15,18-19,41ff.,51ff.; et al.). The Jews accept their own Scripture, but reject Muhammad's:

> And when there cometh unto them a Scripture from Allah, confirming that in their possession—though before that they were asking for a signal triumph over those who disbelieved—and when there cometh unto them that which they know (to be the Truth) they disbelieve therein. The curse of Allah is on disbelievers.... And when there cometh unto them a messenger from Allah, confirming that which they possess, a party of those who have received the Scripture fling the Scripture of Allah behind their backs as if they knew not (*Surah* 2:89,101)

The author of the Quran is especially sensitive about being mocked, derided, and ridiculed by his opponents, so much so that Allah consoles him frequently: "Messengers (of Allah) have been derided before thee, but that whereat they scoffed surrounded such of them as did deride" (*Surah* 6:10; cf. vs. 5; 2:14; 4:140; 9:79-80; 11:8,38; 13:32,43; 15:11; 16:34; 21:41; 30:10; 36:30; 37:12; 40:83; 43:7; 45:33; 46:26).

The Quran fixates on the phrase "deny our revelations": "But they who disbelieve, and **deny Our revelations**, such are rightful owners of the Fire. They will abide therein" (*Surah* 2:39, emp. added; cf. 5:10,86; 6:39,49,150; 7:36,40,146,147,176,182; 29:47, 49; 57:19; 64:10). The term "disbelieve" is used 186 times in 54 surahs. Even the reader who is open-minded in attempting to evaluate the Quran objectively cannot help but feel hounded, pounded, prodded, and intimidated.

Fifth, as expected, Muhammad attempts to muster credibility by cloaking his utterances in the garb of past Scripture, both Jewish (Torah) and Christian (Gospel). He constantly identifies himself with prophets and sages from the past–specifically Hebrew (e.g., Noah, Moses, et al.) and Arabian (e.g., Hud, Salih, Luqman), depicting them as occupying the same position as he. In so doing, he couches his message to Meccans and Jews in historical settings, but crafts and adapts the allusions to urge acceptance of himself (e.g., *Surah* 11:89ff.; 12:109ff.; 28:43ff.,59; 31: 13). He identifies himself as being just like his predecessors, taking the same stance they took, and receiving the same opposition that they received (e.g., *Surah* 7:92,101). For example, Muhammad is no different than Noah (e.g., *Surah* 7:59ff.; 38:13; 72: 1ff.), who likewise was a "plain warner" (*Surah* 11:25), who had no ability to work a miracle (*Surah* 11:31), who was passed off as "but a mortal," (*Surah* 11:27), who was accused of fabricating his revelations (*Surah* 11:35), and who also asked for no remuneration (*Surah* 11:29; cf. 6:91; 10:73; 12:104; 26:109,127,145,164,180; 34:47; 36:21; 38:87; 42:23)–a feature that conflicts with the known facts regarding Muhammad's cut of the spoils. Allah orders Noah to address his unbelieving contemporaries with the prefatory term "say"–the same term given to Muhammad throughout the Quran when Allah tells him what to speak to his contemporaries (*Surah* 11:35).

This same technique of recounting events in the lives of past biblical characters by recasting them to parrot Muhammad's own contemporary circumstances, putting his own words into their mouths, is seen with Abraham (*Surah* 29:16ff.), Joseph (e.g., *Surah* 12:37-40), Moses (e.g., *Surah* 28:36; 43:46; 44:17ff.), Shu'eyb, i.e., Jethro (*Surah* 7:85ff.), and others. In fact, when both Jesus and Moses confronted their contemporaries, they received the same criticism that Muhammad received when he offered his own revelations: "This is naught else than mere magic" (*Surah* 5: 110; 21:6; 10:77; 26:35,49; 27:13; 28:36). And, also like Muhammad, several historical personages accuse their opponents of being liars, including Moses (*Surah* 20:61; 28:34), Abraham (*Surah*

29:17), Solomon (*Surah* 27:27), and the messenger to the tribe of Thamud (*Surah* 54:26). When Moses and Aaron stood before Pharaoh, an Egyptian believer warns Pharaoh and his fellow Egyptians not to form an alliance against Moses, which, coincidentally was precisely what the Arab tribes were doing to Muhammad (*Surah* 40:30). Even as the Meccans charged Muhammad with attempting to turn them from the religion of their fathers, so Pharaoh accuses Moses: "Hast thou come unto us to pervert us from that (faith) in which we found our fathers, and that you two may own the place of greatness in the land? We will not believe you two" (*Surah* 10:79; cf. 7:71; 12:40; 21:54; 34:43).

Instances of this feature of the Quran could be multiplied many times over. The Quran so blends the message of Muhammad with Bible characters, fading in and out of the story, that Muhammad and the historical character are virtually indistinguishable. Noldeke alluded to this feature of the Quran:

> For the most part the old prophets only serve to introduce a little variety in point of form, for they are almost in every case **facsimiles of Muhammad himself. They preach exactly like him, they have to bring the very same charges against their opponents, who on their part behave exactly as the unbelieving inhabitants of Mecca.** The Qur'an even goes as far as to make Noah contend against the worship of certain false gods, mentioned by name, who were worshipped by the Arabs of Muhammad's time. In an address which is put in the mouth of Abraham (xxvi. 75 sqq.), the reader quite forgets that it is Abraham, and not Muhammad (or God Himself), who is speaking (1892, emp. added).

Sixth, one would expect him to be so resentful of, and frustrated by, those who ridicule his alleged revelations that he would issue a childish challenge to them to duplicate his ability by producing comparable revelations:

> And if ye are in doubt concerning that which We reveal unto Our slave (Muhammad), then **produce a surah of the like thereof**, and call your witnesses beside Allah if ye are truthful. And if ye do it not—**and ye can never do**

it–then guard yourselves against the fire prepared for disbelievers, whose fuel is of men and stones (*Surah* 2: 23, emp. added; cf. 6:94; 10:39; 11:12-13; 17:88).

One also would expect him to attempt to link his revelations with previous Scripture, i.e., Moses and the Old Testament, in order to bolster his credibility. He does so (e.g., *Surah* 6:93; 11: 17; 29:47; 46:12). And one would expect him to resort to a childish, retaliatory attitude toward his opponents. The Quran records Noah's response to his enemies: "Though ye make mock of us, yet we mock at you even as ye mock" (*Surah* 11:38).

These six indicators illustrate unmitigated **self-absorption** on the part of the author of the Quran. They provide ample demonstration that he was acting **as a human**, from a strictly human perspective, unassisted by Deity or divine inspiration.

UNBALANCED AND REPETITIVE

A second general observation that one would expect if the Quran is not of divine origin is the tendency to engage in unnecessary repetition–dwelling on and overemphasizing a few ideas. This is precisely what the Quran does: overstatement, overemphasis, and redundant repetition to an extreme degree, harping on a few themes to excess–as if the author had an ax to grind. [NOTE: A chronological arrangement of the surahs brings to light just how much repetition of some concepts takes place at one point in time. Such a sequence also exposes the human side of the author's progression of growth and development over time– a phenomenon that one would not expect to see if God was the author.] Three illustrations of this attribute are noted below.

Polytheism

For example, the Quran is preoccupied, even obsessed, with condemning idolatry and polytheism over and over again–far exceeding the Old Testament prophets. It is monotonous in its constant denunciation of "attributing partners" to Allah (e.g., *Surah* 6:64; 12:106,108; 16:54; 30:33; cf. 6:137-138; 13:16), "associating" other gods with him (*Surah* 6:19,79; 7:33,190; 10:19;

16:1,3; 28:68; 30:35,40; 40:84), "ascribing partners" to him (*Surah* 4:48,116; 5:72; 6:22,149,152; 7:173; 10:29,106; 13:33,36; 16:86, 100; 22:31; 28:87; 29:65; 30:31; 31:13), or setting up "rivals" to him (*Surah* 2:22:165; 6:1; 14:30; 34:33; 39:8; 41:9). Pickthall uses the term "idolater" or "idolaters" 46 times. Related phrases include "beside(s) Allah" (48 times), "beside(s) him" (31 times), "other than Allah" (14 times), and "instead of Allah" (20 times).

The monotony is equally apparent in the accompanying frequent threats of chastisement coming suddenly on idolaters. Repeatedly, the Quran reiterates the same point: that men turn to God in bad times, then back to idolatry in good times (e.g., *Surah* 10:13; 30:33; 39:8). This concept is even couched in the recurring scenario of men whose lives are imperiled in a storm-tossed ship (*Surah* 10:23-24; 29:65; 31:32).

Punishment

The Quran's preoccupation with judgment, retribution, and punishment is likewise boundless and overpowering. As noted in chapter 9, the Quran refers more to Judgment than any other subject, except maybe monotheism. It is positively top heavy and imbalanced on the subject. It stands in sharp contrast with the Bible's own **proper, self-authenticating, proportional balance**–precisely what one would expect if God was its author.

Creation as Signs

The Quran is extremely redundant in referring to various aspects of creation as "signs" or "tokens" or "portents." Several aspects of nature are typically linked together as if the author must continually revert to using the same familiar expressions and phrases to which he has become accustomed. The phrase "heavens and the earth" is used **135 times** in Pickthall's translation. As an example, to feel the full weight of this aspect of the Quran, one would need to secure a copy and read the following verses: *Surah* 2:164; 10:23-25; 14:32-33; 16:3,10-14,65ff.; 29:61-65; 30: 22-25,46-48; 31:26-34; 36:33-42; 40:13; 42:11,28-33; 43:9-12; 45:3-6,12-13; 55:5-29. These verses (and others) blend together the same repetitious phraseology: the creation of the heavens and the Earth, night and day, Sun and Moon, the stars, the winds, the rain water sent down by Allah, the crops that result, and the ships that run on the sea. These phenomena are "signs" for those who will accept them as such. Ali's translation uses "Sign" or "Signs" over **400 times**.

By any measure, the Quran is disjointed, disconnected, extremely redundant, and unbelievably repetitive. One is reminded of the Book of Mormon's anachronistic use of the Hebraism "and it came to pass" (see Miller, 2003a). One would expect an uninspired book to suffer from just this imbalance.

CONFUSION AND IGNORANCE REGARDING HISTORICAL AND BIBLICAL FACTS

Third, one would expect the author of an uninspired document to show ignorance and confusion about historical facts, especially if he was illiterate and lacked access to the broader context of the world. One also would expect him to manifest misunderstanding of previous revelation, i.e., the Bible, if he were unguided by God, since as a mere human, he would both be limited by his own environment and experience, and be unable to master the totality of prior revelation. Once again, the Quran comes through **as expected**.

For example, several historical details in the Quran's account of Moses' life are inaccurate. In the Bible account of Moses' life, God turned Moses' hand leprous to convince him that He would be with him when he went before Pharaoh (Exodus 4:6ff.). This incident took place while Moses was tending livestock in the Sinai desert (Exodus 3:1ff.). However, in the Quran, the incident occurs as Moses is standing before Pharaoh (*Surah* 7:103-108). The Quran claims that **nine** plagues were perpetrated against Egypt: "And verily We gave unto Moses nine tokens" (*Surah* 17:101), one of which was Moses' hand turning white (*Surah* 27:12), while the Bible account records that **ten** were instigated against Pharaoh–not counting the hand incident or the rod being turned into a snake (Exodus 7:10-11:1). Likewise, the Quran identifies one of the plagues as a "flood" (*Surah* 7:133), whereas the ten plagues in the biblical account do not include such. In the Quran, Moses makes a pact with Reuel to marry one of his daughters in exchange for a minimum of eight years service (*Surah* 28:27)—a suspicious resemblance to the pact between Jacob and Laban (Genesis 29:15ff.). When the agreement is fulfilled, Moses sets out with his family and encounters the burning bush (*Surah* 28:29), whereas in the Bible, Moses is still tending the livestock of his father-in-law when the bush incident occurs (Exodus 3:1ff.).

As noted in chapter 4, the Quran contains an erroneous historical allusion to Samaria (*Surah* 20:87). "But since the city of Samaria was not built, or at least called by that name, until several hundred years after Moses' death, the anachronism is at least amusing, and would be startling in any other book than the Quran, in which far more stupendous ones frequently occur" (Tisdall, 1905, p. 113). Additional instances of confusion regarding history include the lack of awareness of the distinction between the tree of the knowledge of good and evil and the tree of life (*Surah* 7:19ff.; 20:120ff.; cf. Genesis 2:9; 3:1ff.,22), as well as the claim that the name of John had not been given prior to John the Baptizer (*Surah* 19:7; cf. 2 Kings 25:23; Ezra 8:12; Jeremiah 40:8). The Quran also manifests a confused conjoining of Christian and Jewish ideas by linking Gabriel with the Holy Spirit (*Surah* 2:87,253; 16:102; 26:193; 78:38; 97:4).

A very serious flaw in the Quran is its manifest ignorance of the overall role of Christianity in the eternal order of things. It projects a lack of awareness of the widespread impact of the Christian religion on the larger world outside of Arabia, as well as an unfamiliarity with the intricacies of prophecy from the very beginning of time, and their fulfillment in the grand scheme of redemption. This ignorance extends to **much—if not most**—of the content of the Bible, the result being that the Quran fails to grasp the broader scope of biblical history. More especially, the Quran is oblivious to the massive chasm that exists between Judaism and Christianity, and the sequential correlation between them. It shows a complete failure to conceptualize the distinction between the Old Testament and the New Testament covenants, and their place in the ebb and flow of redemptive history. Briefly, when one "handles correctly the word of truth" (2 Timothy 2: 15), the Bible teaches that God first dealt with humanity, beginning in the Garden of Eden at the very dawn of human history, by enacting legislation that some have labeled as "patriarchal," in which God interacted with people through a system of patriarchy in which the father acted as the prophet and priest for the family. In approximately 1500 B.C., God began fulfilling the promises He had made to Abraham (c. 2100 B.C.) by setting the nation of Israel apart and giving it a separate and distinct law code. Hence, God continued to deal with the Gentiles (i.e., non-Jews) through the patriarchal laws enacted at the very beginning of time, while He dealt with the Israelites through the Law of Moses. Both the Patriarchal and Mosaic periods of Bible history continued functional (in God's sight) until Christ died on the cross in approximately A.D. 30. Now, God deals with all of humanity (both Jew and Gentile) through a single system of divine religion: Christianity. The entire Bible expounds this framework systematically from beginning to end.

Within this framework resides **the central message of the Bible** in which God worked out His plan by which He could redeem the human race from sin. As noted in chapter 7, the Quran shows abject ignorance–complete disregard for and/or lack of awareness of–this very prominent, core feature of Bible religion: the concept and centrality of atonement. It shows absolutely no awareness of the outworking of God's "eternal" (Ephesians 3: 11) intention to bring Jesus into the world to save mankind.

Additionally, the Quran sends mixed signals regarding the reliability of the Bible, sometimes speaking approvingly, at other times seemingly accusing the Jews and Christians of corrupting their scriptures. Rejecting the Bible as corrupt demonstrates abject ignorance of the facts of textual criticism (Appendix 1), as well as undue influence from the corrupt forms of Christianity and Judaism with which the Quran's author was personally privy–again demonstrating a failure to grasp the bigger context outside his own experience.

The Quran reflects acceptance of the theological mythology that prevailed in post first-century Christendom, including the credence it gives to the legend of the "Seven Sleepers of Ephesus" (*Surah* 18:10-27; see Campbell, 2002; Gilchrist, 1986; Lings, 1983, p. 78). The legend (which predates the Quran) spoke of seven (the number varies) noble Christian youths who fled persecution during the reign of Decius the Emperor, who died in A.D. 251. The youths took refuge in a cave near Ephesus, but then were sealed in to die. Instead of dying, however, their lives were miraculously preserved by falling into a deep sleep that lasted for nearly 200 years–the Quran claiming 309 years (vs. 26). For the Quran to dignify such outlandish tales is to disprove its own inspiration.

Another curious feature of the Quran is its attempt to retell various Old Testament stories. The honest inquirer is forced to ask why, for example, God would impart a narrative about Joseph in great detail (Genesis 37-50), but then do it again (*Surah* 12)? The New Testament certainly refers back to previous revelation (i.e., the Old Testament) for illustrative purposes. It even summarizes past history (e.g., Acts 7; Hebrews 11). But the observant student notices that the New Testament does not **retell** an Old Testament narrative. The Quran, on the other hand, retells stories as if attempting to achieve credibility for the reteller's claim to inspiration by clothing his claim in a narrative that already had been accepted as authentic by those from whom he seeks to gain acceptance.

HUMAN FRAILTIES, ACCOMMODATION, AND INFLUENCE BY CONTEMPORARIES

One would expect the author to manifest human frailties, blunders, and mistakes, thereby exposing his own uninspired status. He would say things that an **inspired** spokesman would not say. He would even, on occasion, accommodate his audience by giving them what they wish to hear. He would, in fact, sometimes be influenced in his thinking (and consequent revelations) by his contemporaries' thinking. The Quran manifests these very tendencies.

As expected, the Quran issues directives that are self-serving and convenient to the desires, needs, and human frailties of Muhammad–even to the point of excusing his inappropriate behavior as exceptional and permissible. For example, as noted in previous chapters, Muhammad received revelations that conveniently permitted him to have more wives than other Muslim men. He received revelations that instructed his followers in showing proper etiquette toward him–even to the point of showering blessings on him (*Surah* 33:56)–what Muslim scholars call "venerating" the Prophet:

> [T]he love of the Prophet lies at the heart of Islamic piety, for human beings can love God only if God loves them, and **God loves only the person who loves His Prophet**. The Quran itself **orders human beings to venerate the Prophet**.... This is **the only act whose performance human beings share with God** and the angels. Traditional Muslims therefore **revere the Prophet** in an inviolable manner and always ask for blessings (*salah*) and salutations (*salam*) upon him. In Muslim eyes, **the love and respect for the Prophet are inseparable from the love for the Word of God, for the Quran, and of course ultimately for God Himself** (Nasr, 2003, p. 47, emp. added).

Also as previously noted, he received revelations that condemn and curse those who resist him, and that allow him to wage war on his enemies. One allowed him even **to break his own oath** in the case of reinstating his physical relationship with the Coptic slave girl (who became the mother of his only male child) after bowing to pressure from his wives: "O Prophet! Why bannest thou that which Allah hath made lawful for thee, seeking to please thy wives? And Allah is Forgiving, Merciful. **Allah hath made lawful for you (Muslims) absolution from your oaths** (of such a kind), and Allah is your Protector. He is the Knower, the Wise" (*Surah* 66:1-2, emp. added). Inserting clarifying remarks like "of such a kind" (Pickthall) or "in some cases" (Ali) does not alter the transparent self-service–in contradiction to the Quran's denunciation of oath-breaking (*Surah* 16:91ff.).

As expected, Muhammad forgets some of his own revelations, and then issues additional revelations that excuse, explain, or justify him for so doing:

> Such of Our revelations as We abrogate or **cause to be forgotten**, we bring (in place) one better or the like thereof. Knowest thou not that Allah is Able to do all things? (*Surah* 2:106, emp. added).

> We shall make thee read (O Muhammad) so that **thou shalt not forget save that which Allah willeth**. Lo! He knoweth the disclosed and that which still is hidden (*Surah* 87:6-7, emp. added).

> And when thou seest those who meddle with Our revelations, withdraw from them until they meddle with another topic. And **if the devil cause thee to forget**, sit not, after the remembrance, with the congregation of wrong-doers (*Surah* 6:68, emp. added).

Both Allah and Satan are credited/blamed for Muhammad's memory lapses.

As expected, Muhammad covers his inability to respond immediately to questioners in order to give himself time to come up with an answer. The surah came in the form of a rebuke from Allah for saying he would give answers to his questioners the next day. It is worded in such a way that he is given an indefinite amount of time to prepare future answers to challengers: "And say not of anything: Lo! I shall do that tomorrow, except if Allah will. And remember thy Lord when thou forgettest, and say: It may be that my Lord guideth me unto a nearer way of truth than this" (*Surah* 18:24). This evasive handling of opponents extends to the attempt to excuse himself for his inability to utter predictive prophecy (*Surah* 10:49ff.; 34:29-30).

As expected, he justifies himself when he has to change a verse by substituting another in its place (*Surah* 2:106; 16:101; cf. 4:82). [NOTE: The Muslim/Quranic doctrine of "abrogation," mentioned briefly in chapter 6, is reflective of the same teaching in the Talmud (e.g., *Hilchoth Mamrim* 2.1.2; cf. Rodwell, 1950, p. 349).] Attention has already been directed to the adjustment the

Quran made regarding the direction of prayer (2:142ff.; see chapter 3). The explanation offered to justify changes is self-evidently insufficient and lacks credibility.

One also would expect the author of the Quran to copy pagan customs on occasion, incorporating them into his own religion, either because he, himself, approves of the practice, or because he figures most followers would be too culturally conditioned to be willing to forego the practice. Hence, circling the Ka'bah as the pagan Arabs had been doing may be continued: "Lo! (the mountains) As-Safa and Al-Marwah are among the indications of Allah. It is therefore no sin for him who is on pilgrimage to the House (of God) or visiteth it, to go around them (as the pagan custom is). And he who doeth good of his own accord (for him), lo! Allah is Responsive, Aware" (*Surah* 2:158). Dietary regulations are ambiguous and accommodative:

> Say "I do not find in the Message received by me by inspiration any (meat) forbidden to be eaten by one who wishes to eat it, unless it be dead meat, or blood poured forth, or the flesh of swine—**for it is abomination**—or, what is impious, (meat) on which a name has been invoked, other than Allah's." **But (even so), if a person is forced by necessity, without willful disobedience, nor transgressing due limits—your Lord is Oft-forgiving, Most Merciful** (*Surah* 6:145—Ali, emp. added; cf. 5:3-5; 6:120; 16:115).

Something that is an "abomination" is acceptable as long as the partaker is not **deliberately, willfully** partaking? While the Bible indicates the reason the Jews were given dietary restrictions was for health and holiness (e.g., Leviticus), the Quran declares, oddly enough, that the reason was their disobedience and rebellion (*Surah* 6:147). Question: If the Jews were given dietary restrictions due to their disobedience, why are the Muslims **also** given dietary restrictions (e.g., *Surah* 2:173; 5:1,3ff.; 6:120)? Another illustration is the way the Arab ritual of ancestral worship is tolerated—though made subservient to the worship of Allah: "And when ye have completed your devotions, then remember Allah as ye remember your fathers or with a more lively remembrance" (*Surah* 2:200).

One would expect accommodation to be made for human inclination and imperfection: "Whoso disbelieveth in Allah after his belief–save him who is forced thereto and whose heart is still content with Faith–but whoso findeth ease in disbelief: On them is wrath from Allah. Theirs will be an awful doom" (*Surah* 16: 106). Unbelievable. If the Quran is correct, the thousands of Christian martyrs who chose to give up their very lives rather than renounce their faith or confess Caesar as Lord, died needlessly! They could have just **pretended** to disbelieve when under compulsion, while secretly retaining their faith. The reader surely is disturbed by the allowance made for deceit. The Muslim may lie and engage in covert deception when facing infidels. This realization sheds considerable light on the behavior of many Muslims and Islamic governments throughout the world. What a contrast with the Bible which sets forth the perfect standard of human conduct, and makes no compromise for infractions. Forgiveness may be sought for sin, but the standard is not adjusted to excuse or justify human frailty. Lying is wrong–under all circumstances–even as God, Himself, cannot lie (Ephesians 4:25; Proverbs 13:5; Titus 1:2; 1 John 2:21).

This aspect of accommodation is common in the Quran. A particular action will be vehemently condemned (like eating blood or forbidding too many wives), but it will then so qualify the prohibition that the original restriction is rendered effectively meaningless. Take, for example, the obligatory fast (*sawm*). The month of Ramadan is a very important observance for Muslims. Much is made out of the fact that fasting is to take place throughout the entire month. So far so good. But "fasting throughout the entire month" means–**during the daylight hours only**. Wait a minute. If you eat breakfast just before daylight (as **many** people do), skip lunch (an increasing tendency of overweight Americans), and then eat supper/dinner after sunset (which **most** people do), you are fulfilling the requirements of Ramadan? Yes. You can eat a huge breakfast, and then stuff yourself in the evening, and thereby comply with the sacred observance. Convenient. The observance evaporates into nothing. It's like a religion that makes one of its requirements to sleep eight hours a day. And, what's more, there are multiple exemptions for Ramadan, including illness, heat, age, and pregnancy. The same may be said for *hajj*–the pilgrimage to Mecca.

CONCLUSION

This chapter has spotlighted four general characteristics of the Quran: inordinate self-absorption on the part of the author, a content that is imbalanced and repetitive, confusion and ignorance regarding historical facts, and manifestations of human frailties, accommodation, and undue influence by contemporaries. Such characteristics cast a fatal shadow over the inspiration of the Quran. Indeed, its author is one whose temperament and psychological state were unquestionably influenced–even governed–by his surrounding circumstances. His approach to his mission was constantly reactive and defensive–imbalanced. Especially during the Meccan years, he manifested a typically human reaction to his contemporaries by being preoccupied with responding to them and coercing them to accept him. In contrast, while Jesus would respond to the questions and behavior of specific individuals, He imparted much information about life unrelated to immediate circumstances–as if written for all time and all people rather than in service to Himself and the temporary trials He faced. Indeed, biblical writers demonstrate an uncanny aloofness, detachment, and objectivity. They were engaged with the profundity of the truths they articulated, and yet strangely reserved as if controlled by a Higher Power–a controlling influence that prevented them from giving vent to their natural emotions (see Appendix 2). In this regard, the Bible and the Quran are worlds apart.

If Muhammad was not inspired, but merely a man who was making it up as he went along, using his own imagination and contemporaneous sources with which he was familiar, what would one expect to observe? Answer: precisely what one encounters in an objective reading of the Quran.

CONCLUSION

Christianity claims to be the one and only true religion. Despite the secularism that has inundated Western civilization, and the pluralistic dilution of the Christian religion throughout Europe and America, the Christianity of the New Testament is an **exclusive** religion. In the very nature of the case, if the New Testament is of divine origin, then Christianity is the only religion acceptable to God, and all other philosophies and religions are false—mere human concoctions. Make no mistake: the Quran claims this same status of exclusivity for itself, insisting that only Muslims—those who embrace Islam—will be saved, and all others will be lost. Read carefully its words: "And whoso seeketh as religion other than the Surrender [Al-Islam—DM] (to Allah) it will not be accepted from him, and he will be a loser in the Hereafter" (*Surah* 3:85). Compare Ali's rendering of the same verse: "If anyone desires a religion other than Islam (submission to Allah), never will it be accepted of him; and in the Hereafter he will be in the ranks of those who have lost (all spiritual good)." The Quran declares that Islam is intended to be victorious over all other religions: "He it is who hath sent His messenger with the guidance and the religion of truth, that He may make it conqueror of all religion however much idolaters may be averse" (*Surah* 61:9). The disparity is deep and far-reaching. Indeed, a **massive** chasm exists between Islam and Christianity, to the extent that they cannot maintain any semblance of agreement with each other.

As stated at the outset of this study, a religion is not to be judged on the basis of how its practitioners conduct themselves. Those who profess Christianity are splintered into a plethora of factions and differing doctrinal viewpoints. And even though the Quran condemns religious division (*Surah* 6:160; 30:32), Islam itself has splintered into factions as well (see chapter 2). So the final test of authenticity, ultimately, is the inspiration of the religion's source and ultimate authority, i.e., the document(s) that it claims to be of divine origin.

This study has been designed to encourage the reader to examine carefully many features of the Quran. Having done so, one must now step back from the details and "get the big picture" by taking a broad, expansive look at Islam and the Quran, lest one fail to "see the forest for the trees." The Quran and the Bible stand in stark contradistinction to each other. Many people refuse to consider the beliefs of others, and simply stick with that to which their family and cultural environment exposed them. But in order to grasp the full extent of the chasm that exists between the Bible and the Quran, one should read **both** thoroughly. Muslims should read the Bible, and Christians should read the Quran. Doing so has caused the author to marvel at the disparity between the two.

Comparing the two books has likewise brought the firm realization that the contrast is stark and astounding. The superiority of the Bible is so transparently evident that one is flabbergasted and dumbfounded that so many human beings have embraced Islam in the last 1,400 years. But think again. Billions of people throughout the thousands of years of human history have opted for many differing religions, philosophies, and ideologies—ranging from the bizarre and ridiculous, to the sinister and evil. The Bible possesses a simplicity that enables the ordinary—even uneducated—person to comprehend its meaning. Yet, it also possesses a level of sophistication, depth, and complexity that transcends human invention and verifies its divine origin. **The Quran lacks this heavenly manifestation of inspiration.**

A FINAL WORD

In one sense, Islam is just another world religion, one among many, that merits consideration and tolerance, however misguided its tenets and precepts are. But in another sense—a very real sense—Islam is unlike all other world religions. Its singular source of authority, the Quran, speaks out in unmistakable terms: Allah intends for Islam to subdue the world— by force, if necessary. Liberal Muslim clerics may deny this conclusion vociferously. However, many Muslims are convinced that they have understood the Quran correctly when they endeavor to engage in terrorist activity and wreak havoc on the world community. They have succeeded in getting the attention of the entire world, and sustaining that attention for years. This "extremist" element may very well turn out to have much more support, sanction, encouragement, and outright assistance from otherwise peaceful segments of the Muslim world than currently imagined by many. In his concluding remarks, Serge Trifkovic issued an urgent warning to the West, whose waning moral and spiritual strength has left it incapacitated and vulnerable to a great threat:

> Western political leaders have every right to pay compliments to Muslim piety and good works, but they should be as wary of believing their own theological reassurances as they would be of facile insults. Islamic populations and individuals draw very different things from their religion, its scripture and traditions, but **anti-infidel violence is a hardy perennial**…. Islam…needs to be understood and subjected to the same supervision and legal restrains that apply to other cults prone to violence, and to violent political hate groups **whose avowed aim is the destruction of our order of life** (2002, p. 295, emp. added).

Some critics warn that Muslim immigrants wish to avail themselves of America's wealth, siphoning all that they can, in order to advance the cause of Islam, but have no desire to share in the moral, spiritual, and religious values and traditions on which America was founded, i.e., the Christian religion. One writer maintains that their deep disdain for the democratic institutions of the host-countries notwithstanding (and just like the members of the communist parties before them), Muslim activists in non-Muslim countries invoke those institutions when they clamor for every kind of indulgence for their own beliefs and customs. They demand full democratic privileges to organize and propagate their views, while acknowledging to each other that, given the power to do so, they would impose their own beliefs and customs, and **eliminate all others** (Trifkovic, 2002, p. 296, emp. added).

During a search of an *Al Qaeda* member's home in England, the Manchester Metropolitan Police found a terrorist manual, described as the "military series" section of the "Declaration of Jihad." The manual sets forth the strategies and tactics employed in *Al Qaeda's* covert operations. A few quotations are apropos: "Islamic governments have never and will never be established through peaceful solutions and cooperative councils. They are established as they always have been—by pen and gun, by word and bullet, by tongue and teeth." The Introduction, a brief history of the spread of Islam after 1924 and the expulsion of the "colonialists," explains how the corrupt, "apostate" Muslim rulers, in league with colonialism, have attempted to "eradicate Muslim identity." Consequently, those loyal to Allah have come to realize that—

Islam is not just performing rituals but a complete system: religion and government, worship and Jihad, ethics and dealing with people, and the Quran and sword.... [A]n Islamic government would never be established except by the bomb and rifle. Islam does not coincide or make a truce with unbelief, but rather confronts it. The confrontation that Islam calls for with these godless and apostate regimes, does not know Socratic debates, Platonic ideals, nor Aristotelian diplomacy. But it knows the dialogue of bullets, the ideals of assassination, bombing, and destruction, and the diplomacy of the cannon and machine-gun.

The manual then quotes the Quran: "Against them make ready your strength to the utmost of your power, including steeds of war, to strike terror into (the hearts of) the enemies, of Allah and your enemies, and others besides, whom you may not know, but whom Allah knows" (*Surah* 8:60).

The single most effective tool in responding to Islam, even in its more sinister aspects, is the Gospel of Jesus Christ. Unless a sizeable percentage of the citizens of the United States of America pulls back from the dogged determination to reject the principles of Christianity in order to embrace pluralism, humanism, moral relativism, "political correctness," and the spiritual depravity that accompanies such ideologies, the country will continue to be a "sitting duck" for hostile and threatening forces from without. A rejection of the God of the Bible inevitably results in moral implosion succeeded by external infiltration (e.g., Old Testament Israel in 2 Kings 17:6-18 and Judah in 2 Kings 17:19-20 and Habakkuk 1:1-11).

America has drifted farther away from its original spiritual, religious, and moral moorings than at any point in the past. Those moorings were identified by French historian and politician Alexis de Tocqueville in his monumental 1835 literary masterpiece *Democracy in America*, published after a visit to America in 1831-1832:

> [T]here is no country in the world where the **Christian** religion retains a greater influence over the souls of men than in America; and there can be no greater proof of its utility and of its conformity to human nature than that its influence is powerfully felt over the most enlightened and free nation of the earth.... **Christianity**, therefore, reigns without obstacle, by universal consent; the consequence is, as I have before observed, that every principle of the moral world is fixed and determinate.... [T]he revolutionists of America are obliged to profess an ostensible respect for **Christian** morality and equity, which does not permit them to violate wantonly the laws that oppose their designs.... [W]hile the law permits the Americans to do what they please, religion prevents them from conceiving, and forbids them to commit, what is rash or unjust.... I do not know whether all Americans have a

sincere faith in their religion—for who can search the human heart?—but I am certain that they hold it to be indispensable to the maintenance of republican institutions. This opinion is not peculiar to a class of citizens or to a party, but it belongs to the whole nation and to every rank of society.... The Americans combine the notions of **Christianity** and of liberty so intimately in their minds that it is impossible to make them conceive the one without the other.... **How is it possible that society should escape destruction if the moral tie is not strengthened in proportion as the political tie is relaxed? And what can be done with a people who are their own masters if they are not submissive to the Deity?** (1945, 1:303-307, emp. added).

Indeed, "how is it possible…?," and "what can be done…?" Contrary to the claim in recent years that the Founding Fathers of America advocated "pluralism" and equal acceptance of all religions, ideologies, and philosophies, the truth is that they feared for the future of the nation should its Christian foundation ever be compromised. Supreme Court Justice James Iredell, who was appointed to the U.S. Supreme Court by President George Washington, reflected this concern in 1788, though he felt confident that Islam would never be allowed to infiltrate America:

But it is objected that the people of America may perhaps choose representatives who have no religion at all, and that pagans and **Mahometans** may be admitted into offices.... But **it is never to be supposed that the people of America will trust their dearest rights to persons who have** no religion at all, or **a religion materially different from their own** (1836, 4:194, emp. added).

Similarly, U.S. Supreme Court Justice Joseph Story, appointed to the Court by President James Madison in 1811, and considered the founder of Harvard Law School and one of two men who have been considered the Fathers of American Jurisprudence, in his *Commentaries on the Constitution of the United States*, clarified the meaning of the First Amendment as it relates to religious toleration and Islam:

The real object of the [First–DM] [A]mendment was not to countenance, **much less to advance Mahometanism**, or Judaism, or infidelity **by prostrating Christianity**; but to exclude all rivalry among Christian sects and to prevent any national ecclesiastical establishment which should give to a hierarchy [of one denomination–DM] the exclusive patronage of the national government (1833, 3:728.1871, emp. added).

The other man who shares the title "Father of American Jurisprudence" in America was New York State Supreme Court Chief Justice James Kent, who, in penning the opinion of the court in *The People v. Ruggles* in 1811, reiterated the national attitude toward Islam that has existed from the inception of the country. In a case that resulted in the punishment of an individual who publicly maligned and denounced the Christian religion, Kent acknowledged the right of "free and decent discussions on any religious subject," but nevertheless insisted:

Nor are we bound, by any expressions in the constitution, as some have strangely supposed, either not to punish at all, or to punish indiscriminately the like attacks upon **the religion of Mahomet** or of the Grand Lama; and for this plain reason, that the case assumes that **we are a Christian people**, and the morality of the country is deeply engrafted upon Christianity, and **not upon the doctrines or worship of those imposters** (8 Johns 290).

The best defense against any sinister ideology, and, for that matter, the ultimate solution to America's internal problems, is so simple–but increasingly unacceptable to more and more Americans:

Blessed is the nation whose God is the Lord, the people He has chosen as His own inheritance. The Lord looks from heaven; He sees all the sons of men. From the place of His dwelling He looks on all the inhabitants of the earth.... No king is saved by the multitude of an army; a mighty man is not delivered by great strength. A horse is a vain hope for safety; neither shall it deliver any by its great strength. Behold, **the eye of the Lord is on those who fear Him,** on those who hope in His mercy (Psalm 33:12-18, emp. added).

Righteousness exalts a nation, but sin is a reproach to any people (Proverbs 14:34).

If My people who are called by My name will humble themselves, and pray and seek My face, and turn from their wicked ways, then I will hear from heaven, and will forgive their sin and heal their land (2 Chronicles 7:14).

"Return to Me, and I will return to you," says the Lord of hosts (Malachi 3:7).

APPENDIX 1

HAS THE BIBLE BEEN CORRUPTED THROUGH TRANSMISSION?

The science of textual criticism is a field of inquiry that has been invaluable in ascertaining the original reading of the New Testament text. Textual criticism involves "the ascertainment of the true form of a literary work, as originally composed and written down by its author" (Kenyon, 1951, p. 1). The fact that the original autographs do not exist (Comfort, 1990, p. 4), and that only copies of copies of copies of the original documents have survived, has led some falsely to conclude that the original reading of the New Testament documents cannot be determined. For example, Mormons frequently attempt to establish the superiority of the *Book of Mormon* over the Bible by insisting that the Bible has been corrupted through the centuries in the process of translation (a contention shared by Islam in its attempt to explain the Bible's frequent contradiction of the Quran). However, a venture into the fascinating world of textual criticism dispels this premature and uninformed conclusion.

The task of textual critics–those who study the extant manuscript evidence that attests to the text of the New Testament–is to examine **textual variants** (i.e., conflicting readings between manuscripts involving a word, verse, or verses) in an effort to reconstruct the original reading of the text. What has this field of inquiry concluded with regard to the integrity and genuineness of the Bible?

IS THE OLD TESTAMENT STILL RELIABLE?

If there are scribal errors in today's manuscript copies of the Old Testament, many wonder how we can be certain the text of the Bible was transmitted faithfully across the centuries. Is it not possible that it was corrupted so that its form in our present Bible is drastically different from the original source?

The accuracy of the Old Testament text was demonstrated forcefully by the discovery of the Dead Sea scrolls. Prior to 1947, the oldest Hebrew manuscripts of significant length did not date earlier than the ninth century A.D. However, when the Dead Sea scrolls were found (containing portions of all Old Testament books except Esther), this discovery pushed the record of the Old Testament text back almost 1,000 years. These copies were produced sometime between 200 B.C. and A.D. 100. One scroll found in the Qumran caves was of particular importance. It was a scroll of the book of Isaiah, which had only a few words missing. What was amazing about this scroll is that when it was compared to the text of Isaiah produced 900 years after it, the two matched almost word for word, with only a few small variations. In commenting on this comparative reading of the two texts, A.W. Adams observed:

> The close agreement of the second Isaiah Scroll from the Dead Sea with the manuscripts of the ninth and tenth centuries shows how carefully the text tradition which they represent has been preserved....We may therefore be satisfied that the text of our Old Testament has been handed down in one line without serious change since the beginning of the Christian era and even before (as quoted in Kenyon, 1939, pp. 69,88).

Amazingly, a comparison of the standard Hebrew texts with that of the Dead Sea scrolls has revealed that the two are virtually identical. The variations (about 5%) occurred only in minor spelling differences and minute copyists' mistakes. Thus, as Rene Paché noted: "Since it can be demonstrated that the text of the Old Testament was accurately transmitted for the last 2,000 years, one may reasonably suppose that it had been so transmitted from the beginning" (1971, p. 191).

Even within the various passages of Scripture, numerous references to copies of the written Word of God can be found. [It would be a gratuitous conclusion to assume that only one copy of the Scriptures existed during the period that the Old Testament covers.] A copy of the "book of the law" was preserved in the temple during the days of King Josiah (c. 621 B.C.), thus demonstrating that Moses' writings had been protected over a span of almost 1,000 years (2 Kings 22). Other Old Testament passages speak of the maintenance of the Holy Writings across the years (Jeremiah 36; Ezra 7:14; Nehemiah 8:1-18).

During Jesus' personal ministry, He read from the Isaiah scroll in the synagogue at Nazareth, and called it "Scripture" (Luke 4: 16-21)—a technical term always employed in the Bible for a **divine** writing. Jesus endorsed the truth that the Old Testament Scriptures had been preserved faithfully. Even though Jesus read from a **copy** of Isaiah, He still considered it the Word of God. Hence, Scripture had been preserved faithfully in **written** form. Furthermore, even though Jesus condemned the scribes of His day for their many sins, in not one instance in Scripture is it recorded where He even intimated they were unfaithful in their work as scribes. Yes, Jesus gave approval to copies (and translations—e.g., the Septuagint) of the Old Testament by reading and quoting from them.

One of the great language scholars of the Old Testament text was Dr. Robert Dick Wilson (1856-1930). A master of over thirty-five languages, Wilson carefully compared the text of the Old Testament with inscriptions on ancient monuments (as these two sources dealt with common material). As a result of his research, he declared that "we are scientifically certain that we have substantially the same text that was in the possession of Christ and the apostles and, so far as anybody knows, the same as that written by the original composers of the Old Testament documents" (1929, p. 8).

IS THE NEW TESTAMENT STILL RELIABLE?

What about the integrity of the New Testament? One may say unhesitatingly and confidently that the uncorrupted preservation of the New Testament has been thoroughly established. In evaluating the text of the New Testament, textual critics work with a large body of manuscript evidence, the amount of which is far greater than that available for any ancient classical author (Ewert, 1983, p. 139; Kenyon, 1951, p. 5; Westcott and Hort, 1964, p. 565). [The present number of Greek manuscripts–whole and partial–that attest to the New Testament stands at an unprecedented 5,735 (Welte, 2003). This figure does not include the other sources of evidence such as the superabundance of patristic citations and ancient versions]. The best manuscripts of the New Testament are dated at roughly A.D. 350, with perhaps one of the most important of these being the Codex Vaticanus, "the chief treasure of the Vatican Library in Rome," and the Codex Sinaiticus, which was purchased by the British from the Soviet Government in 1933 (Bruce, 1960, p. 20). Additionally, the Chester Beatty papyri, made public in 1931, contain eleven codices (manuscript volumes), three of which contain most of the New Testament (including the gospel accounts). Two of these codices boast a date in the first half of the third century, while the third slides in a little later, being dated in the last half of the same century (Bruce, p. 21). The John Rylands Library vaunts even earlier evidence. A papyrus codex containing parts of John 18 dates to the time of Hadrian, who reigned from A.D. 117 to 138 (Bruce, p. 21).

Other attestation to the accuracy of the New Testament documents can be found in the writings of the so-called "apostolic fathers"–men who wrote primarily from A.D. 90 to 160, and who often quoted from the New Testament documents (Bruce, p. 22).

Irenaeus, Clement of Alexandria, Tertullian, Tatian, Clement of Rome, and Ignatius (writing before the close of the second century) all provided citations from one or more of the gospel accounts (Guthrie, 1990, p. 24). Other witnesses to the authenticity of the New Testament are the Ancient Versions, which consist of the text of the New Testament translated into different languages. The Old Latin and the Old Syriac are the most ancient, being dated from the middle of the second century (Bruce, p. 23).

The fact is, the New Testament enjoys far more historical documentation than any other volume ever known. Compared to the 5,700+ Greek manuscripts authenticating the New Testament, there are only 643 copies of Homer's *Iliad*, which is undeniably the most famous book of ancient Greece. No one doubts the text of Julius Caesar's *Gallic Wars*, but we have only 10 copies of it, the earliest of which was made 1,000 years after it was written. We have only two manuscripts of Tacitus' *Histories* and *Annals*, one from the ninth century and one from the eleventh. The *History of Thucydides*, another well-known ancient work, is dependent upon only eight manuscripts, the oldest of these being dated about A.D. 900 (along with a few papyrus scraps dated at the beginning of the Christian era). And *The History of Herodotus* finds itself in a similar situation. "Yet no classical scholar would listen to an argument that the authenticity of Herodotus or Thucydides is in doubt because the earliest MSS [manuscripts– DM] of their works which are of any use to us are over 1,300 years later than the originals" (Bruce, pp. 20-21). Bruce thus declared: "It is a curious fact that historians have often been much readier to trust the New Testament records than have many theologians" (p. 19). In 1968, Bruce Metzger, a longtime professor of New Testament language and literature at Princeton, stated: "The amount of evidence for the text of the New Testament…is so much greater than that available for any ancient classical author that the necessity of resorting to emendation is reduced to the smallest dimensions" (1968, p. 86). Truly, to have such abundance of copies for the New Testament from within seventy years of their writing is nothing short of amazing (cf. Geisler and Brooks, 1990, pp. 159-160).

In one sense, the work of the textual critic has been unnecessary, since the vast majority of textual variants involve minor matters that do not affect doctrine as it relates to one's salvation. Even those variants that might be deemed doctrinally significant pertain to matters that are treated elsewhere in the Bible where the question of authenticity and originality is unobscured. No feature of Christian doctrine is at stake. As Ewert noted: "[V]ariant readings in our manuscripts do not affect any basic teaching of the NT" (1983, p. 145). Old Testament scholar Gleason Archer wrote in agreement:

> In fact, it has long been recognized by the foremost specialists in textual criticism that if any decently attested variant were taken up from the apparatus at the bottom of the page and were substituted for the accepted reading of the standard text, **there would in no case be a single, significant alteration in doctrine or message** (1982, p. 30, emp. added).

Nevertheless, textual critics have been successful in demonstrating that **currently circulating New Testaments do not differ substantially from the original autographs**. When all of the textual evidence is considered, the vast majority of discordant readings have been resolved (e.g., Metzger, 1968, p. 185). One is brought to the firm conviction that we have in our possession the New Testament **as God intended**.

The world's foremost textual critics have confirmed this conclusion. Sir Frederic Kenyon, longtime director and principal librarian at the British Museum, whose scholarship and expertise to make pronouncements on textual criticism was second to none, stated: "Both the authenticity and the general integrity of the books of the New Testament may be regarded as finally established" (1940, p. 288). The late F.F. Bruce, longtime Rylands Professor of Biblical Criticism at the University of Manchester, England, remarked: "The variant readings about which any doubt remains among textual critics of the New Testament affect no material question of historic fact or of Christian faith and practice" (1960, pp. 19-20). J.W. McGarvey, declared by the *London Times* to be "the ripest Bible scholar on earth" (Phillips, 1975, p. 184; Brigance, 1870, p. 4), conjoined: "All the authority and value possessed by these books when they were first written belong to them still" (1956, p. 17). And the eminent textual critics Westcott and Hort put the entire matter into perspective when they said:

> Since textual criticism has various readings for its subject, and the discrimination of genuine readings from corruptions for its aim, discussions on textual criticism almost inevitably obscure the simple fact that variations are but secondary incidents of a fundamentally single and identical text. In the New Testament in particular it is difficult to escape an exaggerated impression as to the proportion which the words subject to variation bear to the whole text, and also, in most cases, as to their intrinsic importance. It is not superfluous therefore to state explicitly that **the great bulk of the words of the New Testament** stand out above all discriminative processes of criticism, because they **are free from variation**, and need only to be transcribed (1964, p. 564, emp. added).

Writing over one hundred years ago in the late nineteenth century, and noting that the experience of two centuries of investigation and discussion had been achieved, these scholars concluded: "[T]he words in our opinion still subject to doubt **can hardly amount to more than a thousandth part of the whole** of the New Testament" (p. 565, emp. added). This means that $999/1000^{th}$ of the text of the New Testament is the same today as when it came from the pens of the inspired writers. The minuscule portion that remains uncertain ($1/1000^{th}$) consists of trivial details that have **no material effect on matters of faith or doctrine**. J.I. Packer, Board of Governors Professor of Theology at Regent College in Vancouver, British Columbia, summarized the facts: "[F]aith in the adequacy of the text is confirmed, so far as it can be, by **the unanimous verdict of textual scholars** that the biblical text is excellently preserved, and **no point**

of doctrine depends on any of the small number of cases in which the true reading remains doubtful" (1958, p. 90, emp. added). Indeed, again in the words of textual scholar F.F. Bruce: "By the 'singular care and providence' of God the Bible text has come down to us in such substantial purity that even the most uncritical edition of the Hebrew or Greek…cannot effectively obscure the real message of the Bible, or neutralize its saving power" (as quoted in Packer, pp. 90-91).

Therefore, the charge alleged by Muslims, that the Bible has been corrupted in transmission, is completely false. Anyone who has taken time to investigate the manuscript evidence that exists for ascertaining the original state of the Bible **knows** that we have the Bible in its near-original condition–a claim that has not been established for the Quran (see chapter 6). The attention given to ascertaining the original state of the Quranic text pales in comparison to that given to the Bible in general, and the New Testament in particular. As John Gilchrist observed:

> [T]here is no translation of the Qur'an to compare with translations of the Bible such as the Revised Standard Version or New American Standard Version. These were done by committees of scholars and the result has been a remarkably consistent and accurate rendering of the original. Every well-known translation of the Qur'an has been the work of an individual and, to one degree or another in every case, the value of the final product is tempered by the presence of the author's own personal convictions and interpretations (1986).

Of course, unsubstantiated claims are made for the transmission of the Quran: "[A]ll Muslims agree that the Quran is the verbatim revelation of God. They also agree about its text and content; that is, **no variant texts are found among any of the schools**" (Nasr, 2003, p. 8, emp. added). The fact that Muslims **claim** unanimity of opinion regarding the purity of the Quranic text does not **prove** that the Quran has been exempt from the peculiar attribute of textual variation to which **all** documents are subject.

Ironically, the Quran itself offers both implicit and explicit endorsement of the integrity of the **biblical** text–at least in its condition at the time the Quran arose in the early seventh century:

> And believe in that which I reveal, **confirming that which ye possess already (of the Scripture)**, and be not first to disbelieve therein, and part not with My revelations for a trifling price, and keep your duty unto Me. Confound not truth with falsehood, nor knowingly conceal the truth…. Enjoin ye righteousness upon mankind while ye yourselves forget (to practice it)? And **ye are readers of the Scripture!** Have ye then no sense?…. O Children of Israel! Remember My favour wherewith I favoured you and how I preferred you to (all) creatures (*Surah* 2:41-42,44,47, emp. added).
>
> Or do they say, "He has forged it"? Say: "Had I forged it, then can you obtain no single (blessing) for me from Allah. He knows best of that whereof you talk (so glibly)! Enough is He for a witness between me and you! And He is Oft-Forgiving, Most Merciful." Say: **"I am no bringer of new-fangled doctrine among the Messengers**, nor do I know what will be done with me or with you. I follow but that which is revealed to me; I am but a Warner open and clear." Say: "Do you see? If (this teaching) be from Allah, and you reject it, and a witness from among the Children of Israel testifies to **its similarity (with earlier scripture)**, and has believed while you are arrogant, (how unjust you are!). Truly, Allah does not guide a people unjust." The Unbelievers say of those who believe: "If (this Message) were a good thing, (such men) would not have gone to it first, before us!" And seeing that they do not guide themselves thereby, they will say, "This is **an (old,) old falsehood!" And before this, was the Book of Moses as a guide and a mercy: and this Book confirms (it) in the Arabic tongue**; to admonish the unjust, and as Glad Tidings to those who do right…. "O our people! We have heard a Book revealed after Moses, **confirming what came before it** (*Surah* 46:8-12,30, emp. added–Ali).

Say: "O People of the Book! do you disapprove of us for no other reason than that **we believe in** Allah, and the revelation that has come to us **and that which came before (us)**, and (perhaps) that most of you are rebellious and disobedient?.... If only they had stood fast by **the Law, the Gospel, and all the revelation that was sent to them from their Lord**, they would have enjoyed happiness from every side. There is from among them a party on the right course: but many of them follow a course that is evil. O Messenger! proclaim the (Message) which has been sent to you from your Lord. If you did not, you would not have fulfilled and proclaimed His Mission. And Allah will defend you from men (who mean mischief). For Allah guides not those who reject Faith. Say: "O People of the Book! You have no ground to stand upon unless you stand fast by **the Law, the Gospel, and all the revelation that has come to you from your Lord**." It is the revelation that comes to you from your Lord, that increases in most of them their obstinate rebellion and blasphemy. But you do not grieve over (these) people without Faith. Those who believe (in the Qur'an), **those who follow the Jewish (scriptures),** and the Sabians and the Christians,–any who believe in Allah and the Last Day, and work righteousness,–on them shall be no fear, nor shall they grieve (*Surah* 5:59, 66-69–Ali, emp. added; cf. 2:62).

And if thou (Muhammad) art in doubt concerning that which We reveal unto thee, then question those who read **the Scripture (that was) before thee**. Verily the Truth from thy Lord hath come unto thee. So be not thou of the waverers (*Surah* 10:95, emp. added).

These verses from the Quran provide confirmation of the accuracy of the Law and the Gospel (cf. *Surah* 87:18-19; 6:155-158). They even appeal to a Jew, contemporary to Muhammad, who verified that the Quran confirmed the Scripture that preceded it. Indeed, the Quran claims to be in unison and harmony with, and complementary to, previous Scripture (the Bible).

The underlying thought in all of these Quranic verses is that the Quran is to be accepted, reverenced, and obeyed every bit as much as the previous Scriptures (i.e., the Bible). These verses are worded in such a way that they **assume** the legitimacy and acceptability of the Bible. The Quranic criticism directed against Jews (and Christians) is not that they corrupted their Scriptures (cf. *Surah* 7:169-170). Rather, they are criticized for not concluding that Muhammad and the Quran were the confirmatory sequel to the previous revelations of Jews and Christians. In fact, when the Jews insisted to Muhammad that they had been given sufficient knowledge by means of the Torah–an admission made by the Quran itself ["Again, We gave the Scripture unto Moses, complete for him who would do good, **an explanation of all things**, a guidance and a mercy, that they might believe in the meeting with their Lord" (*Surah* 7:155, emp. added)]–Muhammad responded with a new surah: "[I]f all the trees in the earth were pens, and the sea, with seven more seas to help it, (were ink), the words of Allah could not be exhausted" (*Surah* 31:27; cf. Lings, 1983, p. 78). If the Quran endorses the integrity of the Bible, and we have in existence manuscripts of the Bible that predate the Quran, then the accuracy and authenticity of the Bible stands vindicated–not only by the voluminous manuscript evidence–**but even by the Quran itself**.

REFERENCES

Archer, Gleason L. (1982), *An Encyclopedia of Bible Difficulties* (Grand Rapids: Zondervan).

Brigance, L.L. (1870), "J.W. McGarvey," in *A Treatise on the Eldership* by J.W. McGarvey (Murfreesboro, TN: DeHoff Publications, 1962 reprint).

Bruce, F.F. (1960), *The New Testament Documents: Are They Reliable?* (Grand Rapids, MI: Eerdmans), revised edition.

Comfort, Philip (1990), *Early Manuscripts and Modern Translations of the New Testament* (Wheaton, IL: Tyndale House).

Ewert, David (1983), *From Ancient Tablets to Modern Translations* (Grand Rapids, MI: Zondervan).

Geisler, Norman L. and Ronald M. Brooks (1990), *When Skeptics Ask* (Wheaton, IL: Victor Books).

Gilchrist, John (1986), *Muhammad and the Religion of Islam,* [On-line], URL: http://answering-islam.org.uk/Gilchrist/Vol1/index.html.

Guthrie, Donald (1990), *New Testament Introduction* (Downers Grove, IL: InterVarsity Press).

Kenyon, Sir Frederic (1939), *Our Bible and the Ancient Manuscripts* (London: Eyre and Spottiswoode).

Kenyon, Sir Frederic (1940), *The Bible and Archaeology* (New York: Harper).

Kenyon, Sir Frederic (1951 reprint), *Handbook to the Textual Criticism of the New Testament* (Grand Rapids, MI: Eerdmans), second edition.

Lings, Martin (1983), *Muhammad* (Rochester, VT: Inner Traditions International).

McGarvey, J.W. (1956 reprint), *Evidences of Christianity* (Nashville, TN: Gospel Advocate).

Metzger, Bruce M. (1968), *The Text of the New Testament* (New York, NY: Oxford University Press).

Nasr, Seyyed Hossein (2003), *Islam* (New York: HarperCollins).

Paché, Rene (1971), *The Inspiration and Authority of Scripture* (Grand Rapids, MI: Eerdmans).

Packer, J.I. (1958), *"Fundamentalism" and the Word of God* (Grand Rapids, MI: Eerdmans), 1976 reprint.

Phillips, Dabney (1975), *Restoration Principles and Personalities* (University, AL: Youth In Action).

Welte, Michael (2003), personal e-mail, Institute for New Testament Textual Research (Munster, Germany), [On-line], URL: http://www.uni-muenster.de/NTTextforschung/.

Westcott, B.A. and F.J.A. Hort (1964 reprint), *The New Testament in the Original Greek* (New York: MacMillan).

Wilson, Robert Dick (1929), *A Scientific Investigation of the Old Testament* (New York: Harper Brothers).

APPENDIX 2

THE INSPIRATION OF THE BIBLE

If the Bible is **not** the Word of God, then all religions and philosophies are equally valid. If the Bible **is** the Word of God, then New Testament Christianity is the only authentic religious reality. As a matter of fact, the divine origin of the Bible can be established beyond dispute. [NOTE: A listing of the sources consulted in the preparation of this appendix is provided after the conclusion].

THE CLAIM TO INSPIRATION

The Bible claims divine origin. The doctrine of the inspiration of the Bible is articulated in a plethora of passages, including the following: 2 Timothy 3:16, 2 Peter 1:19-21; 3:15-16; Acts 1:16ff., 1 Peter 1:10-12, John 10:34-35, Matthew 4:4,7,10, Luke 24:25-27,44-46, Acts 4:25; 17:11, Galatians 1:12; 3:16, Matthew 5:17-20; 22:32,43, 1 Corinthians 2:4-13; 14:37, Luke 21:12-15, John 16:12-13, Acts 1:5,8; 2:1ff., Ephesians 3:1-5, 1 Thessalonians 4:2,15; 2 Thessalonians 2:15; 3:6,14. A thorough study of these passages (and many others) reveals that the type of inspiration that the Bible claims for itself, from beginning to end, is:

(1) "verbal," i.e., inspiration entailed such superintendence by God that even the words themselves came under His influence. [NOTE: That is not to say that the writers merely took "dictation." Rather, the Bible indicates that God adapted His inspiring activity to the individual temperament, vocabulary, and stylistic idiosyncrasies of each writer].

(2) "plenary," i.e., inspiration extends to all of its parts. The Bible is fully inspired in its entirety.

(3) "infallible," i.e., it is incapable of deceiving or misleading. The Bible is therefore completely trustworthy and reliable.

(4) "inerrant," i.e., it is free of error. God used human beings to write the Bible, and in so doing, allowed them to leave their mark upon it, but without making any of the mistakes that human writings are prone to make. God made certain that the words produced by the human writers were free from the errors and mistakes characteristic of uninspired writers. This influence even extended to matters of science, geography, and history.

PROOFS OF THE BIBLE'S INSPIRATION

Having clarified the meaning of the Bible's **claim** to inspiration and transcendence above all other writings on Earth, observe that a mere claim to inspiration is insufficient. The Bible must possess the **attributes** of inspiration. It must contain internal evidence that demonstrates a supernatural origin. What concrete evidence exists to **prove** the inspiration of the Bible? Can a person know for certain that the Bible is God's Word? Yes. Many proofs exist, including the following few.

Absence of Contradiction

First, the Bible does not contradict itself. No genuine error or discrepancy has ever been sustained, though critics have tried for centuries. The fact that the Bible, in its original autographs, is errorless proves its divine origin and places it in a class by itself, since the written productions of mere humans often contain errors. [For a refutation of many of the alleged contradictions of the Bible, see Lyons, 2003; Haley, 1874].

Historical, Geographical, Topographical Accuracy

Second, the Bible possesses stunning, uncanny accuracy in historical and geographical details. Human history books have always required corrections and updates. Not so with the Bible. For example, critics once scoffed at the Bible's frequent (almost 50 passages–Genesis 23:10; 26:34; Joshua 1:4; et al.) allusion to the Hittites, since no known historical sources made reference to such a people. But suddenly, the archaeologist's spade (Hugo Winckler–1906) uncovered at ancient Boghaz-kale in modern Turkey the capital of the Hittite empire. The massive site covered more than 400 acres! The Bible was right, while its critics were wrong.

Luke referred to several minute historical details in Luke 2:1-3 that were once challenged as inaccurate. Luke claimed that Caesar Augustus issued a decree requiring a Roman census (Luke 2:1). Papyrus documents have confirmed that the Romans took a census between 9 and 6 B.C. Luke claimed that Quirinius was governor of Syria at the time (Luke 2:2). Records showed that Quirinius had been governor **after** this time. But an inscription found at Rome in 1828, and Sir William Ramsay's discovery of a monument in Asia Minor shortly before World War I, both confirm that Quirinius held two governorships, one of which could have been during the time Luke said he was governor. Luke also claimed that citizens were required to return to their hometowns for the census (Luke 2:3). Archaeological discovery has confirmed this bit of history as well.

In writing the New Testament book of Acts, Luke referred to 32 countries, 54 cities, and 9 Mediterranean islands. He referred to 95 persons, 62 of whom are not named elsewhere in the New Testament. In so doing, Luke left himself "wide open" to a mistake. Yet every single allusion, when checkable, has been proven to be absolutely accurate. For example, when Luke mentioned that Sergius Paulus was a "proconsul" in Cyprus (Acts 13:7), some scholars were certain the Bible had to be wrong, since Cyprus was an imperial province and the proper title for its ruler would have been "propraetor." However, it was discovered that in 22 B.C., Augustus shifted administration to the Roman Senate and thus, in Paul's day, Cyprus was a senatorial province, and Luke's title was absolutely accurate. Luke's accuracy even extended to orthography in his use of the Latin spelling of Paulus rather than the Greek spelling.

In Acts 14:6, Luke seems to have implied that Iconium was not within the territory of Lycaonia, as were Derbe and Lystra. This implication was once questioned, but Sir William Ramsay's discovery in 1910 of a monument verified Luke's implication. Luke's use in Acts 16:12 of *meris* to refer to a district of Macedonia was once questioned by the great Greek scholar F.J.A. Hort, who insisted that the term never denoted a district. Yet, excavations in Egypt confirmed Luke's use of the term in association with Macedonia. Luke's use of *praetor* to refer to the magistrates of Philippi (Acts 16:20) was pinpointed as inaccurate since such town officials would normally be referred to as two *duumvirs*. However, archaeological inscriptions have confirmed that Luke's term was a courtesy title for the supreme magistrates of a Roman colony and, therefore, completely accurate. Likewise, his use of "politarch" for the rulers of Thessalonica (Acts 17:6,8) was once questioned. But 17 inscriptions have been discovered in that city containing that very term.

Another sample of the Bible's historical accuracy is seen in Isaiah 20:1, where Sargon is mentioned as king of Assyria. Critics once assailed the Bible as inaccurate, insisting that Isaiah must have referred to another Assyrian king. But then, in 1843, Paul Emil Botta, French Consul at Mosul in modern Iraq, in archaeological excavations on the east bank of the Tigris River, 14 miles northeast of ancient Nineveh, discovered Khorsabad—the site of an elaborate, magnificent palace constructed by Sargon II in 706 B.C. The palace covered an area of 25 acres—a space larger than many cities in Palestine today. Instances of the Bible's historical accuracy could be multiplied many times over.

Not only is the Bible geographically and historically correct, it is likewise topographically accurate, i.e., compass directions and elevation allusions are precisely correct. For example, Egypt is said to be "down" from Jericho (Joshua 7:2). The way from Jerusalem to Gaza is said to be "south" of Samaria (Acts 8:26). Bethel is said to be "west" of Ai (Genesis 12:8). In not a single instance of this kind have any of the Bible writers been found in error. How could they have done what learned and careful men throughout the ages have failed to do—unless they were guided by divine wisdom?

Predictive Prophecy

Another proof of the Bible's inspiration is its element of predictive prophecy. Astrologers, psychics, fortunetellers, and self-proclaimed prophets in our day are vague and possess only a degree of accuracy. They are no more gifted than sports prognosticators who simply make educated guesses and miss their predictions as often as they are correct. But the inspired prophets of the Bible were 100% correct. Their prophecies were literally filled with minute detail, and their predictions often pertained to events far removed from themselves by hundreds of years.

In addition to the hundreds of prophecies throughout the Bible that relate to individual people, events, and entire nations, the Bible contains some 332 distinct Messianic prophecies—i.e., predictions pertaining specifically to Jesus Christ. With uncanny precision, Bible writers predicted in minute detail the events of Jesus' earthly life, hundreds of years before they occurred. For example, it was predicted, more than a thousand years before it happened, that Jesus would be a descendant of Abraham (Genesis 22:18; Luke 3:34), through the tribe of Judah (Genesis 49:10; Hebrews 7:14), through the royal family of David (2 Samuel 7:12; Luke 1:32), and from a virgin (Isaiah 7:14; Matthew 1:22). Some 700 years before it happened, Micah predicted that Jesus would be born in Bethlehem Ephrathah (Micah 5:2). Palestine contained two Bethlehems—one in the north, Bethlehem of Zebulun, and one in the south, Bethlehem Ephrathah or Bethlehem of Judah. Micah, in pinpointing the correct Bethlehem, evidenced his possession of supernatural knowledge.

Christ was to appear during the time of the Roman Empire (Daniel 2:44; 7:13-14; Luke 2:1), while Judah still had her own king (Genesis 49:10; Matthew 2:22). He would be betrayed by a friend (Psalm 41:9) for 30 pieces of silver (Zechariah 11:12). That is exactly how it happened (John 13:18; Matthew 26:15). He would be spit upon and beaten (Isaiah 50:6), and His hands and feet would be pierced in death (Psalm 22:16)–which is precisely what occurred (Matthew 27:30; Luke 24:39). Even though He would be killed, it also was predicted that His physical body would not decay since He would be raised from the dead (Psalm 16:10; Acts 2:22ff.). These incredible details simply could not have been anticipated without direct assistance from God.

Scientific Foreknowledge

Still another evidence of the inspiration of the Bible is its fantastic foreknowledge of scientific truth. The writers of the Bible simply did not make the scientific blunders that their contemporaries made. How did Moses (Genesis 15:5) and Jeremiah (33:22) know that the stars are literally innumerable–like the grains of sand on the seashore? For most of the world's history, astronomers came up with figures ranging from the hundreds to about a thousand (Hipparchus–150 B.C.–1,026 stars; Ptolemy–A.D. 150–1,056 stars; Kepler–A.D. 1600–1,005 stars). All of these men lived prior to the invention of the telescope, and so relied upon human eyesight. Astronomers now know that there are billions of stars (and the counting continues). How could the writers of the Bible have known the number of stars to be innumerable?

The Bible writer mentioned the "springs of the sea" and the "recesses of the deep" in Job 38:16. It was not until the 1800s, when technology had made sufficient progress, that scientists began discovering incredible recesses on the ocean floor. In 1873, a team of British scientists, initiating deep-sea exploration, found a trench on the floor of the Pacific Ocean that is over five miles deep. In 1960, the bathyscaph "Trieste" reached the bottom of the Mariana Trench at 35,800 feet–more than 6 miles deep! How did the writer of Job know the ocean contained recesses?

In the field of physics, Bible writers referred to both the First and Second Laws of Thermodynamics. The First Law states that matter is neither being created nor destroyed. This fact is so affirmed in Genesis 2:1, which notes that God "finished" His creative activity (i.e., completed it once and for all). The Second Law of Thermodynamics (or the Law of Entropy) states that the Universe is running down and that energy is being converted into less-usable forms. But passages like Isaiah 51:6, Psalm 102:26, and Hebrews 1:11 long ago indicated that the Earth and the heavens are wearing out. The verses liken the process to clothing that wears out. While the scientific community has only recently recognized these two laws, the writers of the Bible reported these facts long ago.

In the field of medicine, the Bible long ago affirmed that "the life of the flesh is in the blood" (Leviticus 17:11-14). Yet, for centuries, the medical world practiced "blood-letting" on the theory that ailments and sickness are the result of "humors" in the blood. When the first president of the United States, George Washington, was facing death, the doctors attending him contributed to his depleted condition by removing a portion of the quantity of his blood (Wallenborn, 1997; Morens, 1999). Of course, medical science now recognizes that the blood is the key to life. In emergency situations, medical personnel immediately insert an I-V and take measures to bolster the condition of the blood. How did Moses know that blood is the key to life?

Another fascinating medical fact associated with the Bible is its repeated reference to circumcision, and the insistence by God that the procedure be done on the eighth day (e.g., Genesis 17:12; Leviticus 12:3). Why the **eighth** day? In 1935, Professor H. Dam proposed the name "Vitamin K" for the factor in foods that helped prevent hemorrhaging in baby chicks. Medical authorities now know that Vitamin K triggers the liver's production of prothrombin. If Vitamin K is deficient, there will be a prothrombin deficiency and hemorrhaging may occur. Vitamin K begins to be produced in the newborn male only on the fifth through the seventh day of life. But it is **only on the eighth day** that the percent of prothrombin climbs above 100%. The eighth day would therefore be the best day for the ancients to perform surgery. How did Moses know this, unless God told him?

Internal Unity

Another proof of Bible inspiration is its incredible unity. The Bible is actually a compilation of 66 books written by some 40 different people spanning 1,600 years (from 1500 B.C. to A.D. 100). [NOTE: The production of the Quran spanned 22 or 23 years and involved a single author]. The Bible writers came from a variety of cultural and educational backgrounds, and wrote in three different languages (Hebrew, Aramaic, and Greek). They produced a volume that is characterized by such an amazing unity and fantastic continuity as to be inexplicable on the basis of human origin.

Throughout all of their narratives and stories, the writers uniformly attested to the unfolding scheme of redemption, which culminated in the death of Christ. The scheme of redemption is ever present, woven into the fabric of Scripture from beginning to end. One evidence of this feature is the way the Holy Spirit built into Bible history foreshadowing of the coming Christ and the Christian system. Types and shadows abound (Colossians 2:17; Hebrews 8:5; 10:1). The various aspects of the Old Covenant were clearly designed and preordained to prefigure and foreshadow the New—they were "copies of the true" (Hebrews 9:24). Israelite life and worship conducted in 1500 B.C. was preplanned by God and divinely orchestrated to anticipate Christian living after A.D. 30. For example, the ritual activity assigned to the High Priest under the Law of Moses foreshadowed by 1,500 years the redemptive role of Christ (Hebrews 2:14-18; 5:3-5; 7:24-28; 9:6-7,11-14,24-28; 10:19-22). No other book on the planet that claims inspiration possesses this intricate, incomparable attribute.

This fantastic achievement of unity is comparable to 40 people, scattered across more than a thousand years in time, designing 66 separate and distinct metal parts, that are eventually assembled together to form a precision machine that revolutionized the world! The inspiration of the Bible is established on this one point alone.

Stylistic Commonalities

Yet another fascinating piece of evidence exhibited by the Bible is the fact that even though the human writers were permitted to imprint the text with their own natural style, nevertheless, the Holy Spirit–being the ultimate Author of the entire Bible–left **His** imprint. [NOTE: The Quran reflects the personality of Muhammad (cf. Gibb, 1953, p. 22). Though the Bible writers projected their writing style, vocabulary, and educational backgrounds onto their writings, they did not project their **personalities**]. The imprint of the single divine Author of the Bible is evident from a number of stylistic commonalities.

First, observe that the writers were **objective and reserved**. They reported the behavior and activities of their characters without expressing approval or disapproval, or engaging in character analysis typical of human historians. Second, the Bible writers manifested unparalleled **impartiality**. They divulged the sins of themselves and their friends as forthrightly as they did the sins of their enemies. Peter's denial of Christ is presented as forthrightly as the cruelty and hatred of the Jewish hierarchy. Third, the Bible writers reported events with amazing **calmness**. They recorded the most earthshaking, exciting events with the same dispassionate manner that they told of trivialities. The suffering and death of Jesus is set forth with the same objective detachment that they used in noting Jesus taking a seat on a fishing boat to address a crowd. It is as if the writers were functioning under the restraint of a supernatural power that kept them from giving natural vent to the intense feelings and emotions that would have been burning within them. It is as if they were elevated above their normal human inclinations. [NOTE: The Quran does not possess the air of **detached objectivity** that the Bible possesses. The writer of the Quran had an "ax to grind," whereas the writers of the Bible were dispassionate and distant].

And what about the uncanny **brevity** of the Bible? In both the Old and New Testaments, Bible books are incredibly brief—totally unlike the books of average human authors. For example, Matthew, Mark, Luke, and John bore the awesome responsibility of reporting to the world for all ages the momentous events surrounding the life of the Son of God. John even admitted that there were so many activities in Jesus' life that "if they should be written every one, I suppose that even the world itself could not contain the books that should be written" (John 21:25). Luke wrote Acts and, in so doing, preserved for all time the first 30 years of the history of the church and the spread of Christianity. With such cataclysmic, earthshaking subject matter, how did these authors produce such succinct, condensed, concise histories consisting of only a few pages? The answer: the superhuman, over-ruling power and influence of the Holy Spirit was with them.

Their brevity is especially apparent in their reporting of specific incidents. The baptism of Jesus is told in twelve lines by Matthew, and in six lines by Mark and Luke. Of the twelve post-resurrection appearances of Jesus, two are noted by Matthew, three each by Mark and Luke, and four by John. In Acts, the death of the apostle James (which must have been a tremendous blow to the early church, on the order of the assassination of John F. Kennedy to Americans), is noted with eleven words. Entire volumes and multiple movies have been produced addressing the death of JFK!

These observations lead to another wondrous attribute of the Bible: the **omissions** that are made by the writers. What sort of an author, in telling of Jesus the Son of God, would omit the first thirty years of His life—as Mark and John do? Matthew and Luke report only His birth, and Luke reports a single event which occurred at the age of twelve, before skipping to His thirtieth year. Acts is almost totally silent on the activities of ten of the apostles. Paul's activities are described, and yet many of the most exciting events in his labors are omitted in Acts, and only mentioned in passing by Paul in 2 Corinthians 12. Why would a mere human author give us a detailed account of Paul's voyage to Rome, and then omit the trial before Nero, the Caesar over all the Roman Empire? These remarkable omissions are explicable only on the grounds that the authors were constrained by a higher power.

A final stylistic attribute of the Bible is the **air of infallibility** that the writers assume. They addressed themes that have baffled the greatest minds of human history, such as the nature of God, eternality, the nature and purpose of human existence, the source and meaning of human suffering, the afterlife, the future of the Earth, and the final destiny of man. Yet, the writers did not offer speculation; they spoke with unhesitating, matter-of-fact confidence, and admitted no possibility of mistake. They were either the most arrogant, conniving deceivers the world has ever known (next to Jesus Himself)–**or**–they were what they claimed to be: inspired by God to write what they wrote.

CONCLUSION

This appendix merely scratches the surface of the voluminous evidence that exists to substantiate and verify the authenticity of the Bible as the inspired Word of God. [NOTE: For additional information, see Thompson, 2001]. The supernatural origin of the Bible is so overwhelmingly established, one ought to feel every compulsion to be devoted to its truth and to commit the entirety of one's life to Jesus Christ, the Sovereign Lord of the Universe.

The Bible is unlike any other book on the face of the Earth. Indeed, the Bible is the one and only authentic expression of the God of Heaven. It surpasses all other books, and stands as the only reliable guide in life. It is the only source of divine information in the world. I plead with you to give it your full consideration, that you might decide to become a Christian and live your life according to the teachings of the New Testament.

REFERENCES

Albright, W.F. (1949), *The Archaeology of Palestine* (Harmondsworth, Middlesex, England: Penguin).

Archer Jr., Gleason (1974), *A Survey of Old Testament Introduction* (Chicago, IL: Moody).

Bromling, Brad (1989)), "Alleged Discrepancies–The Skeptics' Impotent Axe," *Reason & Revelation* 9:9-12, March.

Free, Joseph P. and Howard Vos (1992), *Archaeology and Bible History* (Grand Rapids, MI: Zondervan).

Gibb, H.A.R. (1953), *Mohammedanism* (New York: Oxford University Press), second edition.

Haley, John W. (1874), *An Examination of the Alleged Discrepancies of the Bible* (Grand Rapids, MI: Baker, 1977 reprint).

Harris, R. Laird (1968), *Inspiration and Canonicity of the Bible* (Grand Rapids, MI: Zondervan).

Jackson, Wayne (1983), "Bible Contradictions–Are They Real?" *Reason & Revelation* 3:25-28, June.

Jackson, Wayne (1983), "Evidences For Bible Inspiration," *Reason & Revelation* 3:7-9, February.

Lewis, Jack P. (1971), *Historical Backgrounds of Bible History* (Grand Rapids, MI: Baker).

Lewis, Jack P. (1975), *Archaeology and the Bible* (Abilene, TX: Biblical Research Press).

Lyons, Eric (2003), *The Anvil Rings* (Montgomery, AL: Apologetics Press).

McGarvey, J.W. (1974 reprint), *Evidences of Christianity* (Nashville, TN: Gospel Advocate).

McMillen, S. I. (1963), *None of These Diseases* (Old Tappan, NJ: Revell).

Miller, Dave (1996), *Piloting the Strait* (Pulaski, TN: Sain Publications).

Morens, D.M. (1999), "Death of a President," *The New England Journal of Medicine*, 341[24]:1845-1850, December 9.

Packer, J.I. (1958), *"Fundamentalism" and the Word of God* (Grand Rapids, MI: Eerdmans, 1976 reprint).

Pinnock, Clark (1977), *A Defense of Biblical Infallibility* (Nutley, NJ: Presbyterian & Reformed).

Ramsay, William (1897), *St. Paul the Traveller and the Roman Citizen* (Grand Rapids, MI: Baker, 1962 reprint).

Thompson, Bert (2001), *In Defense of the Bible's Inspiration* (Montgomery, AL: Apologetics Press), [On-line], URL: http://www.apologeticspress.org/pdfs/e-books_pdf/idobi.pdf.

Wallenborn, White McKenzie (1997), "George Washington's Terminal Illness," [On-line], URL: http://gwpapers.virginia.edu/articles/wallenborn/.

Warfield, Benjamin (1948 reprint), *The Inspiration and Authority of the Bible* (Philadelphia, PA: The Presbyterian and Reformed).

REFERENCES

Abbott, N. (1939), *The Rise of the North Arabic Script and Its Kuranic Development* (Chicago, IL: University of Chicago Press).

Abbott, Walter, ed. (1966), *The Documents of Vatican II* (New York: America Press).

Abdallah, Osama (no date), "When is Polygamy Allowed in Islam?" [On-line], URL: http://www.answering-christianity.com/polygamy.htm.

Al-nasir, Jamal (2000-2003), *Holy Quran Viewer* (London: Divineislam. com), [On-line]: URL: http://www.divineislam.com.

Ali, Abdullah Yusuf (1934), *The Qur'an* (Elmhurst, NY: Tahrike Tarsile Quran), ninth edition.

Amjad, Moiz (1998), "What Was Man Created From?" [On-line], URL: http://www.understanding-islam.org/related/print.asp ?type=article&aid=102.

Arberry, A.J. (1967), *The Koran Illuminated: A Handlist of the Korans in the Chester Beatty Library* (Dublin: Hodges Figgis).

Bell, Richard (1925), *The Origin of Islam in its Christian Environment* (Edinburgh: Gunning Foundation).

Beverley, James A. (1997), *Christ & Islam* (Joplin, MO: College Press).

Braswell, George W. Jr. (1996), *Islam: Its Prophet, Peoples, Politics and Power* (Nashville, TN: Broadman and Holman).

Braswell, George W. Jr. (2000), *What You Need to Know About Islam and Muslims* (Nashville, TN: Broadman and Holman).

Brooks, Geraldine (1995), *Nine Parts of Desire* (New York, NY: Anchor Books).

Bruce, F.F. (1977), *The Defense of the Gospel in the New Testament* (Grand Rapids, MI: Eerdmans), revised edition.

Butt, Kyle (2004), "Martin Luther Speaks on 'Faith Only' and Baptism," [On-line], URL: http://www.apologeticspress.org/modules.php?name=Read&cat=3&itemid=1858.

Butt, Kyle and Dave Miller (2003), "Who Hardened Pharaoh's Heart?" [On-line], URL: http://www.apologeticspress.org/modules.php?name=Read&itemid=2259&cat=7.

Campbell, William (2002), *The Quran and the Bible in the Light of History and Science*, [On-line], URL: http://answering-islam.org.uk/Campbell/contents.html.

"The Challenge the Book of Mormon Makes to the World" (1990), (Euless, TX: Texas Fort Worth Mission).

Cohen, A., trans. (1936), *The Babylonian Talmud: Sotah*, ed. Isidore Epstein (London: Soncino Press).

Cragg, Kenneth (2000), *The Call of the Minaret* (Oxford: Oneworld), third edition.

Cullmann, Oscar (1991), "Infancy Gospels," *New Testament Apocrypha*, ed. Wilhelm Schneemelcher (Louisville, KY: Westminster/John Knox Press).

Dawood, N.J., trans. (1976 reprint), *The Koran* (Harmondsworth, Middlesex: Penguin).

Deroche, F. (1992), *The Abbasid Tradition: Qurans of the 8th to the 10th Centuries AD* (Oxford: Oxford University Press).

Doctrine and Covenants (1981 reprint), (Salt Lake City, UT: Church of Jesus Christ of Latter-day Saints).

Ewing, W. (1956), "Samaritans," *The International Standard Bible Encyclopaedia* (Grand Rapids, MI: Eerdmans, 1974 reprint).

Farrington, Brendan (2001), "FBI Investigates Possible Fla. Links," [On-line]: URL: http://newsmine.org/archive/9-11/questions/stripbar.htm.

Freedman, H. (1938a), *The Babylonian Talmud: Pesachim*, ed. Isidore Epstein (London: Soncino Press).

Freedman, H. (1938b), *The Babylonian Talmud: Shabbath*, ed. Isidore Epstein (London: Soncino Press).

Gasque, W.W. (1975), "Apocalyptic Literature," *The Zondervan Pictorial Encyclopedia of the Bible*, ed. Merrill Tenney (Grand Rapids, MI: Zondervan).

Geiger, Abraham (1896), *Judaism and Islam*, trans. F.M. Young, [On-line], URL: http://answering-islam.org/Books/Geiger/Judaism/index.htm.

Geisler, Norman and Abdul Saleeb (2002), *Answering Islam* (Grand Rapids, MI: Baker), second edition.

"Gemara (Talmud)," [On-line], URL: http://www.ucalgary.ca/~elsegal/TalmudMap/Gemara.html.

Gesenius, William (1847), *Hebrew-Chaldee Lexicon to the Old Testament* (Grand Rapids, MI: Baker, 1979 reprint).

Gibb, H.A.R. (1953), *Mohammedanism* (New York: Oxford University Press), second edition.

Gilchrist, John (1986), *Muhammad and the Religion of Islam*, [On-line], URL: http://answering-islam.org.uk/Gilchrist/Vol1/5c.html.

Ginzberg, Louis (1909-1939), *The Legends of the Jews*, trans. Henrietta Szold (Philadelphia, PA: The Jewish Publication Society of America), [On-line], URL: http://answering-islam.org/Books/Legends/v1_3.htm.

Goldsack, William (1906), *The Quran in Islam* (London: The Christian Literature Society).

Goldsack, William (1907), *The Origins of the Quran* (London: The Christian Literature Society), [On-line], URL: http://answering-islam.org/Books/Goldsack/Sources/index.htm.

Graetz, Heinrich (1891), *History of the Jews* (Philadelphia, PA: The Jewish Publication Society of America).

Green, Samuel (2001), "The Different Arabic Versions of the Quran," [On-line], URL: http://www.answering-islam.org/Green/seven.htm.

Grohmann, Adolf (1958), "The Problem of Dating the Early Qurans," *Der Islam*, [33]:213-231.

Harris, R. Laird, Gleason Archer, Jr. and Bruce Waltke, eds. (1980), *Theological Wordbook of the Old Testament* (Chicago, IL: Moody).

Harris, Rendel (1926), "The New Text of the Kuran," *John Rylands Library Bulletin* [10]:219-222.

Hasan, Suhaib (1994), "Sunnah and Hadith," [On-line], URL: http://www.usc.edu/dept/MSA/fundamentals/hadithsunnah/.

Hertz, J.H. (1934), "Foreword," *Soncino Babylonian Talmud*, ed. Isidore Epstein, [On-line], URL: http://www.come-and-hear.com/talmud/nezikin_h.html.

Hutchison, J. (1939), "Apocryphal Gospels," *International Standard Bible Encyclopedia*, ed. James Orr (Grand Rapids, MI: Eerdmans).

Ibn Ishaq (1980), *Sirat Rasul Allah (The Life of Muhammad)*, trans. Alfred Guillaume (New York: Oxford University Press).

"Is the Quran's Story of Solomon and Sheba from the Jewish Targum?" (no date), [On-line]: URL: http://answering-islam.org.uk/Responses/Saifullah/sheba.htm.

Iredell, James (1836), *The Debates in the Several State Conventions on the Adoption of the Federal Constitution*, ed. Jonathan Elliot (Washington, D.C.: Jonathan Elliot).

Jackson, Wayne (2002), "Did Jude Quote from the Apocrypha?" *Christian Courier*, [On-line]: URL: http://www.christiancourier.com/questions/enochQuestion.htm.

Jackson, Wayne (2003a), "Does the Bible Contain Contradictions?" *Christian Courier*, [On-line], URL: http://www.christiancourier.com/feature/2003_09.htm.

Jackson, Wayne (2003b), "Is It Always Wrong To 'Hate'?" *Christian Courier*, [On-line], URL: http://www.christiancourier.com/questions/hateQuestion.htm.

Jameel, Khuda Hafiz (no date), "King Solomon and the Queen of Sheba," [On-line], URL: http://answering-islam.org.uk/Quran/Sources/sheba.html.

Jeffery, Arthur (1952), *The Quran as Scripture* (New York, NY: R.F. Moore), [On-line], URL: http://www.answering-islam.org/Books/Jeffery/thq.htm.

Jenkinson, E.L. (1931), "Did Mohammed Know Slavonic Enoch?" *The Moslem World*, 21:24-28. (Available on-line at: http://answering-islam.org.uk/Books/MW/slavonic_enoch.htm).

"Jewish Literature in New Testament Times" (no date), [On-line], URL: http://www.bible-history.com/JewishLiterature/JEWISH_LITERATURERabbinic_Chart.htm.

Kateregga, Badru (1981), *Islam and Christianity: A Muslim and a Christian in Dialogue* (Grand Rapids, MI: Eerdmans).

Katz, Jochen (no date), "Who is Going to Pay the Bill for the 'Promise in Overdraft'?" [On-line], URL: http://www.answering-islam.org/Quran/Contra/i001.html.

Keil, C.F. and F. Delitzsch (1976 reprint), *Commentary on the Old Testament: The Pentateuch* (Grand Rapids, MI: Eerdmans).

Kelso, J.L. (1976), "Samaritans," *The Zondervan Pictorial Encyclopedia of the Bible*, ed. Merrill Tenney (Grand Rapids, MI: Zondervan).

"The Largest Muslim Communities" (2000), [On-line]: URL: http://www.adherents.com/largecom/com_islam.html.

"The Largest Shiite Communities" (1999), [On-line]: URL: http://www.adherents.com/largecom/com_shiite.html.

Lenski, R.C.H. (1966), *The Interpretation of I and II Epistles of Peter, the Three Epistles of John, and the Epistle of Jude* (Minneapolis, MN: Augsburg).

Lewis, Jack (1991), *Questions You've Asked About Bible Translations* (Searcy, AR: Resource Publications).

Lings, Martin (1983), *Muhammad* (Rochester, VT: Inner Traditions International).

The Lost Books of the Bible (1979 reprint), (New York: Random House).

Lucado, Max (1996), *In the Grip of Grace* (Dallas, TX: Word).

Lull, Martel (no date), "Of Myths and Women," [On-line], URL: http://www.answering-islam.org/Responses/Azeem/myths .htm.

Lyons, Eric (2003a), "No One has Ascended to Heaven," [On-line], URL: http://www.apologeticspress.org/modules.php? name=Read&cat=2&itemid=523.

Lyons, Eric (2003b), "Who Incited David To Number Israel?" [On-line], URL: http://www.apologeticspress.org/modules. php?name=Read&cat=2&itemid=604.

MacRuaidh, Antoin (no date), "The Compilation of the Text of the Quran and the Sunni-Shia Dispute," [On-line], URL: http:// debate.org.uk/topics/theo/dispute.htm.

"Major Religions of the World Ranked by Number of Adherents" (2002), [On-line]: URL: http://www.adherents.com/ Religions_By_Adherents.html.

Margoliouth, D.S. (1925), "Textual Variations of the Koran," *The Muslim World,* [15]:334-44, [On-line], URL: http://www.answering-islam.org/Books/Margoliouth/variants.htm.

Margoliouth, D.S. (1939), "Some Additions to Professor Jeffery's Foreign Vocabulary of the Quran," *Journal of the Royal Asiatic Society* (London):53-61.

Mark, Brother (1999), *A "Perfect" Quran?,* [On-line], URL: http:// www.answering-islam.org/PQ/index.htm.

Masters, Abu Yusuf Daniel, Abu Maryam Isma'il Kaka, and Abu Iman Robert Squires (2003), "Introduction to Islam," [On-line], URL: http://thetruereligion.org/modules/wfsection/ article.php?articleid=14.

McClintock, John and James Strong (1867), *Cyclopedia of Biblical, Theological, and Ecclesiastical Literature* (Grand Rapids, MI: Baker, 1968 reprint).

Miller, Dave (2003a), "Is the Book of Mormon from God?," [On-line], URL: http://www.apologeticspress.org/modules.php? name=Read&cat=7&itemid=2243.

Miller, Dave (2003b), "Is Denominationalism Scriptural?" [On-line], URL: http://www.apologeticspress.org/modules.php? name=Read&cat=7&itemid=2253.

Miller, Dave (2003c), "Modern-day Miracles, Tongue-speaking, and Holy Spirit Baptism: A Refutation," *Reason and Revelation*, 23:17-23, March, [On-line], URL: http://www. apologet icspress.org/modules.php?name=Read&cat= 1&itemid=2572.

Miller, Dave (2003d), "Things God Cannot Do," [On-line], URL: http://www.apologeticspress.org/modules.php? name=Read &cat=7&itemid=2292.

Miller, Dave (2003e), "The Unique Church," [On-line], URL: http: // www.apologeticspress.org/modules.php?name= Read&cat =7&itemid=2246.

Mingana, Alphonse (1927), "Syriac Influences on the Style of the Koran," *Bulletin of the John Rylands Library*, [11]:77-98. (Available on-line at: http://answering-islam.org/Books/Mingana/ Influence/index.htm).

Mishcon, A., trans. (1935), *The Babylonian Talmud: Abodah Zarah*, ed. Isidore Epstein (London: Soncino Press).

"The Murder of Abel" (no date), [On-line], URL: http://answer-ing-islam.org/Quran/Sources/cain.html.

Nasr, Seyyed Hossein (2002), *The Heart of Islam* (New York: Harper Collins).

Nasr, Seyyed Hossein (2003), *Islam* (New York: HarperCollins).

Noldeke, Theodor (1892), "The Quran," *Sketches from Eastern History*, trans. J.S. Black (London: Adam and Charles Black), [On-line], URL: http://answering-islam.org/Books/Noel deke/quran.htm.

"On the Integrity of the Quran," (no date), [On-line], URL: http: //www.answering-islam.org/Quran/Text/integrity1.html.

Orelli, C. von (1939), "Prophecy," *The International Standard Bible Encyclopedia*, ed. James Orr (Grand Rapids, MI: Eerdmans, 1974 reprint).

Packer, J.I. (1958), *"Fundamentalism" and the Word of God* (Grand Rapids, MI: Eerdmans), 1976 reprint.

Paley, William (1831), *The Works of William Paley* (Philadelphia, PA: J.J. Woodward).

The People v. Ruggles (1811), 8 Johns 290 (Sup. Ct. NY.), N.Y. Lexis 124.

"Pharaoh's Magicians" (no date), [On-line], URL: http://geocities.com/freethoughtmecca/chartumim.html.

Pickthall, Mohammed M. (no date), *The Meaning of the Glorious Koran* (New York: Mentor).

"Polygamy" (no date), [On-line], URL: http://www.answering-christianity.com/islam_polygamy.htm.

Puin, Gerd-R. (1996), "Observations on Early Quran Manuscripts in San'a'," *The Quran as Text*, ed. Stefan Wild (Leiden: E.J. Brill).

"The Quranic Manuscripts" (no date), [On-line], URL: http://www.islamic-awareness.org/Quran/Text/Mss/.

"Rabbinic Chart" (no date), [On-line], URL: http://www.bible-history.com/JewishLiterature/JEWISH_LITERATURER abbinic_Chart.htm.

Rahman, Fazlur (1979), *Islam* (Chicago, IL: University of Chicago Press), second edition.

Rahman, Fazlur (1982), *Islam & Modernity* (Chicago, IL: University of Chicago Press).

Rasool, Butrus, Waleed Quwan, and Faddaan Sinnawr (no date), "Survey of the Quran and Logic," [On-line], URL: http://geocities.com/freethoughtmecca/quranlogic.html.

Roberts, Alexander and James Donaldson, eds. (1951), *The Ante-Nicene Fathers* (Grand Rapids, MI: Eerdmans).

Rodkinson, Michael (1918), *The History of the Talmud* (Boston, MA: The Talmud Society), [On-line], URL: http://www.sacred-texts.com/jud/t10/ht100.htm.

Rodwell, J.M., trans. (1950 reprint), *The Koran* (London: J.M. Dent and Sons).

Roper, Geoffrey, ed. (1992-1993), *World Survey of Islamic Manuscripts* (London: Al-Furqan Islamic Heritage Foundation).

Sale, George, trans. (no date), *The Koran* (New York: Hurst).

Sayfush-Shaytaan, Musaylimaat (2002), "Midrash and the Sword of God," [On-line], URL: http://geocities.com/freethought mecca/sayfallaah.html.

Sayfush-Shaytaan, Musaylimaat (no date), "Thoughts on 'Religious Borrowing' Theories for the Quran," [On-line], URL: http://geocities.com/freethoughtmecca/borrow.html.

Septuagint Version of the Old Testament (1970 reprint), (Grand Rapids, MI: Zondervan).

Shacter, Jacob, trans. (1935), *The Babylonian Talmud: Sanhedrin*, ed. Isidore Epstein (London: Soncino Press).

Shorrosh, Anis A. (1988), *Islam Revealed: A Christian Arab's View of Islam* (Nashville, TN: Thomas Nelson).

Simon, Maurice (1938), *The Babylonian Talmud: Rosh Hashanah*, ed. Isidore Epstein (London: Soncino Press).

Smith, Zach (2003), "The Canon and Extra-canonical Writings" [On-line], URL: http://www.apologeticspress.org/modules. php?name=Read&cat=4&itemid=1972.

Squires, Abd ar-Rahman Robert (2004), "Some Thoughts on the Authenticity of The Qur'an," [On-line], URL: http://the truereligion.org/modules/wfsection/article.php?page=1 &articleid=154.

Story, Joseph (1833), *Commentaries on the Constitution of the United States* (Boston, MA: Hilliard, Gray, & Co.).

Swete, Henry (1911), *Commentary on Revelation* (Grand Rapids, MI: Kregel, 1977 reprint).

"Talmud/Mishna/Gemara" (2004), *Jewish Virtual Library*, [On-line], URL: http://www.us-israel.org/jsource/Judaism/tal mud_&_mishna.html.

"Talmud" (2003), [On-line], URL: http://www.worldhistory.com/wiki/T/Talmud.htm.

"Textual Variants of the Quran" (no date), [On-line], URL: http://www.answering-islam.org/Quran/Text/index.html.

Thayer, Joseph H. (1901), *A Greek-English Lexicon of the New Testament* (Grand Rapids, MI: Baker, 1977 reprint).

Thompson, Bert (1999), *The Bible and the Age of the Earth* (Montgomery, AL: Apologetics Press).

Thomson, J.E.H. (1939), "Apocalyptic Literature," *The International Standard Bible Encyclopedia,* ed. James Orr (Grand Rapids, MI: Eerdmans, 1974 reprint).

Tisdall, W. St. Clair (1905), *The Original Sources of the Quran* (London: Society for Promoting Christian Knowledge), [On-line], URL: http://muhammadanism.org/Tisdall/sources_quran/sources_quran.doc.

Tocqueville, Alexis de (1945 reprint), *Democracy in America* (New York, NY: Alfred A. Knopf).

Torrey, Charles (1933), *The Jewish Foundations of Islam* (New York: Jewish Institute of Religion Press), [On-line], URL: http://answering-islam.org/Books/Torrey/torrey2.htm.

Trifkovic, Serge (2002), *The Sword of the Prophet* (Boston, MA: Regina Orthodox Press).

Watt, W. Montgomery (1961), *Muhammad* (New York: Oxford University Press).

Weingreen, J. (1959), *A Practical Grammar for Classical Hebrew* (Oxford: Clarendon Press).

Williams, John A., ed. (1961), *Islam* (New York: George Braziller).